Contents

Contents

Part One
Introduction

Modernism is a shorthand term for the artistic upheaval that began in the last years of the nineteenth century and ended in the middle years of the twentieth. This volume explores the causes of that upheaval and examines the main literary experiments of the period. The period is defined as being from 1890 to 1950 but we will occasionally be looking back to the mid nineteenth century because this is when the issues discussed in this volume start to make themselves felt. Most of the characteristics of modernity are evident in the final years of the nineteenth century and the early years of the twentieth, and they continue to affect us to this day.

This volume is aimed at those who have little or no knowledge of modernist literature but it differs from other introductions by including readings not just of canonical writers such as Virginia Woolf but also non-canonical ones, such as Saki, who offer a different angle on modernism. It also differs from some other introductions because it offers a unique interpretation of modernism, namely that aspects of it can only be understood by reference to Frederick Winslow Taylor's *The Principles of Scientific Management* (1911). Very briefly, Taylor's experiments with methods of work parallel modernist experiments with forms of literature. We discuss scientific management, along with the intellectual and artistic background of modernism, in Part Two: 'A Cultural Overview', and we occasionally return to it in the chapters on poetry, the novel and drama in Part Three: 'Texts, Writers and Contexts'.

It is helpful, when being introduced to modernism for the first time, to think about its origins, its contexts, its main characteristics and what sort of critical approaches we should take to it. Although we cover each of these areas in the body of the volume, it is useful to rehearse some of the main points here.

We said above that modernism began in the last years of the nineteenth century, but the word 'modern' has been around a lot longer than that. We can trace it right back to the fifth century AD when the term 'modernus', meaning 'now', was used in three ways. The first was neutral. To Pope Gelasius (d. 496) it was a way of distinguishing the present Church fathers from the previous ones. In this context, to be modern was simply to be part of a continuum. The dead, the living and those yet to be born were alike in believing in the one true Christ. The second meaning of 'modernus' was that 'now' is different to 'then'. The Christians, for example, used the term to distinguish their own era of enlightenment from the pagan one of darkness. The word 'modern' now signified that the present was not just different from the past but also better. The writings of Cassiodorus (c. 485–585) lead us on to the third meaning of the term 'modern'. He spent his life trying to reconcile the divisions between the Western and Eastern Churches and between the Romans and the Goths. This is the most complex use of the word 'modern' in the fifth century. It still refers to a break with the classical past but it also refers to a break within what was previously the continuity of the Christian tradition as the differences between the Western and Eastern Church start to become more marked. In response to this potential disintegration, as well as to the culture clash with the Goths, the modern is burdened with the task of finding common ground between these different societies, and different interpretations of the same faith.

The second and third meanings of the term 'modern', rupture and reconciliation, are the ones that we will encounter most in this volume. The Futurists will claim that they have broken completely with the past while the Imagists will uphold the virtues of classical literature. What is most striking, though, is that meanings forged in the fifth century still held true in the early twentieth century. In general, the term modern is used to signify a break with the past when we are thinking about science and technology and reconciliation when we are thinking about the arts and philosophy.

The main contexts of modernism are the industrial revolution, the intellectual and artistic upheavals of the nineteenth century and the rise of mass culture. These are outlined or discussed in the next chapter but there are several others we can mention here. The first is the widespread feeling that the West was in decline. One expression of this view can be found in Oswald Spengler's *The Decline of the West* (1918–23). Spengler's model for the rise and fall of civilisation is the seasonal year. Taking government as an example Spengler claims that spring is a warrior aristocracy, in summer it is absolute monarchy, autumn sees a struggle between the landed class and the commercial class and winter marks the advent of democracy, which is simply the rule of money.

Spengler sums his position up when he declares that Plato stood for a philosophy of becoming, Aristotle for a philosophy of being; the former was in process and would grow, the latter was finished and would decay. He uses the term culture to signify the process of 'becoming' and the term civilisation to signify the product of 'having become'. The relationship between 'becoming' and 'having become' underlies a number of modernist writers, but especially D. H. Lawrence (see Part Three: 'The Modernist Novel in England').

If one view of the West was that it was in decline, another was that it was thriving. This was especially the case with technology, another context for modernism. There were numerous developments between 1880 and 1900, including the first synthetic fibre, the Kodak box camera, the Ford car and the discovery of X-rays. Surely these showed that society was in state of 'becoming' rather than 'having become'? Although technology enabled humans to control nature and delivered a more comfortable lifestyle, it also had a more sinister side. It could be used to control, as it is in George Orwell's *1984* (1949), and to kill in vast numbers, as with the atomic bomb, but the more familiar complaint about technology was that it was dehumanising. This wasn't just a matter of a machine doing the work formerly done by a man, it was that the machine could be a substitute for human contact. The telephone, for example, could be used to arrange a meeting or be used in place of one.

The city, another context for modernist literature, was also seen to be dehumanising. The individual was lost in the crowd and he or she existed in isolation rather than as part of a community. Moreover, the individual was overloaded with stimuli and worn down by constant demands on his or her attention. He or she could respond to these circumstances in different ways. One was to affect an air of indifference and to regard everything as meaningless; another was to adopt a mask as a means of disguising the real self; and a third was to get the real self noticed by standing out from the crowd. The anxiety about the fate of the individual in the city was paralleled in the debate about the nature of the state. Should it be individualist or collective? This was yet another context for modernist literature. The problems of modern society – health, education, the gap between rich and poor and the economic competition from America and Germany – demanded a co-ordinated response. The late 1880s to the end of the First World War (1918) saw an unprecedented growth of state powers as government intervened to improve the lives of its citizens. The debates from that time still resonate today. Should we have a planned economy or should we leave everything to the market?

Such questions may seem far removed from literature. But the work of Franz Kafka (1883–1924) could not have been written without the growth of government power and its associated bureaucracy, while Aldous Huxley's *Brave New World* (1932) shows how completely the state can shape a person's existence. We should also remember that the last years of the nineteenth century and the first years of the twentieth were characterised by women and the working class demanding the right to vote. Their demand to be represented in the political process coincides with the modernist interest in representation, though the artistic meaning of the term is far more complex than the political one.

We have mentioned some of the contexts of modernist literature and there of course others, in particular empire, anthropology and eugenics,[1] but what are the characteristics of that literature itself? First of all, we have to say what we mean by modernist literature. If we are defining it by period then *Tarzan of the Apes* (1912) by Edgar Rice Burroughs is a modernist novel since it falls within our period, but that doesn't seem very satisfactory. Perhaps we should therefore say that modernist literature is characterised by a distinctive set of themes. One of these themes is an interest in the primitive. A variation of that theme, the relation between instinct and intellect, is the subject of Thomas Mann's *Death in Venice* (1912), which was published in the same year as *Tarzan* and is one of the novels discussed in this volume. However, *Tarzan* is also about the relation between primitive and civilised life, so, once again, it passes as a modernist work.

If *Tarzan* is a modernist work, why has no-one hailed it as such? The answer is, and here we come to the crux of the matter, that *Tarzan* is written in a realistic style for a mass audience. By contrast modernist literature questions the conventions of realism and is aimed at a small, select audience. The contempt felt by some modernist artists for trivial forms of entertainment is summed up by Leopold Bloom, one of the central characters of James Joyce's *Ulysses* (1922), who uses a page from the popular magazine *Tit-Bits* as a piece of lavatory paper.

Modernist literature is an attempt to find new forms of representation for a new kind of society, one that seems to be constantly changing. It uses a variety of techniques to do that, from myth to stream of consciousness. But modernist literature is not just an attempt to find a more accurate form of representation, one that is true to individual experience, it also aims to diagnose the ills of modern society and to suggest a cure. Modernist literature therefore has an urgency about it which is reflected in the number of manifestos published by different groups proclaiming their principles. It will be part of the task of this volume to identify some of those groups and some of those principles.

Finally, we come to critical approaches to modernism. This is one of the subjects covered by the four chapters that make up Part Four: 'Critical Theories and Debates'. In very general terms, criticism of modernism has moved from explaining individual works, their allusions, their patterns of imagery, their relation to tradition and so on, to examining the contexts in which modernist literature was written. These include print culture and the First World War. In addition, we can mention feminism and modernism, sexuality and modernism, politics and modernism, postcolonialism and modernism, and consumerism and modernism. One of the things to have emerged from the study of the contexts of modernism is a sense that it is better to use the term 'modernisms' rather than 'modernism'. There do seem to be a plurality of modernisms: Dadaism, Cubism, Futurism, Surrealism and Vorticism to mention but a few. In addition, modernism took different forms in different countries, while Afro-American modernism showed that it could even take different forms in the same country. Presumably these modernisms all have something in common, otherwise they could not all be called modernism: it is that they are all a response to the nature of modern life which conditions how we perceive the world and how we relate to others. They also register the decline of religion, the rise of science and the new democratic institutions, and what these mean for traditional ideas of culture and the self.

These are some of the issues we explore in this volume, which examines a wide range of modernist literature from a number of different angles. The aim is not just to introduce the reader to some key modernist works but also to show how they both relate to each other and engage with contemporary developments. Ideally this volume will give readers the confidence to develop their own reading of modernist works, for one thing is clear about this field of study: it never stands still for long.

Gary Day

Note

1 For a good introduction to some of these and other contexts of modernism, see David Bradshaw (ed.), *A Concise Companion to Modernism* (Oxford: Blackwell, 2003) and Philip Tew and Alex Murray, *The Modernism Handvolume* (London: Continuum, 2009).

Part Two
A Cultural Overview

The forces shaping the writing of the period covered by this book, 1890–1950, were many, but four stand out: the industrial revolution; the intellectual revolution of the nineteenth century; the Aesthetic Movement; and finally, the rise of mass culture. In one way or another, modernist literature appeared in reaction to these developments and those they brought in their wake, particularly the growth of the modern state, the spread of bureaucracy and the rise of scientific management. They all appeared in the nineteenth century, but their effects are still felt today.

We touch upon the rise of mass culture in the following chapters, and because it is more integrated into the discussion of literature than the other three developments, it is not considered separately here. However, we should mention the two main approaches to mass culture that occur in discussions of modernism. The first claims that modern art defines itself against mass culture, and the second, by contrast, claims that there is no great divide between the two.

The Bloomsbury group* is an example of a group of artists and

* The name given to group of friends who began to meet in 1905–6, initially at 46 Gordon Square, Bloomsbury. They included Virginia Woolf (1882–1941), her sister, the artist Vanessa Bell (1879–1961) and Vanessa's husband Clive (1881–1964), the economist Maynard Keynes (1883–1946), E. M. Forster (1879–1970) and the artist Roger Fry (1866–1934). Their association was based on an interest in the arts. They were in revolt against the social, artistic and sexual mores of the Victorian age. Many of their beliefs derived from G. E. Moore's *Principia Ethica* (1903) which stated that conversation and the enjoyment of beautiful things constitute two of the highest goals of social progress.

thinkers who, if they did not actually disdain mass culture, certainly had very little regard for it. At its centre were Leslie Stephen's daughters, Vanessa who married Clive Bell and Virginia who married Leonard Woolf. The values of the group are summed up in the novelist E. M. Forster's essay, 'What I Believe' (1939), in which he lists, among other things, 'personal relationships' and 'an aristocracy of the sensitive, the considerate and the plucky' as the things he believes in.[1]

Clive Bell spoke for the group on art. He argued that the purpose of art is to rouse profound emotion, which it does by 'significant form'.* An artist who concerns him or herself with form is to be preferred to one who does not. This becomes a way of distinguishing between high art and 'popular art'. The one is concerned with form, the other with content.

T. S. Eliot (1888–1965), who seems the very embodiment of high culture, was yet one of those who took pleasure in popular pastimes. He was an avid reader of Sir Arthur Conan Doyle's (1859–1930) Sherlock Holmes stories, enjoyed the music hall and was an ardent fan of the popular actress Marie Lloyd (1870–1922). His poetry contains references, both overt and covert, to all three. While some critics disdained the new art forms others embraced them. The American writer and cultural critic Gilbert Seldes (1893–1970), for example, detailed Charlie Chaplin's artistry, even comparing him to Dickens, and he drew parallels between free verse and jazz – both were 'attractively unpredictable'.[2] Some avant-garde movements also sought to cross the divide between the 'cultivated' and the 'common'. Dada, with its claim that any spontaneous act could be art, was one and Vorticism,† which aimed to be 'essentially popular',[3] was another.

---

* In painting, significant form refers to the arrangement of lines and colours on canvas. The job of the critic, according to Bell, is to point out to the public those parts of a work which unite to produce significant form. The placing of form at the heart of the aesthetic experience separates art from life. What we should respond to in a painting is its form not its content. To appreciate a work of art, says Bell, we need bring with us nothing from life, no knowledge of its ideas and affairs, no familiarity with its emotions. Art transports us from the world of man's activity to a world of aesthetic exaltation.

† Dada, which means 'hobby horse', was randomly chosen from a dictionary to be the name of this movement, also known as Dadaism. The Dadaists said that the First World War had destroyed all moral, political and aesthetic beliefs. They aimed to shock their audience out of the frame of mind

The Industrial Revolution: The Machine and Scientific Management

The industrial revolution began in the latter half of the eighteenth century. Broadly speaking, machines began to perform tasks previously performed by manual labour. For example, the spinning jenny replaced the hand loom, enabling a single worker to more than double his or her output. The introduction of the machine is a defining moment in modern history. It is no exaggeration to say that it changed the nature of society. It led to the establishment of factories and the cities that grew up around them.

The machine is a symbol of progress. It represents human ingenuity, the control of nature and the capacity to satisfy our wants and needs. The machine is also a metaphor for the good society: orderly, purposeful and with every part contributing to the whole. In addition, it alters perception. In the nineteenth century, for example, the train gave people an experience they had not had before: a view of the world at speed.

Those whose only means of transport had been walking or riding on horseback must have been astonished to see towns, factories and countryside flash past from a carriage window. That symbol of modernity, the Eiffel Tower (f. 1889), also changed how humans saw their world. Most people lived at ground level, so to enter the lift, ascend, step out and look down upon Paris must have been breathtaking: the roofs of the city, its historic buildings, its roads, paths and alleyways all laid out like a map.

Both the railway and the Eiffel Tower had an influence on how painters represented the world. The way the Cubists superimposed one image on top of another owes something to the rapid succession of

---

that had led to war. Chance and nonsense were key elements of their art and the movement eventually gave way to surrealism. Vorticism was mainly a movement in painting that flourished between 1912 and 1915. It attacked the sentimentality of Victorian art and celebrated violence and the machine. Vorticist painting consisted of abstract compositions made up of bold lines with sharp angles. See Part Four: 'Literature, Visual and Music' and 'Literature and War' for more on Dadaism and Vorticism respectively.

images seen from a train,* while the view from the tower 'based on frontality and pattern rather than on perspective recession and depth' was the template for 'the characteristic flat, patterned space of modern art'.[4]

The machine also serves as a model for the human. This is particularly true in the case of Frederick Winslow Taylor (1856–1915). His book, *The Principles of Scientific Management* (1911) is, in many ways, a modernist work: it is a manifesto, it is committed to the new and it incorporates different styles of writing† in much the same way that T. S. Eliot combines different voices in *The Waste Land* (1922) (see the Extended Commentary in Part Three: 'Modernist Poetry – America, Ireland and England').

Taylor's main purpose was to increase productivity by the elimination of wasteful practices, in particular the traditional 'rule of thumb methods'.[5] In saying that traditional methods are not suited to the modern workplace Taylor is like those modernists who argue that traditional forms of representation are not suited to the modern world. Both wanted to create something new.

There are four basic steps involved in getting rid of the 'rule of thumb' method. The first is to study the exact series of movements which each man uses in doing his work, 'as well as the implements [he] uses'. The second is to use a stop-watch to determine how long each movement takes. The third is to 'eliminate all false movements, slow movements, and useless movements'. The fourth and final step is to 'collect into one series the quickest and best movements as well as the best implements'.

Taylor gives the example of a bricklayer who had the number of movements he performed reduced from thirty-five to seventeen and whose equipment was also rendered more efficient. The result, however, depended on treating the bricklayer as an automaton. Taylor's most famous case, a man called Schmidt who shovelled pig iron in The

---

* Cubism was an attempt to paint objects as seen from many different angles simultaneously. A cubist picture of a table showed what it looked like from above, below and the sides all at the same time. Pablo Picasso (1881–1973) and Georges Braque (1882–1963) were pioneers of Cubism and the first major cubist exhibition took place in Paris in 1911. See also Part Three: 'Modernist Poetry – America, Ireland and England'.

† Taylor transcribes dialogue with his subjects, making parts of his work read like a play.

Bethlehem Steel Company, was treated in the same way. After being shown the correct method, Schmidt:

> started to work, and all day long, and at regular intervals, was told by the man who stood over him with a watch, 'Now pick up a pig and walk. Now sit down and rest. Now walk – now rest,' etc. He worked when he was told to work, and rested when he was told to rest, and at half-past five in the afternoon had his 47 $\frac{1}{2}$ tons loaded on the car.

Schmidt had to respond like a machine. He was not required to think about what he was doing, only carry out the prescribed movements. In Taylor's words:

> the workman who is best suited to handling pig iron is unable to understand the real science of doing this class of work. He is so stupid that the word 'percentage' has no meaning to him, and he must consequently be trained by a man more intelligent than himself into the habit of working in accordance with the laws of this science before he can be successful.

Taylor's barely disguised contempt is very similar to the intellectual's disdain for the masses summed by philospher Friedrich Nietzsche's statement that 'the mob, the mass, the herd will always be despicable'.[6] That is one of the things that allies Taylor with the modernists; another is his commitment to 'experiment', a word that occurs repeatedly in *The Principles of Scientific Management*.

What primarily concerns us here, though, is his view of the human as a machine, a body without mind programmed to perform tasks in accordance with the laws of scientific management, a view that has parallels in art. The French writer Alfred Jarry (1873–1907) wrote what is often considered to be the first cyborg novel, *Le Surmâle* ('The Superman', 1902). The hero wins a cycle race from Paris to Siberia against a train.

The daughter of an industrialist travelling on the train falls in love with him but, because he is too machine-like, he cannot reciprocate her feelings. A scientist builds him an electric chair to create the emotion of love by enormous jolts from a magneto. But, in a comic conclusion, the superman, zapped by 11,000 vaults, falls in love with the magneto and the magneto with him. Nevertheless, the message is clear: humans will be become more machine-like and human relationships will be replaced by relationships with machines.

Jarry celebrates that development, as does the painter Francis Picabia (1879–1953) who declared, upon arriving in New York, that 'the genius of the modern world is in machinery and that through machinery, art ought to find a most vivid expression ... I mean to work on and on until I attain the pinnacle of mechanical symbolism.'[7] He achieved it in paintings such as *Machine, Tournez Vite* ('Machine Turn Quickly', 1916–18) and *La Fille Née Sans Mère* ('The Girl Born without a Mother', 1916–17). The one marvels at the grace and perfection of the machine form, the other, a modern counterpart to the Virgin birth, implies that the machine is the new religion. It is certainly worshipped in the *Manifesto of Futurism* (1909) whose author, Filippo Tomasso Marinetti (1876–1944) announces that 'we will sing of shipyards blazing with violent electric moons; greedy railway stations that devour smoke-plumed serpents; [and] factories hung on clouds by the crooked lines of their smoke.'[8]

The machine, then, is idealised in both art and scientific management. It is worth stressing this point because one of the commonplaces of criticism is that high modernist art exists apart from the wider culture. But, as we shall see during the course of this book, there were many surprising connections between *The Principles of Scientific Management* and some literary works of the period. In very general terms, both were charged with the redemption of modern civilisation. Art would revitalise the spiritual waste land while scientific management would bring an end to the conflict between employers and employees that created so much economic waste.*

---

* As Taylor writes in the Introduction: 'We can see and feel the waste of material things. Awkward, inefficient, or ill-directed movements of men, however, leave nothing visible or tangible behind them. Their appreciation calls for an act of memory, an effort of the imagination. And for this reason, even though our daily loss from this source is greater than from our waste of material things, the one has stirred us deeply, while the other has moved us but little.'

Not all artists prostrated themselves before the machine. Jacob Epstein's *Rock Drill* (1913–14), for example, which looks like a torso with one arm, is intended as a warning. The sculpture, wrote the artist, is 'the sinister armoured figure of today and tomorrow. Nothing human, only the terrible Frankenstein's monster into which we have transformed ourselves.'[9] Coming as it does on the eve of the First World War this statement proves quite prophetic. One of the inventions of the late nineteenth century was the machine gun, which was to be used to such devastating effect in that conflict.*

We can also see some modernist innovations as a reaction to and indeed a protest against the machine. The irregular rhythms of free verse, for example, disrupt the steady rattle of the assembly line, while the stream of consciousness technique asserts the importance of the mind when humans are in danger of being defined purely in terms of their bodies.† More generally, modern art that was difficult, fragmented and apparently remote from life threw down a challenge to the machine with its unity, simplicity and singleness of purpose. If the machine was predictable, at least some modern art would not be, and if the machine was transparent, if we could see how it worked, then at least some modernist art work would shroud itself in obscurity.

Addressing the contemporary condition, art and scientific management show two sides of modernism: one is the value placed on the individual, the other is the value placed on the system. Taylor's words proved prophetic: 'In the past the man has been first; in the future the system must be first.'

The Intellectual Revolution

The key thinkers of the intellectual revolution were Charles Darwin (1809–82), Karl Marx (1818–83), Friedrich Nietzsche (1844–1900) and Sigmund Freud (1856–1939). They, too, altered the way in which at least the educated saw themselves and their society.

---

* For more on the First World War see Part Four: 'Literature and War'.
† See Part Three: 'The Origins of the Modernist Novel' for more on stream of consciousness writing.

Darwin's theory of evolution proposed that all life had a common ancestor and that it developed along different lines according to conditions such as climate, terrain and natural catastrophes. Those individuals best able to adapt to their environment survive and pass on their genes to the next generation. This bald summary doesn't begin to do justice to the richness, subtlety and complexity of Darwin's 'descent from modification', as he first termed evolution, but our concern is not with the intricacies of his theory but with its impact.

The Origin of Species (1859) questioned the book of Genesis: man was not fashioned complete from clay, according to evolutionary theory, but by gradual descent from other hominids, apes and placental mammals.* The claim challenged centuries of Christian orthodoxy and led to fierce debate. The most famous, in the nineteenth century, was at Oxford in 1860 between the biologist Thomas Huxley (1825–95) and Bishop Samuel Wilberforce (1805–73).

Although no record of the debate exists, it is remembered today partly because of a famous exchange between the two men. Wilberforce asked Huxley if he had descended from a monkey through his grand-father or his grandmother, to which Huxley retorted that he would not be ashamed to have a monkey for an ancestor but he would be ashamed to associate with a man who used his gifts to obscure the truth.

What is Darwin's relevance for modernism? The short answer is that he changed the way human nature was viewed. It was no longer defined by its relationship to God but by its relationship to the animal kingdom. If what Darwin said was true, then traditional conceptions of what man is, from classical Greece to Victorian Britain, had the potential to come crashing down.

This partly explains the modernist interest in the primitive. How hunter gatherers live gives an insight into the development of modern man, but the rest of the human past, all history, all culture, is based primarily on ignorance. What's more, the belief that history is progress does not bear scrutiny from the point of view of evolution, which

---

* Hominids are creatures of the family Hominidae comprising humans and their precursors; placental mammals bear live young, which are nourished before birth in the mother's uterus through a specialised embryonic organ attached to the uterus wall, the placenta.

suggests that a random mutation may lead to the human race being propelled along a quite different trajectory. Darwin became the starting point for a new understanding of human nature.

Karl Marx was another nineteenth century thinker whose work transformed how people saw themselves and the world. He believed that all history was the result of class struggle: 'lord and serf, guild-master and journeyman, in a word oppressor and oppressed, stood in constant opposition to one another [carrying on a fight] that each time ended either in a revolutionary reconstitution of society at large, or in the common ruin of the contending classes.'[10]

The industrial revolution had created two classes: those who owned the means of production, factories, raw materials and so on, and those who owned nothing except their labour power, which they had to sell in order to survive. It was only a matter of time before these two classes, the bourgeoisie and the proletariat, came into conflict, the result of which, according to Marx, would be the establishment of a communist society:

> where nobody has one exclusive sphere of activity but each can become accomplished in any branch he wishes, society regulates the general production and thus makes it possible for me to do one thing today and another tomorrow, to hunt in the morning, fish in the afternoon, rear cattle in the evening, criticise after dinner, just as I have a mind, without ever becoming hunter, fisherman, herdsman or critic.[11]

Marx's view of history stands in stark contrast to Darwin's theory of evolution because Marx thought that history has a goal: the creation of a society where everyone is equal and free to develop as they choose. Marx's concept of the class struggle and his analysis of the workings of capitalism inspired a range of revolutionary movements in the twentieth century, particularly in Russia. He is also important because he put forward the idea that, in his words, 'it is not the consciousness of men that determines their being, but, on the contrary, their social being that determines their consciousness'.[12]

Marx is here overturning a tradition of thought that goes back to Plato and which states, in effect, that humans are rational creatures who use their reason and exercise their will in choosing how to live. It assumes that reason can shape the world and that there are few obstacles it cannot overcome. Marx is saying very nearly the opposite, namely that reason itself is shaped by the environment and that, contrary to the principles of established ethics, we are not as free to act as we fondly believe. In short, our thoughts and actions are largely determined by the class into which we are born. That word 'largely' is crucial. Marx's own words clarify his position:

> Men make their own history, but they do not make it as they please; they do not make it under self-selected circumstances, but under circumstances existing already, given and transmitted from the past. The tradition of all the dead generations weighs like an nightmare on the brains of the living.[13]

Marx's relevance for modernism is that he shows that history is not the result of the actions of great men and women but rather the operation of certain laws arising out of the economic relations between the different groups in society. Marx was one of the first philosophers to grasp the complexity of modern industrial society and how it determines the individual's life. His view that class is the basis of society is the opposite of the eighteenth and nineteenth century view that the individual is the basis of society. The political theory of *laissez-faire* claimed that individuals pursuing their own interests and the invisible mechanism of the market ensured all needs were met.* But by the late nineteenth century it was plain that this model of society was outmoded. It caused too many problems and the state had to intervene to deal with issues such as health, education and welfare.

This not only generated a vast government bureaucracy, but also a new vocabulary of which the chief term was 'citizen'. The word 'individual' respects what is unique about people, but the term 'citizen' emphasises what they have in common. It is a way of seeing people as a mass. Marx's concept of class is also a way of grouping people together,

---

* *Laissez-faire* (literally 'leave to do', or 'leave it be') is the opinion that an economic system should be driven by free market forces, rather than government intervention.

but 'class' is different from 'citizen' because it implies that there are opposing interests which will inevitably lead to conflict.

The strange thing is that, when that conflict comes, neither side uses contemporary idioms or images to describe and justify it. Nor do they invent new ones. Instead they 'anxiously conjure up the spirits of the past to their service and borrow from them names, battle cries and costumes in order to present the new scene of world history'.[14] Marx's claim that 'the tradition of all the dead generations weighs like a nightmare on all the brains of the living' is a pointer to just how hard it would be for modernists to 'make it new'.

Nietzsche was the most radical philosopher of the nineteenth century. In fact it seems a little strange to call him a philosopher at all. He does not write like one, he writes more like a prophet. This is because he was trying to find a form suitable for the expression of his highly individual thoughts. Rather than constructing arguments, he is famous for aphorisms, such as: 'I mistrust all systematists and avoid them' and 'Humanity is finished when it becomes altruistic.'[15] The first utterance shows that he had a different conception of truth from other philosophers and the second that he had a different conception of ethics from them too.

Prior to Nietzsche, philosophers believed, in general, that it was possible to establish the truth about such matters as the existence of God, the external world, free will and so on. These truths were, except in the case of God, verifiable by logic or empirical evidence. Nietzsche, however, disagreed. He argued that philosophers were deceived if they believed that they were governed by reason; instead they were governed by their desires, inclinations and even their physiological needs. We cannot know what is true and what is not true, we can only see things from our own point of view.

Obviously there is a great deal more to say about this aspect of Nietzsche's philosophy, but the key point for our purpose has been made. Nietzsche believed that there is no such thing as objective truth, there are only subjective perceptions. The best we can hope for is multiple perspectives, the kind of thing we find in some cubist paintings where the same object is simultaneously presented from different points of view.

Nietzsche was equally radical in his views on morality. The conventional view of morality is that we choose between good and evil. According to Nietzsche, though, there is no 'I' that chooses. It is 'a fable, a fiction, a play on words'.[16] Here he is in accord with writers such as Johan August Strindberg (1849–1912) who are sceptical about the existence of a real self (see Part Three: 'The European Stage' for more on Strindberg). Nietzsche goes even further than that, for he derides the traditional distinction between good and evil, although this does not mean he thinks that it is acceptable to commit murder.

In the first instance, Nietzsche looks at Western morality historically. Its origins lie in the Judeo-Christian tradition, where Moses gave the Israelites the Ten Commandments and Jesus told us to love God and to love our neighbour as ourselves. Nietzsche argues that this is morality by divine diktat, it is not something we have made for ourselves. Moreover, it was designed for people whose lives were quite different from our own, which means that it has no vital connection with our own existence.

Here we come to Nietzsche's second criticism of conventional morality: it is anti-life. Christian teaching has proved harmful because, in demanding that we subdue the flesh, we have lost touch with our instincts, leaving us in a weakened state with a much diminished capacity to embrace all that life has to offer. In place of morality Nietzsche proposes 'a will to power'. This concept, like many in his work, is not explained in any great detail but, basically, it refers to a desire for a higher, more powerful state of being, free from the pettiness and frustrations of ordinary life.

The person who will embody this will to power is the *Ubermensch* or superman. Once again Nietzsche does not define this term with any real clarity (which made it easy for Hitler to appropriate it to justify his belief in a master race), but the superman is emphatically not someone who wants power over others, rather he is someone who says 'yes' to life and strives to overcome his limitations. In this respect, the superman is connected with Nietzsche's view of art.

This was expressed in his first book, *The Birth of Tragedy* (1872), where he claims that two principles underlay the work of the Greek dramatists, Apollo and Dionysus. Apollo stands for the beautiful appearance of things, Dionysus for intoxication, a transcendence of our 'individual self' and a feeling of oneness with nature. The latter is also, though, an acceptance of the sorrow and suffering which are inescapable facts of our existence. To say yes to pleasure means saying yes to pain. Life, according to this Nietzschean reading, is a continuum and the Dionysian experience affirms it in all its joy and woe. This was expressed in the best Greek tragedy, where the audience saw on stage its own life heightened and transfigured.

Nietzsche helps us to understand modernism by showing us that the traditional foundations of truth and morality are, to say the least, distinctly shaky. Realisation of this is one of the sources of the modernist sense of rootlessness. Nietzsche makes art the central experience of life, as do a number of modernist artists, for example the novelists James Joyce (1882–1941) and Virginia Woolf (1882–1941). They, like Nietzsche, shied away from representational art, but where he demands that art be Dionysian, they are content with its little epiphanies.* Perhaps the novelist who comes closest to Nietzsche's affirmation of the entirety of life is D. H. Lawrence (1885–1930), who also embraced the Nietzschean doctrine of 'becoming'. Put simply, this means that, since all previous systems of belief which helped to define man had been shown, in Nietzsche's eyes at least, to take little account of his true nature, then he must take responsibility for his own being, create his own truths and accept that there is no end to the process of 'becoming' himself.

The 'father of psychoanalysis', Sigmund Freud also had a huge influence on modernist art. André Breton (1896–1966), for example, who launched the surrealist movement in 1924, modified Freud's technique of free association, whereby the patient says whatever comes into his or her head, in order to reveal the true nature of reality.

The technique of free association was developed by Joseph Breuer

---

* The term originally refers to the manifestation of Christ to the Magi (three kings) celebrated on 6 January or Twelfth Night. James Joyce adapted the term to describe the sudden revelation of 'the whatness of a thing'. See also Part Three: 'The Modernist Novel in England', especially the section 'The Modernist Novel and Time'.

(1842–1925) and Freud when they were treating a patient referred to in their case histories as Anna O., but whose real name was Bertha Pappenheim. She developed a range of symptoms including paralysis and disturbances of vision. Both Freud and Breuer asked Anna O. to talk freely about her symptoms and, after thereby revealing the cause – a momentary wish that her father was dead – the symptoms disappeared.

The basics of psychoanalysis are all here: the repressed memory, the illness and the 'talking cure'. It was on this foundation that Freud built his edifice. There are two main stages. In the first, Freud argued that psychological disorders, such as obsessional neurosis, could be cured if the patient could be guided to a knowledge of the event which gave rise to them. Usually this event was of a sexual nature, either real or imagined. In the second stage, Freud accepted that 'the talking cure' did not work as well as he had hoped and that the most psychoanalysis could offer a patient was the means of turning hysterical misery into common unhappiness.

Underlying both stages, though, was Freud's theory of the mind. He distinguished, at the most basic level, between the unconscious and the conscious. The former, for Freud, is dominated by the pleasure principle, the latter by the reality principle. The relation between the two is largely antagonistic. The unconscious is the site of the instincts, principally those of sex and violence, it seeks instant gratification, while the conscious mind, aware that the pursuit of such gratification could easily result in injury or death, strives to keep the instincts in check or, better still, to sublimate them; that is to use their energy for higher purposes: art, music and so on.

Freud argued that dreams were wish-fulfilments, but that the fulfilment was disguised. The conscious mind is off-guard when we sleep, but it is still able to censor material from the unconscious. The instincts are able to by-pass the censor by disguising themselves as seemingly innocuous thoughts and images. The result is a compromise. The instincts are able to find some relief but the censor ensures that they do not appear in their starkest form.

It was Freud's theory of sexual development that shocked his readers, however. The infant, he said, is polymorphously perverse, in other words, taking an auto-erotic (or self-sexualised) pleasure in every part of its body. The sexual instincts themselves go through various stages of development. First there is an oral phase, then an anal one and then, at puberty, the final, genital stage. The sexual instinct can become fixated at any point, leading to neurosis in later life. It was his account of the Oedipus complex, however, for which Freud became best known. Put simply, the little boy wishes to kill his father so he can have his mother, who satisfies all his needs, to himself.

Freud broke with the enlightenment tradition that saw man as rational. In his scheme, man is driven by instincts which, even if slightly deflected from their aim, are likely to result in psychological problems. This kind of nervous illness is one of the minor themes of modernist literature and at least part of that can be traced back to Freud. His idea of man as pulled between the unconscious and the conscious also contributes to the modernist sense that subjectivity is a complex phenomenon, operating on many different levels at once.

In addition, Freud shows the importance of interpretation in coming to a true understanding of dreams, symptoms and even slips of the tongue. The human being is a book that needs to be read very closely. If people have so many layers, then it is no surprise to find this reflected in art, which therefore must also be interpreted carefully. Freud's theories, in other words, validate the notion of the artwork as difficult and elusive, an object that will only yield up its secrets after deep study.

Also of importance are Freud's views on civilisation, by which he means the appreciation and cultivation of the higher mental faculties. It was founded, he claimed, on the renunciation of the instincts, particularly those relating to the Oedipus complex. At the dawn of human history, a group of brothers had conspired to kill the primal father because he denied them the satisfaction of their instincts. They did so, but realised such an act must never happen again. How, though, were future generations to control the aggression that had led to that first murder? One solution was to direct it towards those who did not belong to one's immediate society. Could this be one explanation for the artist's hostility to the reading public, which is one aspect of modernist culture?

A second solution was to internalise violent impulses so that they did not disrupt the social bond. The little boy must suppress his anger at his father for fear of repeating the primal crime. He does so by turning that anger on himself. It takes the form of guilt for his harbouring forbidden desires for his mother. Freud explained the process in detail in *Civilisation and its Discontents* (1930), where he describes the mind as divided into the id, the ego and the super-ego, or 'conscience'.

Freud suggests that first we renounce our instincts (the id) because we fear the father will punish us, and this creates a separate sense of self (the ego), which is policed by the super-ego (the authority of the father) which punishes us with a sense of guilt because, of course, we continue to have prohibited desires. Because it is founded on the renunciation of instinct, civilisation does not bring us pleasure or satisfaction. The fact that it is maintained by the super-ego's constant watchfulness, its constant criticism of the ego, which is also under pressure from the id, does not make civilisation any easier to bear, but it is better than the free-for-all which would ensue should it crumble.

Freud's account of the origins of civilisation is a reminder of how important myth is to the modern sensibility, but the real significance of his theory lies perhaps in the fact that it appears at almost the same time as mass consumerism. Psychoanalysis is above all an account of why desire can never be satisfied. It explains why we always want (and feel that we *need*) more, and that makes it the perfect ally of a system that teaches us never to be satisfied with what we have.

If Darwin, Marx, Nietzsche and Freud were making those who thought about things revise their views on human nature, history and philosophy, developments in science were also showing them that reality was not what they imagined. Ernest Rutherford (1871–1937) had shown that the atom was not, as previously believed, a tiny but solid structure. It was, instead, mostly empty space with a cloud of electrons orbiting the nucleus in the way that the planets go round the stars.

Rutherford's discovery paved the way for quantum physics where subatomic particles behave in an apparently magical fashion. They can pop in and out of existence. It is possible to calculate their speed but not their position, or their position but not their speed. Perhaps the most hair-raising characteristic of the quantum world, though, is that it depends on our observation. Erwin Schrödinger (1887–1961) devised a famous thought experiment to illustrate this point. He asked us to imagine a cat in a box with a vial of poison. The cat, according to the details of this theory, is both dead and alive. It is only when we open the lid and observe the creature that the quantum wave collapses and we have either a live or a dead cat. If that is hard to understand, don't worry. Niels Bohr (1885–1962), one of the pioneers in the field, remarked that anyone who was not shocked by quantum theory has not understood it, while the great physicist Richard Feynman (1918–88) declared that nobody understands quantum physics.

The idea that an object or an organism exists in a state of different potential realities until it is observed, finds an expression in art. As one critic of Virginia Woolf's first published novel, *The Voyage Out* (1915), notes, 'two worlds exist simultaneously: an everyday world of facts where one can plan to marry, take sea voyages, live and die, and an inner world where those events have a different significance and even a different meaning.'[17] It's a similar story in some cubist paintings, where the object is presented from all points of view at the same time. This is intended to give us a more complete picture of, say, a guitar, but it does so at the cost of making it difficult to identify the instrument. Art follows science in making the world strange.

The Aesthetic Movement

It may seem strange to start this section with the German philosopher Immanuel Kant (1724–1804) since he was not part of the Aesthetic Movement either in France or England. Moreover, he was an extremely serious man whereas the English aesthete prided himself on his frivolity. Nevertheless, it is Kant's views on art that provide the intellectual basis for the slogan 'art for art's sake'.

According to Kant, the human being is endowed with three faculties: the faculty of pure reason (understanding), the faculty of practical reason (morality) and the faculty of the aesthetic (appreciation). The aesthetic faculty is different from the other two because it cannot be wholly supported by reference either to reason or to the world. It also contains a contradiction, or what Kant calls an 'antinomy'.

This takes the following form. My perception of beauty is immediate, it is not based on concepts of beauty. If it were, then my perception of beauty would be open to discussion. At the same time, I do not believe that what I perceive as beautiful pleases only me for, after all, I am speaking about the work and not about myself. Hence I seek to justify my opinion with reasons based on whatever it is about the work that strikes me as beautiful.

How does Kant reconcile these opposing views? By pointing out that when we contemplate a work of art, we suspend all our habits and inclinations, all our aims and preferences. If we do not, then we cannot see the work clearly. What's more, if we look at it in the light of our own interests then we are treating it as a means to an end rather than as an end in itself. When we look at the art work as an end in itself, we are looking at it as others too should look at it – from the point of view of reason rather than from the point of view of our likes and dislikes – and since reason is common to all, then we should all agree that what one finds beautiful, all find beautiful.

The free play of imagination is crucial to our contemplation of the work. This means that we neither foist interpretations upon it nor apply it to the real world. What we do instead is attend to its form, which Kant describes as 'purposiveness without purpose'. In other words the work has shape and structure but no specific use. At this point, Kant's theory becomes very complicated.

He argues that the formal organisation of a work is not so much a quality of the work itself as of our perception of it. We experience its unity because our imagination brings our sense of the work under the indeterminate concept of unity, indeterminate in the sense that the concept of unity applies to many other things apart from this particular art work. For example, if I see a set of marks as a pattern, then I bring that set of marks under the concept of 'pattern', a term which is indeterminate because it can be used of so many other sets of marks apart from those in this particular work.

Therein lies the power of the art work: it is at once particular and universal. The English philosopher Roger Scruton (b. 1944) gives an example of how this works in John Milton's *Paradise Lost* (1667): 'When Milton expresses the vengeful feelings of Satan, his smouldering words transport us. We feel that we are not listening to this or that contingent emotion but to the very essence of revenge.'[18]

Kant's claim that the work of art has no practical role to play in society feeds into the Aesthetic Movement, which also denied that art has any utility. His characterisation of the art work as purposiveness without purpose focuses attention on the form of the work, which was the principal interest of the high modernists. Finally, his implied claim that we help to create the work anticipates how readers of, say, Eliot's *The Waste Land* must piece together its different parts to make it whole. However, Kant is also distanced from the modernists, partly by his faith in his reason but chiefly because his vocabulary, in particular the terms 'beauty' and 'sublime', have become outmoded. Even the word 'art' is regarded with suspicion. Marcel Duchamp's *Fountain* (1917), a urinal labelled 'R.Mutt', seems to suggest that anything can be art.

The Aesthetic Movement began in the 1860s and died out in the 1890s after the publicity surrounding the writer Oscar Wilde's trial and his subsequent arrest for gross indecency.* The main people involved in the movement, apart from Wilde, were Walter Pater (1839–94), Algernon Swinburne (1837–1909) and James Abbott McNeill Whistler (1834–1903). The movement was a reaction to the Victorian belief that art should be moral. Its proponents argued that art had its own value which had nothing to do with whether it promoted good or bad behaviour. As Wilde put in his Preface to *The Picture of Dorian Gray* (1891): 'There is no such thing as a moral or an immoral book. Books are well written or badly written. That is all.'[19]

---

* Wilde had brought a case of criminal libel against the Marquess of Queensberry, who had accused the playwright of being a homosexual. The trial collapsed after the defence threatened to bring boy prostitutes to the stand to testify against Wilde and his influence over Queensberry's son, Lord Alfred Douglas. Sentenced to two years hard labour, Wilde emerged a broken man, and died in 1900 at the age of forty-six.

The claim that art was autonomous, that its value resided in itself rather than in any effect it produced, helped shape the modernist view that art had its own sphere of existence. The Aesthetic Movement also bequeathed to modernism its propensity to exclusiveness and elitism. The author and cartoonist George du Maurier (1834–96) satirised this tendency in the pages of *Punch* magazine.* In one issue a young man boasts of how his new acquaintances 'consider me alone to combine, in my own mind and person, Supreme Consummateness with Consummate Supremacy – and I agree with them. We get on uncommonly well together, I can tell you.'[20] The word 'consummate' was frequently used to maintain the aesthete's sense of superiority over his fellow mortals. Other words that served the same purpose were 'blessed', 'precious' and 'utter'. We can hear a faint echo of this attitude in the expressions used by characters in Noel Coward's (1899–1973) plays: 'too divine', 'too tiresome', 'perfectly marvellous', 'most frightful', 'thank you a *thousand* times' and so on.

Another aspect of the Aesthetic Movement which feeds into modernism is the courting of publicity. Aesthetes lived in a highly ostentatious manner. They wore extravagant clothes, adopted exaggerated poses, revered blue china and made a cult of the sunflower. Their work was also highly provocative. Swinburne's *Poems and Ballads* (1866) took as their subject illicit love, blasphemy and sensual indulgence, and he was dubbed by John Morley, a Member of Parliament, as 'the libidinous laureate of a pack of satyrs'.[21]

Nearly thirty years before the controversy surrounding the Post-Impressionist exhibition of 1910,† John Ruskin (1819–1900), Victorian Britain's most respected art critic, described Whistler as a coxcomb who had flung a pot of paint in the public's face. Ruskin was referring to Whistler's *Nocturne in Black and Gold: The Falling Rocket* (1874). The

---

* A weekly magazine of humour and satire published from 1841 to 1992 and from 1996 to 2002.

† Post-Impressionism is a catch-all term for particularly French painting from about 1880 to about 1912. The main artists were Paul Gauguin (1848–1903), Paul Cezanne (1839–1906) and the Dutch artist Vincent Van Gogh (1853–90). Their paintings were quite different but they shared an interest in form rather than content and used colour as an expression of emotion. See Part Three: 'The Modernist Novel in England' and Part Four: 'Modernism and its Critics' for more on this exhibition.

painting is mostly grey black with a splash of yellow and a little spray of gold. It is clearly not in the tradition of moral or realistic painting, and that is why Ruskin took exception to it. When Whistler read Ruskin's comment he sued him for libel. The jury found in his favour but they only awarded him a farthing damages.

The case dramatised the clash between the old and the new, between English tradition and French technique and between art that was serious and art that was playful. It also raised the question of what effect the new mass circulation magazines and newspapers had on art. As artists began to feel more and more marginalised, as they began to feel that their work was increasingly removed from the concerns of wider society, did they feel the need to do something that would put them in the public eye?

From Swinburne's poetry to Duchamp's urinal, modernist art aimed to shock and provoke, but can art that is intended to do that have any real value? Certainly the aesthetes produced little of lasting significance. Wilde is the exception, but we remember him as much for his personality as for his plays. Perhaps the importance of the aesthetes lies more in what they had to say about art rather than in their actual art itself.

Pater said that we can never see the work of art as it really is, all we have are our impressions of it. In making this statement, he has in mind the poet and critic Matthew Arnold's (1822–88) declaration that the aim of criticism is to see the object 'as in itself it really is'.[22] Pater was drawing upon the work of thinkers such as Herbert Spencer (1820–1903) and James Sully (1842–1923) who said that our knowledge of the external world comes through our sense impressions.*

They were also interested in the psychology of the aesthetic response. They argued that all human activity could be divided into two categories: the first goal orientated and the second undertaken for its own sake. It was in this category that the aesthetic response belonged. Kant might have agreed with that but not with Pater's key question about art: 'What is this song or picture ... to me?'[23]

---

* This idea goes back to the philosopher John Locke (1632–1704) and can be found in his *An Essay Concerning Human Understanding* (1689): 'Whence has [the mind] all the materials of reason and knowledge? To this I answer, in one word, from EXPERIENCE.'

Pater's account of aesthetic response begins with the observation that both the physical and the mental world are in a constant state of flux. When we reflect upon either an object or a thought we are left only with our impressions, which 'are in perpetual flight' (p. 152). Because our impressions are so fleeting, it is incumbent on us not to let them pass without realising them as fully as possible. It is by attending to our impressions, sifting and clarifying them, that we become more alert, more alive. 'Not to discriminate every moment some passionate attitude in those about us, and in the very brilliancy of their gifts some tragic dividing of forces on their ways, is, in this short day of frost and sun, to sleep before evening' (p. 153). The role of art in this, according to Pater, is not to educate, it is not to entertain, it is 'to give the highest quality to your moments as they pass' (pp. 153–4).

The key word in Pater's criticism is 'impression'. It is related to living in the city. The crowds, the traffic, the shops, the advertisements and the street vendors all compete for attention. There is no time to dwell on any one sight or sound, we simply move through a blizzard of impressions. This is also connected to another aspect of city life: loneliness. The move from the country to the city involved the break-up of small communities and people living side by side with strangers. Our impressions, says Pater, are the impressions of the individual 'in his isolation, each mind keeping as a solitary prisoner its own dream of a world' (p. 152).

What of Pater's influence? He was not the first to note that modern art was based on the ephemeral, the fleeting and the contingent. That distinction goes to Charles Baudelaire, whose work we look at in Part 3: 'Modernist Poetry – French Origins, English Settings'. But Pater does develop Baudelaire's observation, and the problem of arresting the fugitive moment, of giving substance to the passing impression, is something that also preoccupies Woolf. She is indebted to Pater for her sense that the self is elusive, fleeting and profoundly alone.

Pater could also be seen as an apostle for obscurity, one of the key characteristics of modernist art. If what Pater said was true, that everyone was cut off from everyone else by their own impressions, then any expression of feeling is bound to appear obscure to the audience. It was in precisely these terms that Pater described the work of the painter and poet Dante Gabriel Rossetti (1828–1882): 'His own meaning was always personal, and even recondite ... sometimes complex and obscure [but his words] were always the just transcript of that peculiar phase of soul, which he alone knew, as he alone knew it.'[24]

In conclusion, we can say that the Aesthetic Movement raised all kinds of question about art that modernists would also pose. What is it? Is it form or content? Should it have a role in society? Can only certain people appreciate it? There were no answers to these and other questions, but the search for them was what gave modern art its energy and identity.

Notes

1   E. M. Forster, 'What I Believe' in S. P. Rosenbaum (ed.), *A Bloomsbury Group Reader* (Oxford: Blackwell, 1993), pp. 164–72, pp. 166, 170.
2   Gilbert Seldes, 'Tojours Jazz' in Steven Matthews (ed.), *Modernism: A Sourcebook* (Basingstoke: Palgrave, 2008), pp. 203–5, p. 204.
3   Wyndham Lewis, 'Blast' (1914) in Vassiliki Kolocotroni, Jane Goldman and Olga Taxidou (eds), *Modernism: An Anthology of Sources and Documents* (Edinburgh: Edinburgh University Press, 1998), pp. 291–4, p. 292.
4   Robert Hughes, *The Shock of the New: Art and the Century of Change* (London: Thames and Hudson, 1991), p. 14.
5   Frederick Winslow Taylor, *The Principles of Scientific Management* (New York: Harper Row, 1911). The entire text, from which all quotations are taken, can be found online at www.marxists.org/reference/subject/ economics/taylor/principles/index.htm.
6   Cited in John Carey, *The Intellectuals and the Masses: Pride and Prejudice among the Literary Intelligentsia 1880–1939* (London: Faber, 1992), p. 5.
7   Cited in Robert Hughes, *The Shock of the New*, p. 51.
8   Filippo Marinetti, 'Manifesto of Futurism' in Vassiliki Kolocotroni et al. (eds), *Modernism: An Anthology of Sources and Documents*, pp. 251–3, p. 251.
9   Cited in Robert Hughes, *The Shock of the New*, p. 48.
10   Karl Marx and Frederick Engels, *Marx and Engels: Selected Works* (London: Lawrence and Wishart, 1973), pp. 35–6.
11   Karl Marx and Frederick Engels, *The German Ideology* edited by C. J. Arthur (London: Lawrence and Wishart, 1996), p. 18.

12   Marx and Engels, *Selected Works*, p. 181.
13   Ibid., p. 96.
14   Ibid.
15   Friederich Nietzsche, *Twilight of the Idols* translated by Duncan Large (Oxford: Oxford University Press, 1998), pp. 8, 60.
16   Ibid., p. 28.
17   Susan Rubinow Gorsky, *Virginia Woolf*, 'Twayne's English Authors Series' (Boston, MA: Twayne, 1989), p. 36.
18   Roger Scruton, *Kant: A Very Short Introduction* (Oxford: Oxford University Press, 2001), p. 108.
19   Oscar Wilde, Preface to *Dorian Gray* in Ian Small (ed.), *The Aesthetes: A Source Book* (London: Routledge, 1979), pp. 100–1, p. 100.
20   Cited in 'Introduction' Ian Small, (ed.), *The Aesthetes: A Source Book*, p. xviii.
21   Cited in Josephine Guy (ed.), *The Victorian Age: An Anthology of Sources and Documents* (London: Routledge, 1998), p. 370.
22   Matthew Arnold, 'The Function of Criticism at the Present Time' in Peter Keating (ed.), *The Victorian Prophets: A Reader from Carlyle to Wells* (London: Fontana, 1981) pp. 183–201, p. 194.
23   Walter Pater, *The Renaissance* (Oxford: Oxford University Press, 1986), p. xxix.
24   Cited in 'Introduction' Ian Small (ed.), *The Aesthetes: A Source Book*, p. xx.

Part Three
Texts, Writers and Contexts

Modernist Poetry – French Origins, English Settings: Baudelaire, Mallarmé and the Georgians

There are two ways we can approach modernist poetry. The first is to trace its origins back to Charles Baudelaire (1821–67) whose *Les Fleurs du mal* (1857) has some claim to be regarded as the first collection of modernist verse. The second is to compare so-called traditional poetry with modernist verse. Both approaches complement each other and, in giving us different perspectives, help to clarify modernist poetry and give a sense of its complexity.

The first thing to note about *Les Fleurs du mal* is the title: 'The Flowers of Evil'. This does not accord with our usual idea of poetry, which is supposed to be that '"Beauty is truth, truth beauty" – that is all / Ye know on earth, and all ye need to know', as John Keats (1795–1821) famously said at the end of his 'Ode on a Grecian Urn' (1818).[1] We certainly do not find either of these qualities, nor indeed goodness, another key theme of poetry through the ages, in Baudelaire's 'Preface', the poem which opens the collection.

Thrills and Spectacle

We are preoccupied with 'sin', says Baudelaire, Satan is our puppet-master and we take pleasure in repugnant things.[2] The worst aspect of our nature is not lust, avarice or even cruelty, though we delight in all these, but *ennui* or boredom. It is the monotony of modern life, its tedium, that makes us seek out intense sensations which yet fail to give us any satisfaction. In 'Preface' Baudelaire gives us the image of the 'penniless rake who with kisses and bites / Tortures the breast of an old prostitute' (p. 53). It is a shocking picture of starved lust. The rake is torn between violence and desire; he kisses because he wants to enjoy, he bites because he cannot.

The search for thrills is not new. We can find it – as indeed we can find other aspects of modernism – in the romantics. Keats longed 'for a life of sensations rather than of thoughts'[3] and Byron stated that 'the great object of life is sensation, to feel that we exist, even though in pain'.[4] This preference for the body over the mind can be explained in a number of ways. One is a loss of faith in the Christian religion which taught that the soul was more important than the body.

Doubts about the bible were mostly the product of the educated mind. There had been a number of criticisms of Christianity during the eighteenth century. The philosopher David Hume (1711–76), for example, had argued that belief in miracles requires us to ignore the evidence of our senses which tell us that the blind cannot suddenly see or the dead come back to life. These attacks on Christianity were to intensify during the course of the nineteenth century with the work of the geologist Charles Lyell (1797–1875) and the naturalist Charles Darwin (1809–82). Lyell showed that the earth was much older than was suggested in the bible while Darwin showed that life had evolved, that it had not been created complete as was stated in the book of Genesis.

If the Christian account was not true, if life was arbitrary, then how was one to live? What, indeed, was the purpose of existence if there were no deity, no judgement, no heaven or hell? Why not simply enjoy oneself? Why not relish the senses? Saint Paul had said that 'if ye live after the flesh ye shall die: but if ye through the spirit do mortify the deeds of the body, ye shall live' (Romans 8:13). If Christianity was just a story then these injunctions could be ignored. The sights and sounds of the world could be a source of delight instead of guilt.

Others had a more lofty vision of human endeavour. Both the

American Revolution (1775–83) and particularly the French Revolution (1789–99) suggested that human beings might make their own paradise here on earth if they altered their political systems. The rights of man, the pursuit of life, liberty and happiness were simply a matter of having the right form of government, but the issue of slavery in America and the Terror in France showed that the rhetoric of freedom and equality fell far short of the reality. Consequently people may have lost their ambition to create the perfect human society and settled for the cultivation of their senses instead.

The American and French revolutions may also have generated a taste for drama and spectacle. The violence in Paris and Napoleon's armies marching through Italy, Spain, Germany and even Russia created a sense of excitement as well as fear. The beginnings of industry and the spread of revolutionary ideas spelt the end of old Europe. After such upheaval, people would find it difficult to return to their old ways. Revolution had a bred a desire for constant change and this too may have contributed to the hunger for new sensation.[5]

The Influence of Romanticism and the Experience of Crowds

Baudelaire's attempt to find salvation in the senses can, then, be explained by wider developments, and while similar to what some English romantics were trying to achieve, it is not the same. One difference, apart from the fact that we are speaking of two separate literary traditions, lies in the conception of the poet. Broadly speaking, the romantic poets believed their powers of imagination set them apart from their audience. This was related to a tendency in some poets, for example William Wordsworth (1770–1850), to see themselves as teachers of mankind.

Baudelaire, by contrast, asserts a kinship with the reader –'brother mine' ('Preface', p. 29, l. 40). What they have in common is the 'hideous evil [of] Boredom' (ll. 33, 37). Baudelaire does not claim to teach his readers, merely to know them. He goads them into acknowledging their corruption, their shadow selves, their vagabond inclinations – and embracing them. Nothing is ever quite so straightforward, however. Alongside the poet as the intimate of the reader is another conception of him as an outcast. We see this most clearly in 'Benediction' where the poet embraces his outsider status because it ensures his place in heaven. This of course shows that Christianity is still a live issue in Baudelaire's verse, a point we return to below.

Another difference between Baudelaire and the English romantics is that, by and large, they thought of man in relation to nature while Baudelaire thinks of him in relation to the city. His Paris is composed of roaring streets populated by broken souls. The poet wanders through the city's winding folds, perhaps encountering a passer-by whose sudden glance bestows new life on him; but only for a moment, for she vanishes into the crowd, never to be seen again. Once again, though, it is not a simple matter of contrasts. The poetry of the English romantics sprang from their feelings and so too does Baudelaire's.

Baudelaire is fascinated by crowds. He discusses the artist's relation to them in *The Painter of Modern Life* (1859–60).[6] The poet's 'passion' (p. 105) is to shed his own self, to merge with the crowd, and move incognito through it. He also aims to be its 'mirror' (ibid.), reflecting the crowd in all its multiplicity.

Beauty is also imagined as a form of reflection. She – it appears to be a she – has 'mirrors pure which make all things on earth more beautiful' ('Beauty', *Selected Poems*, p. 53, l. 13). Beauty, it would appear from this, is no more than our image reflected back to us. It therefore has a narcissistic quality which prefigures the obsession with self in modernism.

We discuss beauty further below, but for now we should note that Baudelaire's description of the poet dispensing with his identity recalls Keats's notion of 'negative capability';[7] briefly that a poet should lose his sense of self so that he can more readily take on the identity of others. Again, though, the two things are not the same. Keats is thinking of becoming one with urns or nightingales, not with libertines, harlots or the multitude of common men.

However, the poet is doing something more than merely reflecting the crowd back to itself. He is also looking for that 'indefinable something we may be allowed to call modernity' (*Painter of Modern Life*, p. 106). The problem with contemporary painters, Baudelaire argues, is that they clothe their subjects in the dress of the past. They do so because they believe that it is more attractive than the present.

Baudelaire accuses them of being 'lazy' and says that it is the artist's job to find beauty in the modern world, no matter how 'ugly' – by conventional standards – it may appear (p. 107). He defines modernity as 'the transient, the fleeting and the contingent' (ibid.). These characteristics constitute one half of art, the other being 'the eternal and the immoveable' (p. 103). The dual nature of art, Baudelaire concludes, is a reflection of the dual nature of man, an idea that goes back to the classical world.

Baudelaire tries to heal the divided self partly by eliminating the distance between himself and the reader, partly by disappearing into the crowd and partly by sexual liaisons. In particular he yearns to escape from the oppressive consciousness of self. 'Nothing is sweeter to a mournful soul', he writes in a poem called 'Mists and Rains', than 'On some chance bed to find oblivion' (*Selected Poems*, p. 177, l. 9). However, at the same time that Baudelaire declares that 'the ego is athirst for the non-ego' (*The Painter of Modern Life*, p. 105), he champions the cause of the dandy, who neither seeks love nor wants to be part of the crowd.*

Dandyism is not so much a delight in dress as a protest against triviality and the spread of democracy which threatens to extinguish originality and 'reduce everything to the same level' (p. 108). The dandy, though, is not the complete antithesis of those who want to blend with others, for his satisfaction lies in never revealing himself. By keeping his 'real' self hidden by pretending, indeed, that his appearance is his reality, the dandy never hints at the shattered identity that is such a feature of modern literature.

---

* A dandy is someone who pays a great deal of attention to his dress, manners, language and leisure pursuits. The dandy becomes an important figure in modernity because he – and it is usually a he – is a symbol of individualism in the creeping conformity of mass culture. For further information see Rosalind Williams, *Dream Worlds: Mass Consumption in Late Nineteenth Century France* (Berkeley: University of California Press, 1982).

Baudelaire and Christianity

The dandy is not a prominent figure in *Les Fleurs du mal*, whose presiding spirit is a poetic persona deeply troubled by desire. The volume is divided into different parts, but the section entitled 'Spleen and Ideal' captures its basic dynamic, that though we are still mired in sin, yet we strive for salvation. This basic Christian theme is made more complex by Baudelaire's attraction to what is evil. 'Satan, I worship thee' he cries in 'Possessed' (*Selected Poems*, p. 83, l. 14). He longs for death, for his corpse to be ravished by worms (p. 64) rather than for his soul to fly to heaven.

As in Christian tradition women are viewed by Baudelaire as temptresses, but that very quality, which is what should make him avoid them, is what attracts him. In 'Sed non Satia' ('Never Satisfied') Baudelaire describes a demonic woman in terms usually reserved for God's grace or Christ's entry to Jerusalem. He talks, for example, of her providing 'manna' (p. 69, l. 6) – the bread which God to gave to the Israelites in the wilderness and which later becomes the bread Jesus breaks with his disciples – for his desires.

Baudelaire also hails her lips as 'love's hosanna' (l. 5). In Hebrew, the term means 'please save' and in Christianity it is a cry of praise or adoration. It was used, for example, when Jesus entered the gates of Jerusalem. When we start to think about lips as places of entry, then we begin to realise just how shocking Baudelaire's connection between Christ and the 'Black sorceress' (l. 4) really is. It is very sexual.

So what are we to make of this? Baudelaire is using the signs and symbols of Christianity to negotiate the experience of modernity. He does not use them in a conventional way but inverts their meanings to capture the complexity of contemporary life where it is not so easy to distinguish between good and evil. Sex with the courtesan is the metaphor for communion with the spiritual. That Baudelaire invests women with divinity is seen very clearly in 'To a Madonna' (p. 114) where he wants to build an altar to his mistress and worship her like the Virgin Mary.

Similarly in 'Moesta et Errabunda' ('Grieving and Wandering'), the poet hopes that 'Agatha' can transport him to a 'fragrant paradise' beyond the sea (p. 121, l. 13). Here we touch another theme that finds its way into modernist art and literature, namely the desire to encounter the exotic other, the native living in harmony with nature, contact with whom can revitalise our relationship with our senses which have been dulled by the artificial environment of the city.

The key point, though, is that Baudelaire is working within a symbolic tradition, Christianity, that does not, in the end, quite connect with the contemporary world. Part of the reason for this, as we saw earlier, is that belief in Christianity had declined. At the same time, though, its images and idioms enjoyed a kind of 'after-life', because new forms of expression had not yet emerged.

Poets therefore had to rely on the terminology of a religion that suited the past but not the present. They could either adapt it, as Baudelaire does, or move beyond it, which Baudelaire also does. Phantoms, deserts, oceans, machines, jewels, funerals and even scents are evoked to capture and convey 'the transient, the fleeting and the contingent'.

These and other symbols are used in an attempt to reach some ultimate reality and to transcend the divide in modern man. Symbols speak in 'mystic languages', says Baudelaire in 'Correspondences', uniting infinity with the immediacy of the smell of 'amber' or 'incense' (p. 42, l. 10). They fuse soul and sense, creating a new being, no longer torn between 'good' and 'evil'. Baudelaire's experiment with symbols paves the way for Stéphane Mallarmé's more detailed thinking about the subject. We will come to him shortly.

Beauty

Baudelaire may retain the Christian concept of salvation, albeit in a strange form, but he is also bent on finding beauty in the modern world. In this respect his work marks a mid point between the conventional nineteenth century pursuit of beauty and the modernist rejection of it. Baudelaire's beauty comes close to the 'ugliness' that will be a deliberate feature of much modernist art with its rejection of harmony, proportion and balance.

Baudelaire identifies two forms of beauty, abstract and concrete. However, the distinction is purely formal since they are closely associated – the 'snow-cold heart' (p. 53, l. 6) of the abstract conception of beauty in 'Beauty' chimes with the 'icy majesty' of the concrete conception of beauty in 'Clad in her undulating pearly dress' (p. 70, l. 14). Furthermore, both forms of beauty serve the same function: to transport the poet to a temporary paradise or to grant him temporary oblivion.

We see beauty in the abstract in the aforementioned 'Beauty'. This beauty is 'a reverie of stone' and 'a sphinx not understood' (p. 54, ll. 1, 5). Her 'snow-cold heart' combines with a commitment to the perfection of form since she abhors 'any action which may displace a line' (l. 7). This is an early pointer to what will become a central feature of modernist art: the alliance of formal complexity with intellectual difficulty.*

The beauty depicted in the poem of the same name is rather odd. It is more of an enigma than a display of loveliness. Poets will 'waste their days considering its true significance' (l. 11). The mysterious nature of beauty is the subject of 'Hymn to Beauty', in which the poet cannot decide if it comes from 'the dark gulf or the stars' (p. 57, l. 9). In the end, it doesn't matter whether beauty derives from 'Satan or God, seraph or fiend' (l. 25), what counts is that it makes 'the world less grim, time faster fly' (l. 28).

This is a good example of how Baudelaire moves beyond conventional Christian ideas of comfort to aesthetic ones. Art makes life more bearable, partly because it makes it go more quickly; it hastens the approach of death. Here we come across another latent tendency that will become manifest in modernism, the centrality of art to mediating our experience of the contemporary world.

---

* Examples of this in fine art include Marc Chagall's *Self-Portrait with Seven Fingers* (1913) or Alberto Giacometti's sculpture, *Woman with her throat cut* (1932).

Baudelaire's linking of beauty and death belongs to the dark side of the romantic tradition, as does his mixing of good and evil. Some elements of this tradition find their way into modernist poetry. The desolate landscape, for example, is at the heart of T. S. Eliot's *The Waste Land* (1922), which will be discussed in the next chapter. In general, though, the modernists value art not because it hurries us into oblivion but because it repairs culture, revives the individual or gives insight into life.

We mentioned that Baudelaire considers there to be two kinds of beauty, abstract and concrete. An example of the latter occurs in 'Hair' (p. 60). The speaker in the poem is transported by the dark tresses of his lover to the far continents of Asia, Africa and, eventually, to the 'boundless heaven[s]' (l. 22). Baudelaire focuses on the scent of hair in another poem, 'The Perfume' (p. 85), which restores to the speaker the beauty of past delights. In 'The Living Flame' (p. 93), he praises the woman's eyes which guide his step 'towards the Beautiful' and 'sing' of his 'Resurrection' (ll. 6, 12).

Although the speaker mentions various aspects of a woman's beauty, her hair, eyes and perfume, we never get a clear sense of her physical presence. It is true that these and other poems that deal with beauty are 'concrete' compared to the more 'abstract' ones on the same theme, but they nevertheless fail to give us a fully realised picture of the woman concerned. Parts of her, 'arms, legs, buttocks and loins' ('The Jewels', p. 235) stand for the whole of her without her ever being a 'whole' person.

Baudelaire and the Transformation of Life into Art

Indeed, Baudelaire's women are less like people than like functionaries who precipitate him into heaven or hell – the difference is almost immaterial since each allows him to escape, momentarily, the crushing burden of *ennui*, the feeling of death in life. The transformation of people into functionaries is not confined to poetry. Something similar happens in the factory where each worker is treated as if he or she were a machine.

We looked at this phenomenon when we discussed scientific management in Part Two: 'A Cultural Overview', and it is a part of the 'dehumanisation' that is integral to modernity. In very simple terms it means the individual must be sacrificed to the system. Something similar happens in much of the literature of the early twentieth century where there is less interest in human content than in artistic form.

This interest certainly goes back to Baudelaire. He dedicated *Les Fleurs du mal* to Théophile Gautier (1811–72). Gautier, like Baudelaire, dreaded *ennui*. 'Sooner barbarity than boredom', he is reputed to have declared on one occasion. Gautier coined the phrase 'art for art's sake' which, as we have seen, is the philosophy underlying the Aesthetic Movement in late nineteenth century England (see Part Two: 'A Cultural Overview'). Baudelaire's view of beauty is close to Gautier's understanding of art for both men believe that it should have nothing to do with the practical affairs of the world.

It was an object of contemplation, a means of refining consciousness, a gateway to another realm, anything that was not socially useful or ethically improving. Although this conception of art is most often associated with aestheticism and modernism, we can find hints of it in romanticism, for example Keats's 'Ode on a Grecian Urn' where the work of art is preferred to real life because it is beautiful and because it does not disappoint or decay.

What, then, is Baudelaire's legacy for modernist poetry? He explores the seamy side of life, he portrays the fragmented self, he mixes up good and evil, he moves away from conventional ideas of beauty, he works towards symbolic forms of expression and he looks to art as a form of redemption or transcendence. This list is not exhaustive and some of the things mentioned can, as we have seen, be traced back to romanticism, particularly its dark or gothic side. Baudelaire's depiction of women as destroyers of men has affinities with Keats's 'La Belle Dame Sans Merci' (1820). It is worthwhile remembering these connections because then the advent of French ideas into English poetry does not seem so novel or so innovative.

Baudelaire did not make many formal innovations that could be said, nevertheless, to contribute to modernism. The difficulty in reading him is not so much with his style as his subject matter. The poems have a formal clarity which contrasts with the complexity of their themes. This relationship between form and content changes as we move into modernism. That is to say, the form of the work becomes as complicated, if not more so, than the content.

Towards Modernism

Stéphane Mallarmé (1842–98), along with Paul Verlaine (1844–96), are key figures in developing the modernist poetic. An early indication of what this involves is apparent in Verlaine's poem 'Art Poétique' (1874).[8] Where Baudelaire's focus is mostly on subject matter, Verlaine's is on language. He doesn't want poetry to represent the world, he wants it to transport us to a spiritual realm.

One way in which this is achieved is by abandoning rhyme, which always 'rings false' and the 'wrongs' of which are many ('Art Poétique', p. 173, ll. 5, 28). Verlaine, by the way, does not practise what he preaches. Rhymes abound in his verse. Leaving that to one side, though, his key demand is that it should be 'musical' (l. 1).

Mallarmé elaborates some of Verlaine's points in *Crisis in Poetry* (1896).[9] He says that poetry should not describe, but evoke, allude and suggest. He advocates this manner of proceeding because he believes that the diversity of languages – English, French, Italian, German and so on – can only capture a part of Truth not the whole of it.

Because most of us are fluent in only one language, we are constantly in danger of thinking that our account of Truth is the same as that in every other tongue when, clearly, says Mallarmé, it is not. If we are to approach truth, poetry must become more like music. The sounds of words, their harmony, are more important in Mallarmé's aesthetic than their sense.

Mallarmé is not as hostile to rhyme as Verlaine claims to be. He recommends that we continue to respect the French classical tradition of which rhyme is so integral a part. There are, however, two problems. The first is 'extinction', the second is 'repetition' (p. 123). One period's conception of rhyme is different to another's so a rhyme that is current at one time may disappear in another – a great loss if the poetry has other significant features.

Equally, as there are only a limited number of rhyme schemes, the same ones keep reappearing, particularly the alexandrine, a prominent part of French verse.* Because of these problems, Mallarmé wanted to break free of rhyme just as he wanted to break free from poetry that refers to the world.

What, then, does he put in its place? We have already seen that he doesn't want poetry to describe but to suggest. In part, he wants it to suggest the object of the poem, that is, what the poem is about. Most of the pleasure in reading poetry, he argues, comes from guessing what object it is alluding to.† The poet isn't just evoking the object of the poem, whatever that may be, he is also distilling its essence. He does this by establishing a relation between two images 'from which a third element, clear and fusible, will be distilled and caught by our imagination' (p. 125).

It is difficult to give an example of this rather esoteric account of how poetry works because it is something we experience rather than know. We can sense it, but not point to it. If a poem does not name its object then it certainly won't name the essence of that object. Having said that, though, the interested reader may like to look at 'All Summarised the Soul'[10] where we have lips, cigar smoke and the soul. Mallarmé refuses to say what the relation between them is because 'Meaning too precise is sure / To void your dreamy literature' (ll. 13–14). Nevertheless, we can speculate that the third element may have something to do with the soul. In chemistry, the word 'element' means a substance which cannot be resolved into another substance, and the same applies to the soul.

---

* The alexandrine is the heroic French verse form, used in epic narrative, in tragedy and in the higher comedy. There is some doubt as to the origin of the name; but most probably it is derived from romances, collected in the twelfth century, of which Alexander of Macedon was the hero, and in which he is represented, somewhat like the British King Arthur, as the pride and crown of chivalry. It is a line of twelve syllables divided into two equal parts. An example in English would be: 'I am, my dear friend, very happy to see you'.

† A slightly different version of this idea, incidentally, crops up in Virginia Woolf's *The Waves* (1931), where one of the characters, Neville, remarks that 'nothing should be named lest by doing so we change it'. See further discussion of this book in Part Three: 'The Modernist Novel in England'.

The evocative nature of poetry and the relation between its various parts bring it closer, in Mallarmé's eyes, to music. Verse and music were very closely connected in the ancient world so Mallarmé is, like Verlaine, returning poetry to its roots. He describes poets not as writing but as 'fluting', 'bowing' or 'drumming' (*Crisis in Poetry*, p. 124) and poetry as 'song', 'symphony' or 'orchestra'(pp. 126–7).

Poems are structured like pieces of music. Each theme has its own harmony, each sound its echo. The disposition of the parts, the way they balance one another, their similarities and differences all create a kind of melody. The effect of all this, evocation, relation and music, is to lift us up to heaven where we encounter the essence of things.

Mallarmé's theory of poetry is often obscure, making it difficult to summarise. Nevertheless, this quotation captures some of the important elements we have mentioned:

> When I say: 'a flower!' then from that forgetfulness to which my voice consigns all floral form, something different from the usual calyces arises, something all music, essence and softness: the flower which is absent from all bouquets.
>
> *Crisis in Poetry*, p. 127

We cannot cover all Mallarmé's ideas, although it would be fascinating to pursue some of his assertions. What, for example, does he mean when he says that all literature is simply an amalgamation of age-old truths? What does he mean when he claims that poetry fashions a single new word out of a number of words which is 'total to itself and foreign to the language – a kind of incantation' (p. 127)? On the one hand Mallarmé seems to be saying that poetry has nothing new to offer and on the other hand that it has.

What, though, did he contribute to modernism? There are at least three things. First he separates poetry from ordinary language, second he gives it a highly intricate structure and third he endows it with special powers. Mallarmé divides literary discourse from all other kinds. Many modernists follow his lead – drawing a clear boundary between art and life – and what makes art stand apart is its difficulty.

For Mallarmé poems do not describe, they do not express, they do not tell stories. They are symbols and these symbols are hard to understand. The reader must make the link between the different symbols and also attend to the silences as well as the sounds of the poem. By doing so he or she will come into contact with a higher reality of essences or pure form.

While modernists may not always refer to Mallarmé, his thinking often underpins their views of poetry. Arthur Symons (1865–1945) is credited with introducing French symbolism into England with *The Symbolist Movement in Literature* (1899). We can find there many of the ideas we have already found in Mallarmé, for example that the symbol is a sign of unseen reality. W. B. Yeats and T. S. Eliot were influenced by French symbolism and we will discuss their work in the next chapter. Now we need briefly to consider the kind of poetry being written in England before and during the modernist movement as this will help to bring it into relief.

English Poetry

In the early years of the twentieth century the main, but by no means the only figures in English poetry, were Thomas Hardy (1840–1928), A. E. Housman (1859–1936), Sir Henry Newbolt (1862–1938), Alfred Noyes (1880–1959), Edward Thomas (1878–1917) and, of course, Rudyard Kipling (1865–1936). Each represented different aspects of English verse.

Hardy was a poet of rural life but, more importantly, he represented a certain kind of sensibility, nostalgia, that would play little part in the modernist mentality. Even his titles reveal his characteristic backward glance, 'Reminiscences of a Dancing Man' (1909), 'Saint Launce's Revisited' (1914), 'At Lulworth Cove a Century Back' (1922) and so on.

There is, in Hardy, a sense of something passing, but not quite gone. Or perhaps it is reluctance to let things go. Poems such as 'The Haunter' (1914) show that the dead try to keep hold of the living just as in 'The Voice' (1912) the living try to keep hold of the dead. These highly personal poems are also a way of registering a wider cultural desire to cling to the certainties of the nineteenth century despite their having been undermined.

Geology and the theory of evolution had challenged Christian doctrine and the First World War had dealt a blow to the idea that history was progress. Matthew Arnold (1822–88), in 'Dover Beach' (1867), confronted the insecurity and uncertainty of the coming age and so too does Hardy. 'The Convergence of the Twain' (1912) is about the loss of the *Titanic*, the ship that was supposed to symbolise the new technological dawn, the liner in which we would sail into the future. On its maiden voyage, however, it hit an iceberg, and as it sank to the bottom of the ocean so too, in some minds, did the hopes for the new century. If one of the characteristics of the modern mind is a belief in the power of humans to shape their world then Hardy is definitely not modern. He sees the operation of fate at work in human affairs, 'the Immanent Will that stirs and urges everything'.[11] It is this force which fashioned the iceberg on which the *Titanic* came to grief.

Like Hardy, Housman writes about a rural life which is disappearing. Young men move from farming into the army or crime. Either way, they all die young. Housman shares Hardy's bleak view of existence. Our lives seem cursed. We are doomed to go astray and it is better not to think about things, just to 'laugh and be jolly'.[12] As also in Hardy, there is a strong sense of loss: the 'happy highways' where we went, and where we 'cannot come again' (p. 43, l. 8), as Housman so plaintively puts it in one of his most famous poems beginning 'Into my heart an air that kills'.

Although Hardy and Housman write about the rural world, it tends to be a backdrop for the dramas of life. Thomas is different. He attends to the natural world, its sights, its sounds, its smells. He is alert to sedge warblers, to celandines, to brooks and to nettles in the corner of the farmyard, but he does share with Hardy and Housman a sadness at change.

For a more robust view of life we must turn to Newbolt. Many of his poems celebrate English heroes. 'Drake's Drum' (1895), for example, recalls the defeat of the Spanish Armada and has Sir Francis Drake (?1540–96) say that, should England need him again, they only have to strike his drum and he will return. Newbolt's poems are mini history lessons, stirring evocations of famous battles in which England was victorious.

Newbolt is confident of Britain's right to rule. The speaker in 'A Ballad of John Nicholson' (1897) rebukes one of the leaders of the Indian mutiny with the words:

> Have ye served us for a hundred years
> And yet ye know not why?
> We brook no doubt of our mastery
> We rule until we die [13]

The native 'other' in Baudelaire and, indeed, Verlaine is seen as authentic and living a genuine life in contrast to the artifice and weakened nature of existence in modern civilisation, but, in Newbolt, he or she is a creature to be subdued.

Perhaps Newbolt's most famous poem is 'Vitaï Lampada' (1897; the title translates as 'torch of life'). It links a game of cricket with a battle in the desert. The young schoolboy, who is the last man in, is exhorted to '"Play up! play up and play the game!"' (p. 131, l. 24), words he himself uses years later to inspire the ranks as they are in danger of being overrun by some undisclosed enemy. The implication is that this enemy comprises all those insensible of the benefits of British rule.

Newbolt's poems are rarely read today. If they are, they tend to be dismissed as expressions of imperialism, but they form a useful contrast with modernist poetry, and not just because they rhyme and have a recognisable subject matter. By presenting a heroic view of the English past they encourage readers to take pride in their history, and this forges a sense of national unity. In modernist poetry, however, the focus is on the individual not the nation – wasn't it patriotism that had led to the horrors of the First World War?

Alfred Noyes was a virulent anti-modernist. He was not the only one. The editor of *Modern Poetry 1922–1934* accuses poets such as Eliot of ignoring the reader and of 'avoiding anything that savours of poetic language'.[14] Noyes wrote a poem called 'Art'[15] which is the very antithesis of the modernist use of the term. For example, it envisages the poet still being inspired by the Muse. It makes use of archaic terms such as 'ye' and its themes, for example the immortality of art, are entirely conventional.

Where Verlaine and Mallarmé wanted to make poetry more like music, Noyes wanted to make it more like sculpture. 'Take up the sculptor's tool! / Recall the gods that die / To rule in Parian* o'er the sky' ('Art', p. 15, ll. 55–7). Noyes is more akin to Hardy, Housman and Thomas than to Newbolt because he focuses on the gentle, pastoral side of English life. In poems such as 'A Song of Sherwood' (1906) and 'Shadows on the Downs' (1913) he signals his awareness that a certain way of life is vanishing, and that it is unclear what will replace it.

The most celebrated poet before the modernist revolution was Rudyard Kipling, the first English writer to win the Nobel prize. Again, he tends to be dismissed as an enthusiast for empire, but look at a poem like 'We and They' (1926) and you will soon see that Kipling did not regard Britain as the best or most 'civilised' nation on earth. He understood perfectly well that what is acceptable in one culture may not be so in another. In 'Mandalay' (1890) he portrays life in the East as better than life in the West.

However, Kipling also anticipates certain aspects of modernism, for example the use of common speech in poetry.† The pub conversation at the end of Eliot's 'A Game of Chess', part of *The Waste Land*,§ owes a great deal to Kipling poems such as 'Tommy' (1890), which is highly colloquial. There is also more than an echo of Kipling's 'The Ladies' in Eliot's 'Sweeney' poems. The difference is that Kipling's narrator is matter of fact about his sexual experiences whereas Eliot is repelled by Sweeney's and indeed those of other characters he writes about.

The rural theme was prominent in the five volumes of verse published between 1912 and 1922 known collectively as 'Georgian

---

* Parian relates to the Greek island of Paros famous for its white marble.
† For an example of Kipling's occasional modernist style see 'Epitaphs of War' (1919).
§ See the Extended Commentary in Part Three: 'Modernist Poetry – America, Ireland and England'.

poetry'. The series was edited by Edward Marsh (1872–1953) and published by Harold Monro (1879–1932), founder of the Poetry Bookshop and the *Poetry Review*, both still going strong.

The Georgians wrote mostly about nature but not in a particularly novel or striking way. These lines from James Stephens's (1882–1950) poem 'Check' (1916–17) are typical:

> The night was creeping on the ground;
> She crept and did not make a sound
> Until she reached the tree, and then
> She covered it, and stole again
> Long the grass beside the wall.[16]

The imagery is entirely conventional and there is no sense of an individual voice. Like many Georgian poems, it represents the spent force of the romantic tradition. There is no vision of nature here, no sense of its sublimity or its restorative powers.

Georgian poetry is also a celebration of England – its customs and countryside rather than its military glories. This comes across strongly in poems such as Rupert Brooke's (1887–1915) 'The Old Vicarage, Granchester' (1911–12) which contains the famous lines 'Stands the church clock at ten to three? / And is there honey still for tea?'[17] Monro's poem 'Weekend' (1916–17), extols the joy of escaping to a cottage in the country. It is seen as a haven from 'the careful clock … the officious train',[18] symbols of paid employment that cage the soul. The Georgian capacity to take delight in the ordinary activities of life is evident in poems such as Martin Armstrong's 'Miss Thomson Goes Shopping' (1920–2) which recounts her washing up, cleaning the grate, putting on her bonnet, searching for her basket and so on. It is a poem not merely devoid of drama but also of incident.

The celebrations of England should be seen in relation to the fair number of Georgian poems which deal with other lands. 'The Child and the Mariner' (1911–12) by William H. Davies (1871–1940) depicts abroad as a source of adventure which contrasts with the office bound existence that Monro chafes against. Similarly we find in Walter de La

Mare's (1873–1956) 'Arabia' (1911–12) a longing for a place where the senses can be indulged, where the body can take its pleasures in a guilt free fashion. These are the sort of sentiments that we found not just in Baudelaire, but also in Kipling. The conclusion we can draw from this is that though there are vast differences between English poets and their continental counterparts, there are also some continuities.

The focus on nature and England in Georgian poetry is due to a number of factors, the empire and the romantic tradition being prominent among them. There is also, as we have seen, a desire to escape from the city to the country. To that extent Georgian poetry was in flight from the key experience of modernity – urbanisation and its effects – and although there are some poems dealing with the First World War, that traumatic event goes largely unremarked.

Since Georgian poets did not engage with the problems of modern civilisation the way was opened for poets who would. In any case, writing within the exhausted idiom of romanticism, the Georgians simply did not have the linguistic or conceptual resources to negotiate the difficulties of contemporary culture.

Extended Commentary: Imagism

Imagism was a reaction to what Ezra Pound (1885–1972) called the 'doughy mess of Keats, Wordsworth, heaven knows what, fourth-hand Elizabethan sonority blunted, half-melted, lumpy'.[19] Its leading exponents, in the early days, were Pound, T. E. Hulme (1883–1917), F. S. Flint (1885–1960), Hilda Doolittle (H. D.) (1886–1961) and Richard Aldington (1892–1962). There were four Imagist anthologies, *Des Imagistes* (1914) and *Some Imagist Poets* (1915, 1916 and 1917) and their several prefaces outline the main aims of the 'movement', if we can use that term of a group that seemed more divided than united. Flint and Pound quarrelled over when Imagism began and the arrival of the cigar-smoking Amy Lowell (1874–1925) in 1914 precipitated an even more serious crisis. Her insistence on using the term Imagism to describe her own brand of free verse, known as 'polyphonic prose' (use of assonance, alliteration, rhythm, return of images etc.) so annoyed Pound that he left the movement.

Imagism was one of a number of poetic developments designed to revitalise English poetry. Others included Vorticism and Futurism. These two are difficult to distinguish because they both celebrated violence, energy and the machine. The situation becomes even more complicated when we realise that Pound was an Imagist and a Vorticist, indeed he gave the latter movement its name. The vortex was the centre of energy that was to blast away the complacency of established tradition.

The basic aim of the Imagists was to present, as clearly as possible, an image which also conveyed the poet's feelings. Here's an example from Aldington's poem 'Images' (1914):

> The flower which the wind has shaken
> Is soon filled again with rain:
> So does my heart slowly fill with tears
> Until you return[20]

It would be mistaken to see the image as a symbol of the poet's feelings. Although the early Imagists claimed to be influenced by French Symbolists, particularly in respect of poetry as a form of music, the two movements were quite different from one another. The image directly portrays the object whereas the symbol merely alludes to it. The image defines, the symbol suggests; the image deals with the real, the symbol with the ideal.

Pound thought that Imagists and Symbolists were similar to the extent that they both believed in art as an expression of the individual; though of course this was also a key tenet of romanticism. However, Pound also sought to differentiate Imagism from Symbolism. Contrary to the notion expressed above, Pound claimed symbols have a fixed value while images have a variable one. Mallarmé would have disagreed. The high priest of Symbolism took great pains to argue that the symbol works by suggestion, evocation and allusion. The idea that it is like a mathematical sign would have been wholly alien to him.

The 'Preface' to *Some Imagist Poets 1916* notes that Imagism was more concerned with how something is presented rather than with what is presented. It was an attempt to revolutionise poetic form not content. Flint stipulated a number of rules that imagists should follow in composing their verse: 'direct treatment of the thing', no superfluous words and composing 'in sequence of the musical phrase, not in sequence of the metronome' (*Imagist Poetry*, p. 129). This third guideline was an attack on rhyme. Flint thought it artificial, a form imposed on the object, when it is the poet's job to render in words its natural form.

These basic guidelines were fleshed out by Pound, culminating in his famous definition of the image as 'that which presents an intellectual and emotional complex in an instant of time' (p. 130). The presentation of this complex frees the reader momentarily from the limitations of time and space with the result that he or she feels a sudden sense of growth, 'which we experience in the presence of the greatest works of art' (ibid.).

Imagist poems, however, do not conform to the rules laid down by Flint and Pound, partly because it is very difficult, if not impossible, to treat an object directly. One of the most famous imagist poems is Pound's 'In a Station of the Metro' (1913). It consists of two lines, comparing faces in a crowd on a wet day to petals on a branch (p. 95). The poem may not have any superfluous words but it does contain a comparison and a half rhyme (crowd/bough).

To compare is not to treat directly, while the half rhyme flouts Flint's third rule, and while many imagist poems do not rhyme, they do deploy metaphors and sometimes even similes. The moon is not the moon, it is the goddess Venus ('Evening', 1914, p. 58) or a petal ('Green', 1915, p. 84). Is saying that a rose is as hard like hail ('The Garden', 1915, p. 66) a direct treatment of the rose? Does it even convey a clear picture of the rose? The answer is no.

Pound's definition of the image as a fusion of intellect and emotion also has its problems. His demand that poets 'consider the way of the scientist' ('A Few Don'ts by an Imagiste', *Imagist Poetry*, p. 132) and his insistence on 'objectivity and again objectivity' (Letter to Harriet

Monroe, 1915, *Imagist Poetry*, p. 141) suggest that emotion is a distorting feature. He would respond to that charge by arguing that he wants a genuine rather than literary expression of emotion – an idea which again derives from romanticism. An emotion that is expressed in a poem, though, is by definition literary. Feeling is never immediate, it's always mediated.

Pound's claim that an image is an intellectual and emotional complex in an instant of time is also hard to sustain when we start examining some of the poetry. John Gould Fletcher's 'Irradiations' (1916), for example, is a long poem that contains not one but many images and it takes time to work out what they mean and how they relate to one another. Other poems, such as H. D.'s 'The Pool' (1917), do not present us with a clear image but rather a series of questions, so that not just the identity but also the significance of the image are constantly deferred.

Two further principles of the movement are mentioned in the 'Preface' to *Some Imagist Poets 1915*. The first is to use the language of common speech – to which we will come in a moment – and the second is absolute freedom of subject matter. It is rare, though, to find 'subject matter' substantially different from that found in the Georgian anthologies. The dominant topic is nature. How different to Baudelaire, for whom modernity was essentially an urban experience.

Even poems that take the city as their subject present it in terms of nature. Newspapers are compared to fragrant spring flowers in 'Spring Day' (1916, p. 88). This is an example of how imagist poets 'aestheticise' life, that is give it a value only in so far as it can be turned into art. Flint's poem 'Beggar' (1917) offers a succinct illustration. It turns destitution into beauty just as the beggar turns his bronze whistle into a 'silver' tune (p. 76). We admire the art at the expense of the reality, and this, in one form or another, is one of the features of some modernist literature. In place of raw contingency it puts the highly wrought aesthetic.

Let's not forget that the bulk of imagist poetry was published during the First World War, but there is barely any reference to it in the several anthologies. Those poets who do mention the war have a curiously distant attitude to it. We do not hear the whiz of bullets, or the cough of mortars, nor do we see soldiers drowning in gas or the wounded thrashing in no-man's land as we do in the poems of Wilfred Owen (1893–1918) or Siegfried Sassoon (1886–1967). They batter the senses whereas Flint and Aldington sooth them with tranquil images.

Thus, we encounter a faultline in the poetry of this period. Imagist poetry is technically innovative but traditional in subject matter while First World War poetry is technically traditional – Owen wrote sonnets – but its subject matter is highly contemporary. Why, though, despite its formal experimentation, is Imagism so conservative, even timid in its choice of topics?

One answer is that it is constrained by its relation to romanticism. The significance that, for example, Wordsworth attached to nature made it difficult for succeeding generations to focus on anything else. We noted above that one of the later principles of Imagism was to use ordinary speech and this echoes Wordsworth's aim, stated in his preface to the *Lyrical Ballads* (1798) to use 'the real language of men'.[21]

Mallarmé thought the opposite: poetry should be distinguished from common language because it is concerned with uncommon things, and, indeed, many writers shared his view. It is one source of the notorious 'difficulty' of modern art. If Imagists were committed to ordinary speech, however, some of them had a very peculiar notion of what that was. In Pound's 'Priapus' (1914, p. 61) for example, we find talk of being flayed by blossoms: not the sort of remark you would be likely to overhear in a pub, not even in 1914. Kipling captured the demotic (or everyday) far better than any Imagist. If they did manage to tone down the rather archaic diction then there was still the problem of their subject matter, touching as it did on the classical world.

This brings us, yet again, to Imagism's tangled relation to tradition. On the one hand its proponents declare they represent a new departure while at other times they claim to be merely reasserting the principles of good poetry throughout the ages. Hulme, writing in 1911, distinguished clearly between romanticism and classicism. The former assumes that man's nature is limitless and that he would be able to fulfil his infinite potential if only he could break free from the artificial restraints imposed by convention. The latter assumes that man's nature is fixed and that he is only able to achieve anything by virtue of custom, tradition and social organisation.

In literary terms, romanticism tends to be rather vague. It is not concerned with the here and now but with the beyond. The contrast between the frustrations of the present and the hoped for future fulfilment give romanticism a somewhat gloomy air. In many cases, complains Hulme, it is little more than the expression of an unsatisfied emotion. Unlike romanticism, classicism is based on recognising that there are limits to human aspiration. This means it focuses more on this world than on some fantasy realm, and, in doing so, it accurately describes what lies around us.

Here, in summary form, is the intellectual basis for Imagism. It is precise, controlled and definite. It does not squander words but uses them sparingly and to good effect. It gives a disciplined expression of emotion compared to the vaporous exhalations of romanticism. However, as we have already noted, Imagism bears more than a trace of romanticism within it. Two things can be said about this. First that Hulme presents a simplified picture of romanticism for polemical purposes and second that it is hard for any art to break completely with the past. Indeed, one of the themes of modernist literature is its relation to what went before and whether it should be preserved or discarded.

However, we shouldn't just look at Imagism in terms of its relation to tradition. We should also see it as symptomatic of certain developments in modern society, particularly advertising and scientific management. The logic of the image is the logic of the advertisement. Ideally both are short, striking and get their message over in an instant. Although Imagism seems to be rather remote from the business of ordinary life – see Pound's 'Ts'ai Chi'h' (1914, p. 95) with its falling petals – its very form echoes the jingle and the billboard. Imagism, in short, is part of the commercial idiom of consumption.

It also partakes of the logic of production. The emphasis on the method of writing poetry parallels the emphasis on the method of working that we found in scientific management (see Part Two: 'A Cultural Overview'). Frederick Winslow Taylor, whose 1911 book gave us the term, does not think that work should be a form of self-expression any more than the Imagist thinks that poetry should. Taylor is as impatient of tradition as Pound, and for the same reasons: it is wasteful. The worker must be retrained so that all his movements are as streamlined as those of a machine.

Pound said to would-be imagists: 'Use no superfluous word, no adjective, which does not reveal something' ('A Few Don'ts by an Imagiste', p. 131). This is the literary equivalent of removing all those actions that do not contribute to the efficient execution of a task, whether it be transporting pig iron or fitting a wheel on a Model T. Not only that, but the imagist poem also resembles a little machine. It has all the characteristics of the perfect mechanism. It is accurate, impersonal and all its parts are geared to one end.

Scientific management encapsulates one of the main characteristics of modernity, a concern with the means rather than the end. There is a retreat from the big questions of existence as public culture gives way to a mass culture more committed to entertainment than to disseminating and discussing the latest developments in the arts and sciences.

The space to raise questions about the nature of society, its structures, values and institutions, has shrunk. If there is little opportunity to discuss the ultimate ends and purpose of human society, then there is little left but to concentrate on maintaining, as efficiently as possible, its present state. Imagism, by being more concerned with technique than truth, by isolating the image instead of integrating it, by making the poem in the image of the machine, reflects this particular aspect of modernity.

Should this make the relation between Imagism and the wider society seem somewhat tenuous, consider Pound's 'The Garden', which berates the children of the unwashed poor (p. 95). Such an utterance expresses a vicious, anti-democratic prejudice that is also, unfortunately, one of the many facets of modernism. Artistic experimentation was not necessarily accompanied by political liberalism.

Notes

1   John Keats, *Selected Poems* (Harmondsworth: Penguin, 1999) pp. 167–9, p. 169, ll. 49–50.

2   Charles Baudelaire, 'Preface' to *Selected Poems* translated by Joanna Richardson (Harmondsworth: Penguin, 1975), pp. 27–9. Quotations from Baudelaire's poems in this chapter are from this edition.

3   John Keats, 'Letter' in Daniel G. Hoffman and Samuel Hynes (eds), *English Literary Criticism: Romantic and Victorian* (London: Peter Owen, 1966), p. 111.

4   Cited in Mario Praz, *The Romantic Agony* translated by Angus Davidson (Oxford: Oxford University Press, 1988), p. 74.

5   See George Steiner, *In Bluebeard's Castle: Some Notes Towards The Redefinition of Culture* (London: Faber, 1971) esp. pp. 17–27.

6   Quotations from this work are taken from the extract in *Modernism: An Anthology of Sources and Documents* eds Vassiliki Kolocotroni, Jane Goodman and Olga Taxidou (Edinburgh: Edinburgh University Press, 1998), pp. 102–9.

7   John Keats, 'Letter' in Peter Kitson (ed.), *Key Documents in Literary Criticism: Romantic Criticism* 1800–25 (London: Batsford, 1989) p. 103.

8   Paul Verlaine, *Selected Poems* translated by Joanna Richardson (Harmondsworth: Penguin, 1975), pp. 173–4.

9   Quotations from this work are taken from the extract in *Modernism: An Anthology of Sources and Documents* eds Kolocotroni et al., pp. 123–7.

10   This poem, and others, is available at www.poetryintranslation.com/PITBR/French/Mallarme.htm.

11   Thomas Hardy, *Selected Poetry* (Oxford: Oxford University Press, 1998), p. 73, l. 18.

12   A. E. Housman, *The Collected Poems* (London: Jonathan Cape, 1979), p. 53, l. 1.

13   Henry Newbolt, *Collected Poems 1897–1907* (London: Thomas Nelson and Sons, 1908), pp. 101–7, p. 105, ll. 55–8.

14   Maurice Wollman (ed.), *Modern Poetry: An Anthology 1922–1934* (London: Macmillan, 1939), p. viii.

15   Alfred Noyes, *Collected Poems: Volume 1* (Edinburgh: William Blackwood and Sons, 1925) pp. 13–16.

16   *Georgian Poetry 1916–17* (London: The Poetry Bookshop, 1917), p. 19, ll. 1–5.

17   *Georgian Poetry 1911–12* (London: The Poetry Bookshop, 1912), pp. 33–7, p. 37, ll. 126–7.
18   *Georgian Poetry 1916–17*, pp. 82–6, p. 86, verse 9, l. 6.
19   Cited in Frederick R. Karl, *Modern and Modernism: The Sovereignty of the Artist 1885–1925* (New York: Atheneum, 1985), p. 369.
20   Peter Jones (ed.), *Imagist Poetry* (Harmondsworth: Penguin, 2001), p. 47. All quotations of imagist poetry and prose are from this anthology.
21   William Wordsworth and Samual Taylor Coleridge, *Lyrical Ballads* (London: Routledge, 2007) p. 296.

Modernist Poetry – America, Ireland and England: Stevens, Williams, Yeats and Eliot

Modernism was an international movement. What happened in France affected English poetry. Part of the reason for the international character of modernism was that it was an art which responded to cities: Paris, Berlin, Moscow, New York, Chicago and, of course, London. No matter whether you lived in Prague or St Petersburg, the city posed the same problems of crowds, perception, mass culture and the dissolution of traditions.

It is strange, therefore, to find that a good deal of what we would call modernist poetry does not portray the city at all. Of course there are exceptions, such as T. S. Eliot's *The Waste Land* (1922) and William Carlos Williams's epic *Paterson* (1963) but, in general terms, we do not find too many modernist poems that focus on the city per se; though that doesn't mean it can't shape poetry in quite specific ways.

The switch from one seemingly unrelated image to another, for example, which is a feature of a good deal of modernist verse, captures the experience of walking down a busy street where attention constantly switches from one sight to another. The motor-car, soon to become an integral part of city life, alters poetic rhythm. It was still possible to write regular rhymes after its arrival – many did – but such rhythms seemed slightly unreal because they were increasingly at variance with the stop–start progress of the car, its jerky journey along the road.

The American poet Wallace Stevens (1879–1955) does not write directly about the modern urban environment but it finds its way into his poetry nonetheless. It structures his existence and shapes his conception of the art. Stevens worked as an insurance lawyer for most of his life. Poetry was something he wrote in his spare time, but his famous declaration, 'I have no life except in poetry',[1] draws attention to a key aspect of modernity: the division between the public self and the private self and the lack of connection between them. 'I certainly do not exist from nine to six, when I am at the office … At night I strut my individual state once more' (p. ix).

The city, then, particularly the experience of work, helps precipitate the split in the self which is a such a key feature of modernity. We should also note the implications for art. In making a clear distinction between his poetry and his career in insurance, Stevens suggests that art has nothing to do with the workaday world. If art is, as Stevens indicates, the medium in which the individual can flourish, then he is also implying that he or she cannot do so at his or her place of employment.

Stevens's identification of art with the private realm represents a change from the nineteenth century where literature and painting had a public role. They represented Victorian society and criticised its shortcomings. By such means they upheld the notions of a common experience and shared values despite quite often clear evidence to the contrary, for example the conflict between masters and men in the new factories. It wasn't just the rise of mass production, however, that threatened art's ability to speak for all. New technology, innovations in communication and the rise of mass culture seemed better equipped to assume some of art's traditional functions. The cinema could tell a story like the novel and seemed poised to surpass painting as the visual art form par excellence, while the mass circulation magazine would express a far wider range of concerns than the Poet Laureate ever could.

Its historic role threatened, out of touch with the public and not needed by business, art was in crisis. What were poets, painters and novelists to do? One option was to examine the nature of art itself and this, together with art's separation from the wider society, gave modern art its rarefied character. Art was now primarily something that had to be interpreted. It was not about the artist's feelings, it did not portray a recognisable reality and it was not intended to make us act or become better people. Of course to say this is to exaggerate; if modernist art did none of these things then it would be completely beyond our grasp.

The Poetry of Wallace Stevens and Modernism

The point does need to be made, however, that modernist art is difficult and needs to be interpreted. This difficulty arises in part from artists exploring the nature of art rather than using art to explore the world – though again we are not dealing in hard and fast distinctions, for any artist who delves into his or her medium is also enquiring about the world: he or she is, for example, implicitly asking questions about the relation between representation and reality. Stevens's poetry sometimes takes as its theme the nature of poetry. 'Thirteen Ways of Looking at a Blackbird' (1917) is not really about a blackbird, it is about the power of the imagination – which of course places it firmly in the romantic tradition. Yet to say that it is 'about the power of the imagination' hardly does justice to the rich complexity of the poem.

It consists of thirteen short verses, some of which are clearly indebted to Imagism (see especially line 17, with its dramatic and compressed description of sharp and glassy icicles, *Poems*, p. 16; see the Extended Commentary in the previous chapter for more on Imagism). A blackbird is mentioned in each of the verses, giving the poem the appearance of unity. This appearance is strengthened by the mention of snow in the opening and closing stanzas, and the tone of the poem – calm, considered and rational – is uniform throughout. Yet we struggle to make sense of it. What does the blackbird represent? Why are there only thirteen ways of looking at it? What is the connection between the poet's mind and the bird? Who are the mysterious riders in their glass coach in lines 41–2? Does this glass refer back to the glass of the icicles? If so, how?

We could go on but enough has been said to establish the enigmatic quality of 'Thirteen Ways of Looking at a Blackbird'. This poem is a puzzle which points to another characteristic of modernist verse, that it is more intellectual than emotional. In one way 'Thirteen Ways of

Looking at a Blackbird' is like a cubist painting. This art form, whose principal practitioners were Georges Braque (1882–1963) and Pablo Picasso (1881–1973) revolutionised painting because it presented the object not from one but from multiple perspectives – all at the same time. So, for example, in Braques's *The Table* (1910), we see the object simultaneously from the front, from the back, from the sides, from underneath and from above. The cubist 'thesis' was that reality is the sum of all the different ways we can perceive it, but since we cannot see it in this manner, it will forever elude us. Even paintings like *The Table* can only gesture to the numerous angles from which the simplest object can be viewed.

'Thirteen Ways of Looking at a Blackbird' is the poetic equivalent of a cubist painting in that it presents various views of the bird without privileging any. Try reading the verses in a different order and see if that fundamentally changes your understanding of the poem – it may give you new ideas but it will still be equally puzzling. Stevens's poem not only alludes to Cubism, it also incorporates a technique from the new art form of cinema. The very first stanza presents us with a distant view of mountains and then we suddenly zoom in to the blackbird itself (ll. 2–3) in an example of the cinematic close up used in poetry.

So, in addition to learning that, at least in the case of Stevens, modernist poetry is difficult to understand, we have also learnt that it has a relationship with both the avant-garde and popular culture. This is an important point because we often hear that one of the characteristics of modernism is that its art is hostile to popular culture; the cubist painter, for example, is contemptuous of the naive idea of representation found in the poster and the photograph. In Stevens, however, we find evidence of a possible reconciliation between the high and low of contemporary culture.

Stevens, Poetry and the Modern Workplace

We also find in Stevens traces of the transformation of the culture of work which is another characteristic of modernism. The mechanisation of labour and the need to be more productive created a culture in which ordinary activities took on some of the characteristics of work itself. In the 1930s, for example, the principles of scientific management (see Part Two: 'A Cultural Overview') were even applied to ironing. These principles chimed with the Protestant work ethic to confer a high value on a person's industry and sense of vocation. In this climate, then, it's not surprising to find Stevens putting his readers to work. He does not give them 'the meaning' of 'Thirteen Ways of Looking at a Blackbird', rather the reader is called upon to participate in the construction of the poem; to labour at the language, to link the different images and ideas and research its references and allusions. To the extent that the reader is expected to exert him- or herself, he or she becomes associated with the workforce at large and shares some of its anxieties.

In particular, he or she only ever produces a partial reading of the poem in the same way that a man at a conveyor belt only ever has a partial relation with what passes in front of him. Of course the two activities, reading and working on an assembly line, are very different. One is creative and intellectual, while the other is repetitive and manual. The point is they are both forms of labour, and in each case this labour adds to something but does not complete it, and therein lies a cause of anxiety.

We could push the analogy a little further and say that Stevens's detached style of writing reflects the alienation of the worker – meaning that he or she is forced to work for someone else, and has no say in what is produced nor any control over how. Stevens is as emotionally removed from his subject matter as the factory operative is from the task of moving pig iron from one part of the floor to another. In 'The House Was Quiet and the World Was Calm' his description of the summer night is thinned out to become a perfect thought (*Poems*, p. 69, l. 9) almost empty of feeling; it is primarily an abstract idea rather than a concrete image.

Once again, the analogy can only be taken so far. The poet is not told to write a poem and he or she decides upon the subject and how it will be treated. However, the comparison at least encourages us to question the conventional view that modernist art is defined partly by its distance from the wider culture. Is it really the case that it is more concerned with self than with society, with aesthetics rather than politics?

One of the aims of this book is to show that modern art is deeply implicated in the transformation of work and the growth of the bureaucratic state. Fossil experts can reconstruct an extinct creature from a fragment of bone. Similarly, a small poetic detail can give us an insight into the shape of society as a whole. We are used to hearing the claim that modern art, by virtue of its difficulty, stands apart from the rest of the culture, but such statements gloss over how that same art validates, replicates and reinforces notions of, say, human identity. T. S. Eliot's remark that poetry is 'an escape from personality'[2] chimes with Frederick Winslow Taylor's view that a worker's personality is not important, only his function (see Part Two: 'A Cultural Overview).

Moreover, the modernist poet's preoccupation with form rather than content finds a parallel in scientific management's obsession with formalising habits of work, imposing uniform methods of working on different individuals. We need to be careful here, though, for it is possible to turn the argument around and say that the form of modern art is not the same as the form of modern work. In both cases we find an interest in formal procedures, but the form of art is complex, while that of work is simple; the form of art is organic, while that of work is mechanical; and the form of art *could* be seen as an expression of the individual self while that of work suppresses the individual self.

Manufacture and art share one other characteristic: they both transform raw material into a finished product. The fibre that grows round the seed of the cotton plant, for example, is spun, woven and dyed to make clothes while the artist processes events or experiences and turns them into art. Once more we need to appreciate the limits of the comparison – a factory is a very different place from an artist's studio. Moreover, in contrast to artists, industry produces goods that have a practical function. Having said that, of course, there are many products on the market which do not have a particular use, such as garden gnomes, and even those that do, such as clothes, have an aesthetic aspect.

Stevens, 'The Man with the Blue Guitar' (1903)

Stevens looks at how poetry transforms reality in 'The Man with the Blue Guitar', a poem he wrote apparently after viewing Picasso's *Old Guitarist*, painted during his 'blue period' (1901–4). The blue guitar of the title is a symbol of poetry, and has the power to change and transform the world around it, just as the poet does with his or her words (*Poems*, p. 28, l. 31). We noted the connection between modernist poetry and music in the previous chapter and it is one Stevens dwells on at some length in this poem and, indeed, in 'Thirteen Ways of Looking at a Blackbird'. Poetry originated in song and, although it developed as an autonomous art form, the link with music persisted.

Some modernist poets, and Stevens is among them, were attracted to the close association between poetry and music because they were looking for different ways to validate their work in the contemporary world. Previously, the value of poetry lay in its ability to instruct or entertain, to express an emotion, or evoke a person or place. In modern society, though, other media could do all this more easily. Poets therefore looked to music, with its dense formal patternings, as a model for their work. What particularly appealed to them was that music, particularly of the classical variety, did not refer to anything outside itself. Its existence was justified by its own internal organisation rather than by any role it fulfilled – an argument that could be applied to poetry, whose own social role had diminished.

There are two basic claims made about music in 'The Man with the Blue Guitar'. The first is that the instrument plays things as they are and the second is that it changes them, and the poem plays back and forth between these two propositions. Music is also a means of binding people together (p. 29, ll. 31–2). If the blue guitar is a symbol of poetry, though, it is also the case that verse transcends whatever is played upon the instrument (pp. 29–30, ll. 46–8). The clear suggestion is that poetry takes the place vacated by God. In the nineteenth century, the poet, critic and school inspector Matthew Arnold (1822–88) had made a similar claim, that we must look to poetry rather than religion to comfort and console us.

Equally grand but more plausible is the statement that the poetic persona and the blue guitar 'are one' (p. 33, l. 134). The notion that a poet 'becomes' what he or she writes about goes back at least to John Keats (1795–1821). The poet, he wrote, should cultivate what he called 'negative capability', the state 'when a Man is capable of being in Uncertainties, Mysteries, doubts, without any irritable reaching after fact & reason'.[3] This, then, allows him to assume the identity of whatever he describes. 'If a Sparrow comes before my Window', writes Keats, 'I take part in its existence and pick about the Gravel'.[4] What pains him in 'Ode to a Nightingale' (1818), is being recalled from the bird's reverie back to his 'sole self'.[5]

The speaker's claim in 'The Man with a Blue Guitar', that he fuses with the instrument, has its roots, then, as does a great deal of modernist poetry, in romanticism. It is also a constant theme of Stevens's poetry. We find it, for instance, in 'Thirteen Ways of Looking at a Blackbird' – where a man, a woman a blackbird are one (p. 16, ll. 9–12) – but why do we find this trope in poetry from the romantics to the modernists? That is a huge question but a very schematic answer would take the following form. One of the characteristics of modernity is a feeling that man is alone, cut off from God, Nature and society itself. He is cut off from God because biblical criticism and evolution have cast doubt on the truth of the scriptures; he is cut off from Nature because science has reduced it to a set of laws and the industrial revolution has forced more and more people to work in factories rather than on the land; and he is cut off from society because he exists as part of a crowd rather than as part of a community.

Stevens, 'Esthétique du Mal' (1947) and the Nature of Art

All this gives rise to feelings of anxiety, sadness and rootlessness. 'Poetry', Stevens writes, 'is a form of melancholia'.[6] Again, we can find these feelings in the romantic period. A good example would be Keats's 'Ode on Melancholy' (1819), or Coleridge's 'Dejection: A Letter'

(1802), but where the romantic could look to nature for remedy, the modernists cannot. How, then, do they address the condition of being isolated, with all its attendant problems? The particular version of the modernist angst that Stevens explores in 'Esthétique du Mal' concerns the relationship between words and world.

The poem starts with a man writing letters home, so straight away we have the modernist theme of displacement, of someone outside an environment that would sustain, identify and support him. The man is a writer but he can only write about things if they are 'ancient' (*Poems*, p. 57, l. 8). How have we arrived at a point where writers feel unable to engage with the contemporary world? Stevens suggests that Christianity, by making us focus on the hereafter rather than the here and now, has weakened our perceptions of things and our ability to describe them (p. 58). He also claims that the growth of science has attenuated our senses. We operate more on the level of ideas than of instincts (p. 65, verse 12, l. 1), and consequently fail to experience it in all its splendour. Stevens may very well be right that, to quote Wordsworth, 'Our meddling intellect / Mis-shapes the beauteous form of things: / We murder to dissect'[7] but his own poetry, so conceptual and self-conscious, seems to perpetuate the very problem of which he complains.

What can we do to create an art that revives our senses, refreshes our perceptions and renews our apprehension of the world? Stevens rejects the romantic turn to nature (p. 59, verse 4, ll. 11–12). If he dispenses with one key romantic notion, however, he embraces another: the imagination. 'The imagination', he writes, 'is the romantic' (*Opus Posthumous*, p. 163). It is, however, in crisis, and one reason is the death of Satan, which he describes as a tragedy for the imagination ('Esthétique du Mal', *Poems*, p. 62, verse 8, ll. 1–2). This seems to be a reference to Baudelaire, for whom Satan, as we saw in the previous chapter, is a key figure in rendering the experience of modern life. Moreover, the very title of Stevens's poem, 'Esthétique du Mal', recalls *Les Fleurs du Mal*. We have moved from flowers of evil to an aesthetic of evil; or, to put it another way, we have moved from nature to art.

We must look, in other words, to art to replenish us and give significance to life. The imagination may be dead but it can be resurrected and we are compelled to create anew a world without God or his substitute, Nature with a capital 'N'. Poetry is the highest form of fiction ('A High-Toned Old Christian Woman', *Poems*, p. 4, l. 1), and fiction, Stevens opines, is all there is. 'The final belief is to believe in fiction, which you know to be a fiction, there being nothing else' (*Opus Posthumous*, p. 163). As fiction, poetry fulfils a number of functions: it leads us to life and completes it, it is the attempt to find some form of satisfaction, it contributes to happiness and so on. We choose between poems on the basis of how well they meet these goals.

How, though, does poetry achieve these various aims? That is a more difficult question to answer. The first step is to disengage from reality. The second step is to invent a trope, a figure of speech that will lift us above the commonplace routines of everyday existence. 'Reality', Stevens memorably wrote, 'is a cliché from which we escape by metaphor' (*Opus Posthumous*, p. 179). This remark also gives us a clue about what Stevens considers to be most important about a poem, namely its artistry, or aesthetic aspect, and the aesthetic, he writes, 'is the measure of civilisation' (p. 171). So while it is normal for a poem to have some sort of theme, its value resides in how that theme is rendered.

At times, Stevens goes further, claiming that 'a poem need not have meaning and ... often does not have' (p. 177), which underlines the point that it is the management of words, the patterns, the linguistic invention that takes our breath away. Lines from 'Esthétique du Mal' which describe falling soldiers mowing a lawn may not make much sense but the sheer impossibility of the image is what delights us (*Poems*, p. 64, verse 11, ll. 2–4). On the subect of what makes sense, we should note that Stevens offers many definitions of poetry, so many in fact that it is difficult to know exactly what his view of poetry is. It should, for example, be an escape from reality and at the same time recognise that 'reality is the ultimate value' (*Opus Posthumous*, p. 166).

However, this is the very strength of poetry. By being so various, so incorrigibly plural, it escapes those categories by which we 'dispose' of the world. We shouldn't forget, though, that while poetry is 'the gaiety (joy) of language' it is also 'a form of melancholia' (*Opus Posthumous*, pp. 160, 174). The 'mal' in 'Esthétique du Mal' doesn't just refer to Baudelaire's 'Flowers of Evil' but to 'pain', 'ache' and 'disease'. They are the raw material of the modernist aesthetic, but whether the resulting art object brings relief from these states or merely reflects them in its own dissonant intricacies is still very much a matter of debate.

The Poetry of William Carlos Williams and Modernism

Another American, William Carlos Williams (1883–1963) was writing at approximately the same time as Stevens and he, too, was a part time poet. As a doctor, a paediatrician in fact, putting pen to paper was only something he could do after he had finished his rounds. His output was prodigious, however. Williams wrote novels, short stories and essays but it is as a poet that he is probably best remembered. He was a friend of Ezra Pound (1885–1972) and Hilda Doolittle (1886–1961). Like Pound, Doolittle, known more familiarly as 'H. D.', was an important figure in the development of Imagism (see the Extended Commentary in Part Three: 'Modernist Poetry – French Origins, English Settings'). It is therefore not surprising to find imagist elements in Williams's work such as references to nature and the classical world.

A poem like 'The Cold Night' (1921), clearly illustrates the Imagists' influence on Williams with the comparison of the 'white moon' to 'the bare thighs of / The Police Sergeant's wife'.[8] The simile has all the strengths and weaknesses of Imagism. It is striking but collapses under closer inspection. Why the Police Sergeant's wife and not some other woman? Also the stars around the moon are likened to the woman's children, but the moon is a symbol of chastity.

Williams's poetry can be said to expand the possibilities or expose the limitations of imagist verse depending on your point of view. Certainly Williams could write long, reflective poems in which bold images played an integral part. After him, Imagism can have narrative and political punch. 'Proletarian Portrait' (1935), for example, uses all the 'objective' description characteristic of imagist poets to make a point about poverty. It describes a young woman looking in her shoe for the nail 'that has been hurting her' (*Collected Poems 1*, pp. 384–5, l. 11). The poem shocks by its simplicity and directness and succeeds admirably in conveying, through clever use of a single detail, the privations of the woman's life. There is also a fine tension between the politics of the title (the Marxist term 'proletarian')* and the concrete image used to portray the woman's downtrodden condition. In other words we are shown suffering but with the suggestion of how it might be eased.

At the same time there are many poems which seem to describe such simple, everyday things that the reader might wonder what they are 'for'. Such a one is 'Poem' (1930) which just describes a cat climbing over the top of the 'jamcloset' (*Collected Poems 1*, p. 352, l. 4). It's very similar to one of Williams's most famous poems 'This Is Just To Say' (1934) in which the speaker apologises for eating plums that were left in the icebox (fridge). These poems, and to some it would be heresy to say this, are frankly banal. They are the verbal equivalent of a photograph of your pet. The picture may mean something to you but very little to anyone else. This is not to dismiss Williams's work, however; on the contrary, it's to pinpoint its significance.

In the first place Williams's focus on the commonplace paves the way for the contemporary phenomenon of reality TV. Our culture's fascination with programmes like Big Brother has its origins in art that puts the mundane aspects of life at its centre. Williams, like Stevens, writes in an almost neutral way about his subjects. We get very little sense of what either poet feels about what they write and the tone of the poems rarely varies. It is emotionally flat and intellectually detached. Williams especially comes close to being like a camera that indiscriminately records whatever passes in front of it, and it is precisely this refusal to select or pass comment that characterises reality TV.

What we might call the 'inanity' of some of Williams's poetry is also significant because it breaks decisively with the art of the past. In effect, by describing a waitress, a woman sitting at a window, a drunk or a laundryman, Williams is breaking with an artistic tradition that insisted

---

* See Part Two: 'A Cultural Overview' for more on Marx.

on a high subject matter, written in a high style with high morals. To be exact, he is doing precisely what Wordsworth did in *The Lyrical Ballads* (1798) – rejecting grand themes and elevated expression in favour of common incidents related in 'a selection of language really used by men'.[9] Williams, therefore, is as much for one tradition as he against another. Like Wordsworth he writes about ordinary things in a conversational manner, but he differs from the earlier poet in not drawing a moral. Williams is also different from Wordsworth in the way he puts his poems on the page. They are not divided into verses, they do not rhyme, they often do not begin with a capital letter, they can contain shopping lists and even illustrations (see 'April', *Collected Poems 1*, pp. 335–6).

The dissolution of traditional forms is carried much further by another American modernist, e. e. cummings (1894–1962) whose poems are characterised by typographical experiment and the abandonment of syntax. A flavour of the style can be found in the first section of a poem which, like all cummings's, has no title:

> sh estiffl
> ystrut sal
> lif san
> dbut sth[10]

It is possible to work out the words – or some of them: 'she stiffly struts all if sand' – but that doesn't bring us much closer to understanding what the poem is about. This little extract underlines the point we have been making: that while modernist poetry liberates itself from the verse of the past it sometimes does so at the expense of sense, structure and value.

There is another way of looking at the matter, however. If Williams is indeed breaking with tradition, it is because he wants to give voice to a distinctly American experience. He is distancing himself from the literature of Europe in order to create a wholly American style of writing. The creation of a national identity is one of the ways of countering the loss of established communities as people move from the country to the city. This is one of the themes of Williams's essay 'The American Background' (1934).[11] He argues that the loss of what he calls a primary culture of craft by a secondary culture of wealth has left people feeling lost and disorientated. It is the job of the artist to create a common culture out of this changed condition, one that is based, as Williams puts it in 'Paterson' (1927), not in ideas 'but in things' (*Collected Poems 1*, p. 23, l. 25).

His epic, five volume poem *Paterson* (1963)* illustrates this principle, being an account of the history and locale of the people of Paterson, New Jersey. The language of not only this poem but also of many others resembles the journalistic ideal: the clear reporting of facts. Here we see another point of contact between modernist poetry and the wider culture. The tendency in Britain was for poetry to separate itself from the idioms of the popular media because of their limited expressive power, but for Williams at least such speech had an energising effect on verse.

In the 'Introduction' to his volume *The Wedge* (1944) Williams wrote that 'a poem is a small (or large) machine made of words'.[12] Once more we encounter a poet who likens his art to that of a mechanism and, in so doing, he brings the world of art closer to the world of work. The idea of poetry as a machine allies it with scientific management, the aim of which is to make humans function like machines. Once more we find notions of poetry underpinning conceptions of the human found in the workplace. In this respect poetry is more an ideology than an aesthetic. It supports the views and values of those who govern and who, through the use of the media, persuade the rest of us that those views and values are true. It is as well to remember this claim when we hear that modernist art considers itself to be separate from the rest of society and critiques it.

---

* Williams wrote a poem called 'Paterson' in 1927. He also wrote a multi-volume epic called *Paterson*. The five books of *Paterson* were published separately in 1946, 1948, 1949, 1951 and 1958, and the entire work was published as a unit in 1963.

The Poetry of W. B. Yeats and Modernism

At first glance there doesn't seem to be much similarity between Williams and the Irish poet W. B. Yeats (1865–1939) and yet they were both engaged in the same project, the creation of a national identity. Both poets felt the need to shake off English influence and assert the integrity and validity of their own culture. The task was somewhat easier for Williams because America had gained political independence from Britain in 1783; it was harder for Yeats because Ireland was still under English rule.

Yeats's early work evokes Ireland's Celtic past. In 'To the Rose Upon the Rood of Time' (1893) he announces his intention to 'sing the ancient ways: Cuchulain* battling with the bitter tide; / The Druid, grey, wood nurtured, quiet-eyed, / Who cast round Fergus dreams, and ruin untold'.[13] These remote figures, belonging to a largely mythological past, do not seem to have much relevance to the modern world, but Yeats is one of a number of poets (Eliot is another) who looks back to the past to revive the present. Not all modernists sought to overthrow tradition, some needed it to nourish their own work and believed it had an important part to play in the wider society.

'From the great candle of the past', wrote Yeats, 'we must all light our little tapers'.[14] By this, he meant that a knowledge of Irish literature and folklore would enlarge the vision of his fellow countrymen who, he believed, were too set on making money to appreciate the beauties of the past. Yeats was a leading light in the Irish Revival (*c.* 1875 to *c.* 1925), a movement which aimed to promote a national identity and culture. His proposal for the creation of an Irish National Literary Society was part of this process and its goal was to create 'a nationality that is above party ... and to assert those everlasting principles of love of truth and love of country that speak to men in solitude and in the silence of the night' (*Selected Criticism*, p. 19).

---

* Cuchulain (pronounced 'cuHOOlin') is the central figure in a series of ancient stories known as the Ulster Cycle.

A similar idea lay behind the Abbey Theatre (f. 1904) co-founded by Yeats and Lady Isabella Augusta Gregory (1852–1932). Lady Gregory was another important figure in the Irish Revival. She helped popularise Irish legends with her translations of *Cuchulain of Muirthemne* (1902) and *Gods and Fighting Men* (1904). She also collected folktales from the tenants on her Coole Park estate and from the surrounding area, which she published with the title *Visions and Beliefs in the West of Ireland* (1920). Ideally, these were to be the basis of a play staged at 'The People's Theatre', as the Abbey was dubbed but, as Yeats wrote in a letter to Lady Gregory, this did not happen.

To understand why, we need to know a little bit about Yeats's ideas about poetry, which also applied to his ideas about drama. Yeats was part of the symbolist tradition which we discussed in the previous chapter. One of the main characteristics of symbolist writing is that it suggests a mood, emotion or higher reality; it does not represent the world. Yeats makes a similar point when he says that by pattern and rhythm, the symbol enables us to see a beauty which escapes our normal vision. The rose, for example, is his symbol of ethereal loveliness – though more straightforwardly it signifies Ireland to him. Because it gives access to a spiritual realm, the symbol also has great power to move us. Its effects ripple through time. It is like music, a favourite comparison of modernist poets. 'I am certainly never sure', Yeats writes, 'when I hear of ... anything that fills the ear of the world, that it has not all happened because of something that a boy piped in Thessaly'.[15]

Yeats is one of the few modern poets to promote the idea of beauty. One of the aims of art, from its earliest days, was the creation and contemplation of beauty, but there was a retreat from that aspiration in the modern age as painters, writers and musicians became more interested in whether what they were doing was or wasn't art. Yeats's explanation for this state of affairs is that the rise of democracy and mass culture cut the Irish off from their past and fostered a new way of thinking that is primarily practical and goal orientated.

The effect on art is twofold. Either it results in work that focuses on the external nature of things without any regard for their internal nature or else it results in the rejection of art altogether. Yeats was disappointed by plays submitted to the Abbey Theatre because they copied life too closely, because they were made from 'observation, never from passion [or] lonely dreaming',[16] while in his poem 'The Fisherman' (1919), he writes of 'great Art' being beaten down by the wider culture of modern Ireland (*Collected Poems*, p. 146, l. 24).

Yeats's solution to this situation was to establish a small select group of like-minded people who would 'read poetry for pleasure and understand the traditional language of the passion' ('A People's Theatre', p. 190). The word 'passion' occurs a lot in Yeats's writing and has a number of different meanings, but the chief one is that 'it is the straining of man's being against some obstacle that obstructs its unity' (p. 187) and unity, Yeats believed, was an important, if not the most important quality of beauty.

One of the things that Yeats saw as an obstacle to unity in his society was political division, which is why he 'hated the literature of the point of view'[17] – it excluded rather than included. The political divisions occurred over the question of Irish independence and how best to obtain it. Yeats did not believe in armed insurrection but his attitude to the Easter Rising of 1916, which was ruthlessly suppressed, nevertheless displayed some admiration for those who had organised it. The recurring phrase in his poem 'Easter Rising' (1921) – 'A terrible beauty is born' (*Collected Poems*, p. 176, l. 16) – is ambiguous. Yeats aspired to a spiritual beauty rather than a worldly one and that is why it is 'terrible', but the fact this is a terrible *beauty* means that it has some attraction.

The high value Yeats places on unity is in contrast to some modernist artists, such as the composer Arnold Schoenberg (1874–1951) who rejected all forms of unity in his music. 'Away with harmony' he cried,[18] but what does Yeats mean by this? In part he means the unity of his own poetic self. The poet 'is never the bundle of accident and incoherence that sits down to breakfast' ('A General Introduction for My Work', p. 255). The act of composition draws the different parts of himself together, the continuity of images, the development of a theme, give his poetic persona a coherent identity. Writing, we might say, is one response to the broken, divided self of modernity.

Another aspect of unity is the poet's relation to his audience. Yeats found this quality in the poems of Thomas Davies (1814–45), who dedicated his life to Irish nationalism. They 'spoke, or tried to speak out of a people to a people' ('A General Introduction for My Work', p. 256). In other words, what united the poet and his audience was a shared history but English rule, disagreement about how to end it and divisions about what kind of society Ireland should be, all undermined the poet's relation to his readers.

In the end, Yeats looked to European literary tradition for an ideal of unity. He was particularly taken with Dante Alighieri (1265–1321), author of *The Divine Comedy* (*c.* 1314–20) whose study, Yeats claimed, was 'the unity of being, the subordination of all parts to the whole as in a perfectly proportioned human body' ('A People's Theatre', p. 186). This view of the human body also served, in Dante's time, as a model of society in which everyone knew their place. The little toe was not as grand as the head, but it served a necessary purpose, just like the peasant in the strictly hierarchical society of the middle ages. Dante's idea of unity could not apply to modern, democratic society where, in principle, everyone was equal. Yeats despised his society and his attitude to the people is summed in his phrase 'the barbarous crowd' ('His Phoenix' (1919), *Collected Poems*, p. 150, l. 25)). In adopting Dante's idea of beauty, he was also adopting his idea of society. To say that Yeats was an authoritarian would be an understatement. He flirted with fascism and was an admirer of the Italian dictator Benito Mussolini (1883–1945), as indeed was his friend Pound.

The crowd, the character of modern society and the contentious nature of Irish politics meant that unity, and therefore beauty, had to be sought elsewhere. The nature of the self also plays a part in Yeats's pursuit of these qualities in his art. Throughout his work there is a strong sense of the division between the mind and the body and how they seem to demand different things. In an early poem, 'The Dawn' (1919), Yeats declares that 'knowledge' is 'not worth a straw' (*Collected Poems*, p. 144, l. 13), clearly implying that the life of the senses is fulfilling. He is denied experience of this, however, because the woman whom he loved, Maud Gonne (1886–1953), did not love him, at least not in the way he wanted. Therefore one of the themes of his poetry was, as he called it in 'Presences' (1919), 'that monstrous thing / Returned and yet unrequited love' (p. 153, ll. 7–8). As he grew older he leant as he writes in 'The Tower' (1928) towards the life of the mind – 'I must ... / Choose Plato and Plotinus for a friend' (p. 200, ll. 12–13) – but there is regret at the fading of the flesh.

'Sailing to Byzantium' (1928), starts with a restatement of the division in Yeats's work between thinking and feeling. The 'sensual music' of the young is contrasted with the 'intellect' of the old (*Collected Poems*, pp. 199–200, ll. 7–8). The speaker of the poem feels there is no place for him in the modern world and therefore sets out to Byzantium, capital of the Byzantine or Eastern Roman empire. His desire is to be gathered 'into the artifice of eternity' (p. 200, l. 24), to escape nature and be 'such a form as Grecian goldsmiths make' (p. 200, l. 27). The poem's speaker, then, seeks to escape the opposition between mind and body by becoming a form of art.

In 'Among School Children' (1928), there is a different solution to this problem. In the final verse Yeats finds a way of reconciling all the oppositions that haunt his poetry. As he looks back over his life, as he thinks about the state of childhood and adulthood, he realises that he needs to think of them as a whole, not as separate parts of his life. The symbols he uses for this are first a chestnut tree and then a dance:

> Oh chestnut tree, great-rooted blossomer,
> Are you the leaf the blossom or the bole?
> O body swayed to music, O brightening glance
> How can we know the dancer from the dance?
>
> *Collected Poems*, p. 224, ll. 57–60

The tree stands for stability, the dance for movement and a tree itself can be said to 'dance' as the wind rushes through its branches. Art, in the form of a symbol, has given Yeats his vision of reality that everything is one, against which the ordinary business of life, as he wrote in another poem, 'A Meditation in Time of Civil War' (1921), is mere 'fantasy' (p. 187, l. 5).

In many ways, Yeats is more of a romantic than a modernist poet. He writes of unrequited love, of the Celtic past and, despite altering traditional metres, he remained committed to their essential forms: 'even what I alter must seem traditional' he wrote ('A General Introduction for My Work', p. 267). To call Yeats romantic, though, is really a way of calling him a modernist since, as we have seen, the two are intimately related. Yeats follows Wordsworth's trajectory: he starts out trying to make the language of poetry 'coincide with that of passionate, normal speech' (p. 265), but ends by groping for symbols that will reveal the true nature of reality. More generally, he shared the romantic distrust of reason and its interest in folk art.

Yeats was writing after romanticism, though, and his contempt for the masses and his desire to make art an exclusive affair place him firmly in the modernist era. What complicates his relation to it, however, is his ambiguous relation to the nature of modernist art. Its key characteristic, in so much as we can say of art so various that it has a 'key' characteristic, is 'difficulty'. While Yeats is committed to writing in the symbolist tradition, he also laments that:

> The fascination of what's difficult
> Has dried the sap out of my veins, and rent
> Spontaneous joy and natural content
> Out of my heart.
>
> 'The Fascination of What's Difficult', *Collected Poems*,
> p. 89, ll. 1–4

The absence of feeling in modernist art is what finally separates it from romanticism.

Extended Commentary: Eliot, *The Waste Land* (1922)

The Waste Land is the quintessential modernist poem because it seems to have no clear narrative, there are no obvious connections between the different sections and it is full of references to works that most readers will not have heard of. The first readers of the poem were so bewildered that Eliot had to supply, reluctantly it should be added, a series of notes explaining the more difficult parts of the poem. Whether that makes it any easier to understand, however, is a moot point.

Perhaps the best way to approach such a work is by acknowledging its difficulties and then trying to deal with them. We can note first that it has five parts: 'The Burial of the Dead', 'A Game of Chess', 'The Fire Sermon', 'Death By Water' and 'What the Thunder Said'. This gives the work a structure similar to that of an Elizabethan play, which had five acts. The question of whether *The Waste Land* is more like a tragedy or a comedy is one we will come to shortly. For now, the connection with drama helps us to appreciate the multitude of speakers in *The Waste Land*.

Hugh Kenner relates this aspect of the poem to the arrival of the telephone. The numerous voices in the poem are words without context, exactly the experience of speaking to someone on the phone.[19] We can't see where they are, nor can we see their gestures or facial expression which, psychologists tell us, account for ninety-five per cent of communication; consequently we can never be sure if we have understood them correctly.

Because there is no face to face interaction on the telephone, it is easier for speakers to dissemble, to pretend that something is the case when it is not. In that respect, the telephone is associated with acting. Eliot originally wanted to call the poem 'He Do The Police in Different Voices' which, with the idea of impersonation, further reinforces *The Waste Land*'s relation to drama. The notion of performance is a central part of Eliot's early work. The speaker in 'The Love Song of J. Alfred Prufrock' (1917) talks about meeting an audience of faces,[20] while in 'Portrait of A Lady' (1917) he complains that he must enact a series of transformations in order to express himself (*Complete Poems and Plays*, pp. 18–21, p. 21, verse 3, ll. 26–7).

This is similar to what Eliot is doing in *The Waste Land*, using scraps of myth, religion and popular culture to convey the condition of modern civilisation as he sees it. Our sense of self is intimately bound up with the habits of thought, ways of feeling and frames of reference for the society in which we live. If they, for whatever reason, begin to fall apart, then we become anxious about who we are. *The Waste Land* is in part about this crisis of identity.

The rise of mass society, the horror of the First World War and the increasing mechanisation of daily life undermined the traditional culture by which people made sense of themselves and their place in the world – though there is a strong argument for seeing modernity as intensifying rather than initiating this process. After all, the industrial revolution began to gather speed in the late eighteenth century.

We certainly get a strong sense of disintegration in *The Waste Land*. In 'The Burial of the Dead' and 'The Fire Sermon' the speakers talk of a fragmented experience of life and an inability to connect, instead finding only nothingness (*Complete Poems and Plays*, p. 61, ll. 1–2 and p. 70, ll. 301–2). The claim that things have fallen apart and cannot be put back together is dramatised in the poem itself, for we jump from one topic to another without any apparent reason. What, for example, is the relation between the woman sitting in the chair, and the conversation in the pub in 'A Game of Chess'?

Before we can answer that question, we should consider a remark near the end of 'What the Thunder Said' and thus near the end of the whole poem (p. 75, l. 430), which implies that though traditional culture has crumbled, it can still maintain our sense of self, if we can gather up enough of its scraps. However, the emphasis is on propping up the self, on preventing it from collapsing, not on its authenticity or its expressive powers. Compare this to Picasso, who used the shards of a shattered culture not just to shock and amuse his audience but to suggest new ideas, new values, new ways of looking at the world.

We need to remember, though, that it is only the speakers in the various sections who talk about fragments. While it is true the poem shifts from subject to subject and even seems disjointed, it is also true that these different subjects are united by common images and themes. In 'A Game of Chess' the lady sitting in the chair is compared to Cleopatra (69–30 BC), through the simile linking her chair with a throne' (p. 64, l. 78). This same image forms part of a description of the Queen's royal barge in Shakespeare's *Antony and Cleopatra* (II.ii.191).

The reference to Cleopatra suggests that the woman in 'A Game of Chess' has the same power to destroy a man through her beauty as Egypt's most famous queen.

We move from Cleopatra to Philomel, a character in Ovid's *Metamorphoses* (AD 2–8), who was raped by King Tereus of Thrace. In order to prevent her telling anyone what he had done, Tereus cut out her tongue. The poem, thus, has gone from woman as vanquisher of man, to woman as victim of man. We next move to a rather tense exchange between an unidentified couple which could be Eliot and his neurotic wife Vivien. The woman seems to need reassurance (p. 65, ll. 111–12) which the man does not give her. This couple also play chess which, given the title of this section, suggests that their relationship is the most important of this part of *The Waste Land*.

What does chess signify? It is a game where the most powerful player is the queen, which is a reminder of Cleopatra. Also, the fact that each player is intent on defeating the other underlines what we have already learnt, that relationships are a struggle for power. Finally there is the scene in the pub which presents the relation between men and women from a working class point of view and the emphasis here is on having children, remaining attractive and possible adultery.

Sex and relationships are the common threads linking the different parts not just of 'A Game of Chess' but of the whole of *The Waste Land*. Think, for example, of the clerk and the typist in 'The Fire Sermon'. His assault (p. 68, l. 239) is not as violent as that of Tereus on Philomel but we are clearly meant to see a parallel between the contemporary and the classical world. Eliot presents sex in *The Waste Land* as something that is either violent or distasteful, perhaps because it has lost its connection to reproduction. The creation of new life is associated with the image of water, which also 'flows' through the poem, as is evident from the frequent references to rain, the river, pools, fishing and, of course, thunder.

Without water nothing grows. At the beginning of 'The Burial of the Dead' the speaker does not want it to rain because it will bring forth the same sterile routines and forms of life that have made contemporary society a 'waste land'. The various sections of the poem chart aspects of that 'waste land' (see, for example, the first 'verse' of 'The Fire Sermon') and at the same time explore ways in which it can be transformed. We can defy custom and convention, through what Eliot terms a daring surrender (p. 74, l. 403), and we can also look to tradition to refresh and renew the cultural landscape.

Of particular importance here is religion, and Eliot looks at both Western and Eastern varieties. All religions share certain common features, particularly the idea of death and rebirth. This feature is also a key part of the grail myth. An important figure in that myth is the Fisher King who presides over a barren kingdom. He appears in 'The Fire Sermon' and 'What the Thunder Said' (pp. 67, 74). The basic story is that the Fisher King has been wounded in battle and therefore nothing grows in his kingdom. He is the keeper of the holy grail and the lance which pierced Christ's side when he hung on the cross. Knights who come to the castle see these objects and if they ask the right questions about them, for example why the lance bleeds, then the king will be cured and the land will be fertile again.

We said earlier that *The Waste Land* had a dramatic structure, and we said that helped us to appreciate the different voices in the poem. We could also have added that it was an example of how modernist artists mixed different genres. Painters, for example, would stick objects onto their work, blurring the line between sculpture and pictures. However, the five act structure of *The Waste Land* is more fundamental than that, for it reflects the religious element which is present in all drama.

Plays grew out of religious ritual. As far as we know the first religions celebrated the harvest with a sacrifice of thanks to the gods. So we can see, in the earliest forms of worship, both life and death. Tragedy, which ends in death, is based principally on the sacrifice, while comedy, which ends in marriage, is based principally on fertility. *The Waste Land* contains both tragedy and comedy. It starts with death and ends with life, with the coming of rain. Eliot himself, in his notes to the poem, said that much of it was based on Jessie L. Weston's book on the grail legend, *From Ritual to Romance* (1920). He also said, however, that *The Waste Land* 'was only the relief of a personal grumble and wholly insignificant grouse against life'.[21] Before that, as we noted earlier, he declared that poetry is 'an escape from personality' ('Tradition and the

Individual Talent', p. 21). The two statements are very different. Which are we to believe?

There are many more things we could say about *The Waste Land*, such as how it collapses time by making the past contemporaneous with the present, both influencing each other, but that would take a whole book. Suffice it to say that beneath the apparent random movement of the poem are a number of themes and images to do with death and new life that give it more of a unity than is apparent at first reading.

Notes

1   Wallace Stevens, *Poems* selected and with an Introduction by John Burnside (London: Faber, 2008), p. vii.
2   T. S. Eliot, 'Tradition and the Individual Talent' in *Selected Essays* (London: Faber, 1976), p. 21.
3   John Keats, 'Letter' in Peter Kitson (ed.), *Key Documents in Literary Criticism: Romantic Criticism 1800–25* (London: Batsford, 1989), p. 103.
4   Keats, 'Letter' in Daniel G. Hoffman and Samuel Hynes (eds), *English Literary Criticism: Romantic and Victorian* (London: Peter Owen, 1966), p. 111.
5   John Hayward (ed.), *The Penguin Book of English Verse* (Harmondsworth: Penguin, 1956), pp. 293–5, p. 295, l. 72.
6   Wallace Stevens, *Opus Posthumous: Poems, Plays, Prose* edited with an Introduction by Samuel French Morse (New York: Alfred Knopf, 1957), p. 161.
7   'The Tables Turned' in William Wordsworth and Samuel Taylor Coleridge, *Lyrical Ballads* (London: Routledge [1798] 2007), p. 149.
8   William Carlos Williams, *Collected Poems 1 1909–1939* (Manchester: Carcanet Press, 2000), p. 154, ll. 1, 3–4.
9   William Wordsworth and Samuel Taylor Coleridge, *Lyrical Ballads*, p. 296.
10 e. e. cummings, *Complete Poems 1904–1962* (New York: Liveright, 1994), p. 444, ll. 1–4.
11 William Carlos Williams, *Selected Essays* (New York: New Directions Publishing Corporation, 1969), pp. 134–61.
12 William Carlos Williams, *Collected Poems II 1939–1962* (Manchester: Carcanet Press, 2000), p. 54.

13   W. B. Yeats, *Collected Poems* edited and with an Introduction by Augustine Martin (London: Vintage, 1992), p. 27, ll. 1–5.

14   W. B. Yeats, 'The Irish National Literary Society' in *Selected Criticism* edited with an Introduction by A. Norman Jeffares (London: Macmillan, 1970), p. 20.

15   W. B. Yeats, 'The Symbolism of Poetry' in *Selected Criticism*, p. 47.

16   W. B. Yeats, 'A People's Theatre' in *Selected Criticism*, p. 185.

17   W. B. Yeats, 'A General Introduction for My Work' in *Selected Criticism*, p. 256.

18   Cited in Peter Gay, *Modernism: The Lure of Heresy From Baudelaire to Beckett and Beyond* (London: William Heinemann, 2007), p. 250.

19   Hugh Kenner, *The Mechanic Muse* (Oxford: Oxford University Press, 1987), pp. 34–5.

20   T. S. Eliot, 'The Love Song of J. Alfred Prufrock' in *The Complete Poems and Plays of T.S. Eliot* (London: Faber, 1978), pp. 13–17, p. 14, ll. 26–7.

21   Quoted in Peter Ackroyd, *T. S. Eliot* (London: Abacus, 1985), p. 116.

The Origins of the Modernist Novel: Flaubert, Mann, Kafka and Joyce

James Joyce's *Ulysses* (1922) is the modernist novel par excellence, but what makes it so? There are a number of answers. First we have, in Leopold Bloom, not a hero but an anti-hero; second there is no plot in the traditional sense of the term; third there are a number of references to bodily functions, for example defecation, that are normally taboo in art; fourth *Ulysses* draws heavily on the tradition of European literature; fifth it constantly draws attention to its fictional status; and sixth it is characterised by the stream of consciousness style.

Even the most cursory knowledge of the history of the novel, however, shows that many of these elements have been around almost since the inception of the genre. The hero of George Gascoigne's *The Adventures of Master F. J.* (1573), for example, with its immature, over-emotional author surrogate is hardly a beacon of morality. Neither is Daniel Defoe's *Moll Flanders* (1722), a woman who cheats, lies, steals, has several husbands and abandons her children. The spotless hero is more likely to be found in melodrama or romance stories than in the novel.

We tend to take it for granted that a novel has a plot – which we can briefly define as how or why things happen in a story. Plots were originally a part of drama – Aristotle makes them the most important element in his theory of tragedy – and they did not become a prominent feature of the novel until the nineteenth century. Prior to that time most 'novels' simply recounted the adventures of a rather roguish hero or heroine who lived by his or her wits. The term most commonly used to describe such novels was 'picaresque'* and they were episodic in structure, that is they were composed of a sequence of events that happened largely to one person. The first English example of a picaresque novel is Thomas Nashe's *The Unfortunate Traveller* (1594) and the form was still popular in the eighteenth century, as the popularity of Tobias Smollett's *The Adventures of Roderick Random* (1748) proved.

By then, though, the novel was beginning to develop in new directions. Samuel Richardson's *Pamela, or Virtue Rewarded* (1740) is an example of the psychological novel. It tells the tale of a young servant girl who succeeds in becoming the wife of a young rake rather than his mistress. Throughout, the focus is less on what the character does than on what she sees, feels and thinks. This is also the case in Richardson's masterpiece, *Clarissa* (1747–8), which tells the story of the eponymous heroine's persecution by the immoral Lovelace as a means of revenging himself on her family. The psychological novel, with its focus on the interior life of the hero or heroine, is a clear precursor of the modernist novel which explores the inner workings of a character's mind.

It is true that we do not find many references to bodily functions in the nineteenth century novel but if we go back to François Rabelais's story of a giant and his son, *The Life of Gargantua and Pantagruel* (1564), we find a great deal of crudity and obscene humour. We learn, for example, how often the baby Gargantua soils himself, while elsewhere a crowd flees from the urinating Pantagruel as if trying to escape a great flood. We find similar scenes in the eighteenth century novel where the hero, in Jonathan Swift's *Gulliver's Travels* (1726), suffers the indignity of a herd of cattle defecating on his head. Eighteenth century authors are also quite comfortable with sex. Smollett generates a great deal of humour from the sexual frustration of a spinster in *Humphrey Clinker* (1771). Joyce's description of Bloom evacuating his bowels does not seem either new or daring when we look at the larger history of the novel.

* From the Spanish *picaro*: a wily trickster.

Nor is there anything particularly innovative about Joyce drawing on the myth of Odysseus in his account of Bloom's day. Greek tragedy retold ancient myths while Shakespeare was famous for adapting old stories for his plays. More specifically, the critic Samuel Johnson (1709–84) updated the Roman Poet Juvenal's Tenth Satire for his poem 'The Vanity of Human Wishes' (1749), while Jane Austen (1775–1817) parodied the conventions of Gothic fiction in *Northanger Abbey* (1818). All these authors make varied use of literary traditions; they serve as a standard by which to judge current literature; they act as a means of revitalising the contemporary world; and they help build bridges between the past and the present.

The modernist novelist's self-consciousness about his or her art-form also has its precedents. Laurence Sterne's *The Life and Opinions of Tristram Shandy, Gentleman* (1759–67), with its erratic time scheme, anticipates experiments in modernist fiction. If we go back even earlier we find that another concern of the modernist novel, the relation between truth and fiction, lies at the centre of *Don Quixote* (1605 and 1615). Written by Miguel Cervantes (1547–1616), it tells the story of how the eponymous hero reads so many books of chivalry that he goes mad. Imagining that he is a real knight he sets off with his squire, Sancho Panza, in search of adventure. His love and knowledge of chivalric tales means that he interprets reality in terms of his reading. Hence windmills are giants, inns are castles and flocks of sheep are opposing armies. Cervantes seems to be suggesting that our imagination is more important in determining what we see than things themselves.*

Other features of the self-conscious nature of Cervantes's fiction include how he comes to write the novel and the purpose of its interpolated tales. Cervantes presents himself as both the author of *Don Quixote* and someone who merely tracks down the manuscript of the tale, and this raises all kinds of question about the writer's relation to his work: is he an inventor, or a chronicler? Does he stand apart from his

---

* See T. S. Eliot's poem 'Burnt Norton' (1934), which comments on mankind and its relationship with reality.

tale or is he somehow part of it? How is the story put together? The interconnected stories told by characters encountered by Don Quixote and Sancho Panza, are often straightforward romances that are satirised in the main body of the work – so how are we to interpret them? As a reminder of why the chivalric world is being made the subject of laughter, or as a restatement of its integrity, of its ability to survive satire and criticism?

Without doubt the tales disrupt the narrative and, in so doing, they turn our attention away from action to narration. We become less interested in what happens than in how it is reported. This, too, is part of our experience of modernist fiction, which is characterised more by little epiphanies, the revelation of the nature of things, than by the drama of great events. Don Quixote and Sancho Panza spend a lot of time listening to the stories of characters they encounter. This conceit, of the central character being more of an audience than an actor, finds its way into the novels of Franz Kafka (1883–1924). In both *The Trial* (1925) and *The Castle* (1926), 'K.' spends a lot of time listening to stories in the hope that they will throw some light on the bewildering situations in which he finds himself.

Stream of Consciousness

We have argued that most of what is regarded as distinctive about the modernist novel can be found in earlier manifestations of the genre. We should not, however, overlook how modernist authors bring these different elements together to create something new. There is one element that we have not yet discussed which, perhaps more than any other, is associated with the modernist novel, and that is the 'stream of consciousness'. It is true that this device is anticipated by the free-flowing speech of characters such as Miss Bates in Jane Austen's *Emma* (1816) or Mrs Nickleby in Charles Dickens's *Nicholas Nickleby* (1838–9) but in both cases it is confined to minor characters and marks them as either eccentric or sexually frustrated. In the modernist novel, by contrast, the stream of consciousness technique is central to our experience of all the characters. Far from being an individual idiosyncrasy, it is the structuring principle of the work as a whole.

The term 'stream of consciousness' was first used by William James in his *Principles of Psychology* (1890) where it describes the unbroken flow of perceptions, thoughts and feelings in the waking mind, but it has long since been used to describe a narrative method in modern fiction in which the narrator records in detail what passes through a character's consciousness. M. H. Abrams usefully defines stream of consciousness as 'a mode of narration that undertakes to reproduce, without a narrator's intervention, the full spectrum and continuous flow of a character's mental process, in which sense perceptions mingle with conscious and half-conscious thought, memories, expectations, feelings and random associations'.[1] Incidentally, the first writer to use the stream of consciousness technique in England was not, as might be expected, James Joyce or Virginia Woolf (both 1882–1941)* but Dorothy Richardson (1873–1957), whose contribution to modernism has recently been recognised.† She preferred the term 'interior monologue' and used it in her *Pointed Roots* (1915), the first of an autobiographical sequence of novels known as *Pilgrimage* (1915–67).

Joyce's *Ulysses* contains many examples of stream of consciousness writing. One such occurs when Stephen Dedalus, one of the three major characters in the novel (the other two are Bloom and his wife Molly), is walking along a beach.[2] His thoughts range from noticing his thirst, and observing the weather changing, before moving into more obscure terrain, then returning to comment on the evening drawing in. Apart from reproducing the jerky rhythms of internal life, this extract also contains a Latin phrase and a literary reference. Some critics accuse Joyce, as well as Eliot, of being elitist because they expect their readers to be familiar with the canon of Western literature. However, as we noted above, authors referring to, incorporating or even rewriting works by their predecessors is nothing unusual in literary history. In any case, why should readers demand that writers come down to their level?

---

* See Part Three: 'The Modernist Novel in England' for more on Woolf's writing style.

† Édouard Dujardin (1861–1949) was the first person to use the stream of consciousness technique in his short novel *Les Lauriers sont coupés* (1887).

Part of the encounter with art involves our stepping outside what we already know to learn new things and experience new ways of seeing. The determined reader should be able to track down these translations and references for him- or herself.

However, Joyce is not simply trying to exclude readers who may not be familiar with an ancient language (roughly translated, the Latin phrase Stephen speaks in the passage referred to above means 'Lucifer, tell me, who unknown falls into the West?'), or with Milton's *Paradise Lost* (1667), to which the phrase alludes. Like his predecessors, he is trying to enrich ordinary life by drawing upon well established literary and cultural traditions. A more interesting question than whether or not Joyce is elitist is why the stream of consciousness style came to prominence in the early twentieth century.

One answer is that it was a reflection of a general interest in mental life best exemplified by Sigmund Freud (1856–1939), whose *The Interpretation of Dreams* was published in 1900. Why, though, was there this general interest in mental life? There are at least three possible and related explanations. The first is a need for privacy, the second is to find some part of life free from state or social control and the third is the failure of the conventional novel to cope with rendering society in its full complexity.

The need for privacy is part of the response to living in the city. We have to remember that, historically, most human beings lived their lives in small villages. It was only in the late eighteenth and nineteenth centuries that they began to live in cities in large numbers, due mainly to the industrial revolution. One of the most striking features of urban life is the crowd. The sense that one's personal space is constantly under threat in the street, the roads and the shops forces the individual back into his or her own consciousness. This tendency is reinforced by the sense of loneliness that is also a feature of city living. Despite being surrounded by so many of one's fellow creatures in the factory and in rented apartments, it is not easy to get to know them. There are no guidelines for converting strangers into friends and, in any case, the population of an area is often transitory, making it difficult to form lasting relationships.

If crowds make the individual consciousness both a place of isolation and, strangely, comfort, the development of the modern state establishes it as a place of freedom. At the beginning of the twentieth century there were two main conceptions of the state. The first was known as *laissez-faire*, basically the idea that individuals should be free to pursue their economic interests without interference from the state. The second was known as 'interventionism' or 'collectivism', basically the idea that the state should take a more active role in regulating not just the economy, but also society itself. The early years of the twentieth century saw an expansion of the British state as it sought to deal with a whole host of problems ranging from the poor physical conditions of British soldiers to the country's need to compete with the new economies of America and Germany.

The 1902 Education Act and the 1905 Unemployed Workmen's Act are just two examples of how the state stepped into the lives of individuals.* Despite such changes actually benefitting the population there was nevertheless a great deal of opposition to them, particularly to the introduction, in 1907, of the compulsory return of income tax forms. The debate surrounding the rights and wrongs of state intervention hinged, then as now, on the question of individual liberty. Was the extension of state power a threat to freedom or a necessary response to the needs of modern society?

One of the provisions of the 1911 National Insurance Act required doctors to treat all those who paid into the scheme, but the British Medical Association disliked the prospect of doctors effectively becoming state employees and refused to treat insured people unless their income was over £2 a week. The BMA eventually backed down but the case dramatises, in a small way, the issues that were at stake. Doctors wanted to retain their independence, their right to treat whom they chose; the state thought this less important than ensuring the health of the population as a whole.

---

* The 1902 Education Act saw the creation of Local Education Authorities with the power to establish new secondary and technical schools and to develop the existing system of elementary education. It also gave funding to voluntary schools, bringing them under government control. The 1905 Unemployed Workmen's Act provided the means to give work and training to the unemployed.

It may seem tenuous to relate such matters to the stream of consciousness style in modernist fiction. The fact remains, however, that the technique came to prominence at the very time that the state was expanding its activities. It is at least possible to argue that, as people felt the impact of legislation in their daily lives, their sense of freedom became internalised. They were free to think, if not to act, in the way they chose.

The early twentieth century also saw the rapid growth of the nation state. The promotion of a national identity inevitably emphasised what people within a clearly defined territory had in common rather what separated them and this too may have played a part in the development in the novel's interest in inner life. If we are deemed to be the same as others in the discourse of nationalism we can at least be different from them in the flow of our consciousness. Although we can never demonstrate the truth of such claims, they at least have the virtue of making us think about the relation between modernist art and the wider culture.

Another possible explanation for the stream of consciousness style is as the logical culmination of the nineteenth century novel's interest in the relation between the individual and society. The hero or heroine of the eighteenth century commonly undertook a journey round Britain. This was partly a reflection of developments in transport, roads, canals, coaches and so forth, but it was chiefly a means of trying to understand the changes being wrought by the new commercial society that was emerging. The nineteenth century novel also focused on social change, particularly that brought about by the industrial revolution and how it affected the individual.

The aim of the nineteenth century novelist was to balance the needs of the individual against the demands of society. As the century wore on, however, this proved to be too great a task. In the first place, authors retreated from the eighteenth century ambition to understand society in all its complex relations. George Eliot's *Middlemarch* (1871–2) is probably the last attempt to grasp the whole of English society in microcosm. After that date, the sheer scale of the modern world and its speed of change proved too much for the novelist's imagination. In the second place, the individual was becoming less 'knowable'.

The nineteenth century novel had, by and large, focused on a character's outer rather than inner life, reflecting the Victorian ideals of duty and service. The isolation of the individual in the crowd, and the growth of a mass culture promoting private pleasure rather than public service were just two of the factors responsible for the reconfiguration of the self. Accordingly, novelists had to find new ways of rendering this new self. In addition, they were spurred on by the fact that they needed a new subject matter, given that the traditional functions of storytelling and depictions of character in action had been taken over by the cinema and popular fiction.

Flaubert, *Madame Bovary* (1857)

It would be too much to say that *Madame Bovary* is the first modernist novel, even if it was published the same year as Baudelaire's *Les Fleurs du mal* (see Part Three: 'Modernist Poetry – French Origins, English Settings). The author, Gustave Flaubert (1821–80) uses few formal innovations but, nevertheless, his most famous work is, in terms of themes and temperament, distinctly modernist.

The story centres on the eponymous heroine, or rather anti-heroine, Emma Bovary's longing for a more fulfilling life than the one she shares with her husband, the provincial doctor Charles. Incidentally, the figure of the doctor is quite an important one in modernity. He or she represents the new scientific outlook and, like the detective, is charged with righting society's wrongs. Just think of how many television programmes today have a hospital or a police station as their main setting. That they do can be traced back to the appearance of the professional as a major figure in a number of stories at the end of the nineteenth century, for example the solicitor Jonathan Harker in Bram Stoker's *Dracula* (1897). Dracula himself, Harker remarks at one point, would have made a good solicitor. The growing prominence of the professional protagonist marked modernist literature off from the gentrified hero of the eighteenth and indeed nineteenth century novel.

What modernist elements does *Madame Bovary* contain? Flaubert anticipates Joyce's fascination with bodily secretions when he mentions 'the little drops of sweat' on Emma's shoulders.[3] There's also the sense of excitement about city life: 'From that dense packed humanity she inhaled something vertiginous, and it gorged her heart' (p. 245). At the same time, however, there is a desire not to be part of the crowd: 'Emma was inwardly satisfied to feel that she had reached ... that ideal exquisite pale existence, never attained by vulgar souls' (p. 36). There's a celebration of the new: 'Everywhere commerce and the arts are flourishing; everywhere new means of communication, like so many arteries in the body politic, opening therein new relations' (p. 132).

There is support for a scientific rather than a religious outlook: Charles Homais, the pharmacist, criticises priests because they 'dull the understanding' (p. 193) while praising every form of scientific advancement because they sharpen the intellectual faculty. As well as keeping up with the latest developments in his field Homais also takes an interest in 'pisciculture [the cultivation of fish], the manufacture of rubber and the railways' and when he dies he intends to bequeath his body 'to a hospital that it may subsequently benefit Science' (pp. 310, 322). Moreover, it is in *Madame Bovary* that we find the origin of one of the most enduring attitudes in modernist art: a pronounced hostility to the bourgeoisie (middle class), to its stupidity, greed, complacency and philistinism. The audience at the opera house, for example, may have been there to 'seek some respite in the fine arts from the cares of business, but money was ever uppermost, and they were still talking about cotton, liquor or indigo' (p. 206).

Finally, before we briefly consider Emma herself as an emblem of modernity, there is the question of form. Flaubert despised the idea that literature should be useful. To that extent he belongs to the tradition of art for art's sake (see Part Two: 'A Cultural Overview'). He seems to contradict himself, however, because he also thinks that art does have a use, namely to challenge the bourgeois view of the world, as he does in *Madame Bovary*. He takes the predictable plot of a bored housewife and rewrites it in a style that combines the erotic, the naturalistic, the sentimental and the ironic. This was in marked contrast to Flaubert's predecessors, for example George Sand (1804–76) who wrote in a more flowing, uniform style.

It took Flaubert five years to write *Madame Bovary* even though he often spent up to sixteen hours a day on the novel. He was extremely particular about his craft. Each sentence had to be finely balanced, each phrase perfect. Flaubert was not merely being fussy or fastidious, he was determined to distinguish the artistry of his writing from that of the new, mass produced, formulaic fiction. This was 'literature' versus the mass market. Flaubert's mother said the effort desiccated his heart, an observation that recalls Yeats's comment, noted in Part Three: 'Modernist Poetry – America, Ireland and England', about how the fascination of what's difficult had dried the sap out of his veins.

One aspect of Flaubert's artistry is his development of free and indirect style. This rather grand sounding term refers to the merging of the narrator's voice with that of a character. So instead of Flaubert telling us how long ago Emma sat with Léon, her long term lover, in the chimney corner, the information comes from both himself and his character: 'What a long time it was now since she had sat with him, on the stool in the chimney corner, burning the end of a stick in the big flames from the crackling reeds' (p. 160). We can detect Flaubert's presence in 'since *she* had sat', but the feelings of loss and nostalgia are clearly coming from Emma, as it is she who is doing the remembering. The free and indirect style, by dispensing with the omniscient or all-knowing narrator, by blending him or her with the character's thoughts, feelings and perceptions, paves the way for the development of the stream of consciousness style. At least one critic claims that Joyce 'explicitly modelled his technique on Flaubert's'.[4]

However, Flaubert was and remains a nineteenth century novelist, and while he may not overtly condemn his heroine in the manner of a Dickens or a Thackeray he nevertheless shapes our response to her. Mostly he does this by taking us into her mind, but he also uses other strategies. At the agricultural show, for example, he makes the conversation of several characters overlap (p. 138), much in the manner of the pub talk at the end of T. S. Eliot's 'A Game of Chess'.* By juxtaposing

* See the Extended Commentary in Part Three: 'Modernist Poetry – America, Ireland and England'.

the exchanges between Emma and Rodolphe Boulanger, her upper class seducer, with announcements from the platform, Flaubert not only highlights their separation from ordinary decent life but he also conveys the animal-like nature of their liaison, which is quite different from how Emma imagines it.

Emma herself is an anti-heroine, a woman whose actions, chief of which is adultery, we are expected to understand but not approve of. She suffers from boredom, the theme of Baudelaire's *Les Fleurs du mal*: 'boredom, quiet as the spider, was spinning its web in the shadowy places of her heart' (p. 42). That the experience of *ennui* should be integral to the modernist temperament is strange given the range of entertainment provided by the new mass culture. One answer to this apparent conundrum is that increased regulation, the imposition of working practices and the passive nature of new forms of amusement such as the cinema combined to prevent the individual from exerting him- or herself which would lead to a sense of fulfilment, a sure way of banishing boredom.

Emma is certainly passive. Like Estragon and Vladimir in Samuel Beckett's *Waiting for Godot* (1955) she was 'waiting for something to happen' (p. 58).* Emma is well aware that, as a woman, she is more trapped by circumstances than a man in her position. 'A man at least, is free; he can explore each passion and every kingdom .... But a woman is continually thwarted [by] the inequity of the law' (p. 82). The boredom that lies so heavily upon her, however, cannot be reduced to her gender – as Baudelaire so amply testified, it weighs equally heavily on men. Emma takes refuge from 'the boring countryside, the imbecile petits bourgeois [and] the general mediocrity of life' (p. 55) by reading, mostly romantic fiction and magazines for women. The latter, with their court gossip, foreshadow our own culture's obsession with celebrity.

Since Emma spends so much of her time with a book in her hand we can say that *Madame Bovary* is, in part, a novel about reading; about what we read, how we read and the effects of reading. We find similar issues in *Don Quixote* and, indeed, there is a case for claiming that

* See the Extended Commentary in Part Three: 'The British Stage and Theatrical Thinkers'

Emma is a female version of literature's most famous knight. At times she conflates romantic creations with real life, identifying with the characters in a story so that the 'voice of the heroine seemed to be simply the voice of her own consciousness' (p. 207). This, indeed, proves to be her undoing. She judges life by fiction and finds it wanting. Why can't her existence be as exciting as those she reads about in books?

Flaubert seems to be warning his readers against indulging in cheap fiction because it creates unrealistic expectations about life and relationships. At the same time he is making a plea for literature whose value lies in its distance from cliché. The language of the best-seller, to use a contemporary expression, 'is a machine that continually amplifies the emotions' while the language of literature registers the anguish of speech that is 'like a cracked cauldron on which we knock out tunes for dancing bears, when we wish to conjure pity from the stars' (pp. 177, 218).

The danger of popular fiction is that it gives the impression that we can know things quickly and express them easily. It presents a simplified picture of the world which pays no regard to how complex we and the world really are, nor how difficult it is to convey that complexity. One of the defining features of modernity is the rise of mass culture and the effect it has on traditional art. *Madame Bovary* provides an early instance of how the artist responds to this challenge: chiefly by showing how mass culture promises a life we can never really lead.

Mann, *Death in Venice* (1912)

Thomas Mann's novella, *Death in Venice* is not an obvious contender for the modernist canon and yet it is every bit as profound as another key work of the period, Joseph Conrad's *Heart of Darkness* (1902).* Both texts peer into the abyss of the human heart. Mann's central

---

* Conrad's novel describes the narrator Marlow's journey to find Kurtz in the Congo. Kurtz is an employee of a Belgian trading company and nothing has been heard from him for a while. Marlow discovers that Kurtz has been indulging in rites involving sex and violence. The novel is a symbol of how contact with Africa reawakens the primitive nature of human beings. Many critics have pointed out the racism of the novel and its failure to address, despite mentioning them, the evils of colonialism.

character is Gustav Aschenbach, an author who has written a history of Frederick the Great, a novel and a treatise on aesthetics, *Mind and Art.* His devotion to intellectual matters has been built on the denial of his instinctual life. He experiences this in all its chaos and confusion when he goes on holiday to Venice and becomes infatuated with a young Polish boy called Tadzio. Aschenbach has a dream of Dionysus, the Greek god of wine, and the inspirer of ritual madness and sexual ecstasy.* He dreams he is caught up in a wild procession of Dionysus's female followers, maenads, who dance in animal skins and worship phallic objects. He tries to resist the tambourines and the flute music but is drawn into the frenzy and wakes 'unnerved, shattered and powerless in the demon's grip'.[5]

The split between the mind and the body is not a particular characteristic of modernity since it is an essential distinction in most of the world's religions, but in this period it received a new meaning and expression. The moderns were beginning to break free of a nineteenth century, middle class culture – sober, austere, frugal, respectable – and they weren't very well equipped to cope with the consequences. How do you deal with desires that have been repressed for years but are now acknowledged, even approved of? Wasn't the new popular culture based on the pleasure principle?

Freud was the scientific explorer of this new terrain, but artists such as Mann were also drawn to map this strange landscape. His fear, like Conrad's, is not only that our instincts will overwhelm us but that that is what we passionately desire. We have, thinks Mann, 'an inborn, natural, and even incorrigible preference for the abyss' (*Death in Venice*, p. 363). A character who portrays such feelings is Kurtz in *Heart of Darkness*. He is an ivory trader who has set himself up as a god over the natives and overseen obscene rites. Well might Mann echo Kurtz's dying words: 'the horror, the horror'. T. S. Eliot used another phrase from Conrad's novel, 'Mistah Kurtz – he dead', for his poem 'The Hollow Men' (1925) which conveys a picture of ghostly humanity inhabiting a twilight world on the verge of a feeble apocalypse.

---

* He was also the patron deity of agriculture and theatre.

Mann, Conrad and Eliot all project a sense of imminent destruction. It stems from a surrender to the most base promptings of our nature, to abandon culture and civilisation for a life of riotous and ruinous instinct. This is in contrast to the traditional account of the relation between mind and body, that the flesh should be either subdued or brought into harmony with the spirit. The desire for self-destruction is not just an individual affliction, it also seems to affect society as a whole. Mann's novel, we remember, was published during the First World War (1914–18), the most devastating, at that time, of any in history.

Aschenbach's disintegration is caused by his infatuation for Tadzio, who is less a character than a work of art. He is compared to a 'godly sculpture' (p. 332) and emerges from the sea in a manner that recalls Sandro Botticelli's painting *The Birth of Venus* (*c*. 1482–6). Indeed Aschenbach compares him to a 'beautiful [and] tender deity' (p. 321). Tadzio has a feminine appearance and this also associates him with Dionysus, whose long hair and slim figure give him a womanly look. Some may argue that to present Tadzio as a pagan divinity or work of art is simply to disguise an inappropriate sexual desire: a man in his fifties should not 'fall in love' with a fourteen year old boy.

In that respect Mann's novel resembles Vladimir Nabokov's *Lolita* (1955) which tells the story of the middle aged Humbert Humbert's obsession with a twelve year old girl, Dolores Haze. Nabokov's defence against any possible charge of paedophilia is that Humbert's attraction to Dolores is not sexual but aesthetic. We are starting to go round in circles here, though, for the claim is that an interest in art is a cover for an interest in sex. We cannot resolve this matter here except to point out that desire takes many forms, so while Aschenbach is struck by Tadzio's beauty, it does not follow that he wants sexual relations with him. It is true that Aschenbach behaves like a lover – having his hair dyed, his eyebrows plucked and his cheeks rouged – but, by this time, he is suffering from fever and is not himself. Moreover, there is another component to Aschenbach's love for Tadzio: he is the son he never had (p. 300).

As a work of art – which he is, literally, since he is a character in a novel – Tadzio becomes the focus of Aschenbach's reflections on the nature of art. First the boy symbolises the living, breathing beauty that Aschenbach has never managed to achieve in his own writing, which particularly in his later years, has become 'conventional, conservative, formalistic, even formulaic' (p. 299). Second Tadzio prompts Aschenbach to think about the nature of beauty. Beauty rather than knowledge, Aschenbach considers, is at the heart of the experience of art because beauty draws things together while knowledge pulls them apart (pp. 297–9).

In his early work, however, Aschenbach does not rely on beauty to unify a work but ethics, which 'transcends knowledge, transcends the hampering and disintegrative force of cognizance' (p. 298). However, the problem with ethics, or what Aschenbach calls 'moral resoluteness' (ibid.) is that it presents a simplified picture of the world and the psyche. It is only when he encounters Tadzio that Aschenbach starts to think about beauty. At first he takes the traditional line that beauty 'is the only form of the spiritual that we can receive with our senses' (p. 334) but later comes to the conclusion that beauty is 'truly a path of sin, a path that is bound to lead you astray' (p. 363). Since Aschenbach judges beauty in terms of its ethical effects alone, he is not really considering it in its entirety. By imposing a moral grid on it, he simplifies beauty in the same way that he simplified the world and the psyche, by only looking at them in terms of good and bad.

Leaving those considerations to one side, does the corrupting power of beauty lie in the work of art or in the beholder? The answer would seem to be both. We have seen that Aschenbach's habit of self-denial makes him susceptible to sensory indulgence but there is also something repellent about Tadzio, whose teeth are 'pale and jagged, without the sheen of health, and particularly brittle and translucent' (p. 323). There is something rotten in the state of beauty. The god is revealed as sickly human (and humanity as a whole is sick in this novel). The cholera that kills Aschenbach is a symbol of a creeping fog of filth that will infect all civilisation. The irony is that this arises from the pursuit of beauty.

The modernity of Mann's tale lies principally in its theme rather than its form. What it shows is that old ideas about art – truth, beauty and ethics – are not suited to the new world. They belong to a conception of humanity that has ceased to exist. Only an art that is itself broken and fragmented can address a broken and fragmented humanity. The discussion of art is picked up again in Joyce's *A Portrait of the Artist as a Young Man* (1916, see Extended Commentary) where, once again, it is based on an attraction to an other, though one not as deadly as that suffered by Aschenbach or even, for that matter, Emma Bovary.

Kafka, *The Trial* (1925)

Franz Kafka (1883–1924), a German Czech, is probably the most enigmatic writer of the modernist period. He recounts the most extraordinary events in the most matter of fact style. Take the opening of his short story, *Metamorphosis* (1913), which begins as follows: 'When Gregor Samsa awoke one morning after troubled dreams, he found himself changed into an enormous cockroach'.[6] There is no sense of shock or surprise, just irritation that his new condition is going to make it very hard for him to continue his job as a travelling salesman. It is almost comic, a dimension of Kafka's writing that has yet to be explored. Comedy, we might add, is in short supply in modernist literature.

The Trial also opens with the hero, K., in bed. He is waiting for his breakfast but instead an official enters and informs him he is under arrest, though he doesn't say why. The bed is a recurrent image in Kafka. Many of his characters, particularly the official ones, conduct business from their beds, although the reason for this is never explained. Indeed, in Kafka's work there are rarely, if ever, any answers. We don't know why K. is arrested, we don't know of what he is accused, nor do we know why he is 'executed', as he is at the end of the novel. If modernity prides itself on the advance of knowledge, Kafka is there to remind us that some things, perhaps the most important things, can never be known, no matter how many questions we ask.

To return to the subject of beds, throughout *The Trial* K. is described as being 'tired', 'tired out' or 'utterly tired'.[7] It seems that characters are in bed because they are tired, and they are tired because of the burden of work which, in modernity, seems to sap the spirit more than in previous ages. Even so, is it normal to conduct business from the depths of your bed? The strangeness of such behaviour is rendered even more strange by its being presented as if it were normal. One of the most bizarre episodes in the novel occurs when K. discovers, in a cupboard at the bank where he works, a man whipping the warders who came to arrest him. They are apparently being punished because he complained about them.

K.'s reaction is puzzling. He does not ask why they are at the bank, he does not ask why they are in the cupboard, he does not report them nor does he ask them to leave. He just wonders if the cane is painful. That seems a decidedly odd reaction to finding a sado-masochistic scene being enacted at your place of work. K.'s response is reasonable to the extent that he observes, asks questions and draws conclusions, but it is unreasonable because he does not query the legitimacy of such behaviour, nor why it is taking place in the bank. This blend of the rational and the irrational is the essence of Kafka. It is apparent in one of his most frequent expressions – 'as if'* – for that implies something both is and is not: in those two words is the ghostly world of Kafka.

Kafka was a great admirer of Flaubert, as is evident from his use of the free and indirect style which he takes to its logical conclusion by making it almost impossible to separate K. from the narrator: each seems as bewildered by events as the other. Why, if K. is under arrest, is he allowed to continue to live a 'normal' life? Why, when he attends court, is it in a block of flats? Why does the judge have pornographic drawings on the bench? Is there a connection to 'The Whipper' here, and how does it relate to K.'s casual sexual encounters with most of the women he meets in the novel?

One way of explaining all this is to say that the novel demonstrates Freud's assertion that we are dominated by our sexual desires; it is they which drive our behaviour. That would be another feature of the novel's modernity. The recourse to Freud may also help us interpret *The Trial*. K. has sex with a number of women, most of whom are attached to

---

* This comment depends on the translation from the original German.

someone else: a husband, a lover or a relation. Is his arrest anything to do, not with his promiscuity, but with what it represents? Freud argues that all males go through the Oedipus complex. That is they harbour unconscious wishes to sleep with their mothers and kill their fathers, wishes which also give rise to guilt.

It is possible to argue that the women with whom K. sleeps represent the mother figure to the extent that they nurture him and are married to or are with someone else. If that is so then the law represents the father, for K. is indeed hostile to all aspects of the legal process, refusing to accept its authority over him. Again, if we accept this line of reasoning, it follows that what K. is accused of is the cultivation of Oedipal desires. The law tries to make him acknowledge his guilt so that he can transcend them, but his constant refusal to do so leaves open one course of action – death.

This interpretation is convincing, but so are many others. The problem with Kafka is that he offers the reader signs and symbols that can be read in many ways that are equally plausible. Read *The Trial* carefully and you will see that each explanation of an event is followed by another which negates the previous explanation, and so on. Kafka is the supreme modernist because he tells us that *symbols* cannot be interpreted. They will possess us, baffle us and eventually destroy us without us ever finding out what they mean. If that sounds like the experience of bureaucracy, it is. Officialdom is Kafka's great subject, a world of complicated rules which refer only to themselves.

Extended Commentary: Joyce, *A Portrait of the Artist as a Young Man* (1916)

Kafka is a typical modernist to the extent that his work requires interpretation – even if it ultimately refuses it. Modernist literature was more difficult, more demanding and required more effort than the adventure stories of John Buchan, author of *The Thirty Nine Steps* (1915); 'Sapper', real name Herman Cyril McNeile, author of *Bull-dog*

Drummond (1920); or P. C. Wren, author of *Beau Geste* (1924). However, that was the intention, for modernist authors felt themselves engaged in a much more serious enterprise: preserving the soul of art in an age that seemed to prefer entertainment to education.

The nature of art is part of the subject matter of Joyce's *A Portrait of the Artist as a Young Man*, the novel which precedes *Ulysses*. It is a transitional work, belonging partly to the nineteenth century tradition of *bildungsroman*,* and partly to new, experimental modes of writing. The novel centres on the childhood and youth of Stephen Dedalus, who also appears in *Ulysses*. 'Stephen' refers to the first Christian martyr who was stoned to death for blasphemy while 'Dedalus', refers to Daedalus, a figure in Greek mythology famous for his craftsmanship and engineering skills. Both names reflect aspects of Stephen's character. While he is not blasphemous Stephen does reject the Catholic church, and like his Greek namesake, he is devoted to elaborate constructions.[8] Since Stephen is Joyce's alter ego, we can regard *Ulysses* and the even more exacting *Finnegans Wake* (1939) as the fulfilment of that ambition.

As with Yeats, Ireland features strongly in Joyce's work. His basic position is that the Irish are oppressed not just by the British or by the Catholic church but also by themselves. There are numerous references to Ireland's troubled past in the *Portrait*. One of the most famous scenes in the novel is an argument at a Christmas dinner between Dante Riordan, an aunt of the Dedalus children and John Casey, a friend of Mr Dedalus, over Charles Stewart Parnell (1846–91), a strong advocate of Home Rule and Land Reform. Parnell was cited as co-respondent[†] by William O'Shea when he divorced his wife Katherine O'Shea, an action which split his supporters and set back the cause of Irish independence. There were those, like Dante, who felt that Parnell was morally unfit to lead the Irish Parliamentary Party and those, like John, who felt that his private life was separate from his politics.

---

* A German term applied to novels where the hero is educated to a new understanding of himself and the world.
† A co-respondent is the man or woman cited in divorce cases as having committed adultery with the wife or husband.

The scene dramatises the divisions between the Irish themselves, particularly between supporters of the Catholic church and the nationalists. Part of what Stephen is searching for is a language free of internal conflict (p. 204). He also wants to subvert the language of the coloniser, English. This comes across most strongly in the episode where Stephen goes to see his dean of studies, who is English (p. 205). Stephen is aware how alien their supposedly common language is to him, and how unnatural words seem to sound when pronounced in his Irish accent. The invention of new words, the multi-lingual punning, the chopping up of sentences, the abandonment of the conventional plot and a host of other features characteristic of *Ulysses* and *Finnegans Wake* are not only declarations of war on the English tongue, they are also an attempt to create a specifically Irish literary language.

We can see Joyce starting to experiment in the *Portrait*. This is evident from the very first sentence, which starts off in the familiar 'Once upon a time' format, but proceeds in a very unconventional vein in terms of content, vocabulary and syntax (p. 3). First, Joyce breaks with nineteenth century convention by not setting the scene for what will follow. Second, the sentence has no punctuation. Third, the lack of punctuation anticipates the stream of consciousness style because it partially recreates how the young Stephen remembers/experiences the story. Fourth, the image of a father telling his son a story is a symbol of the Irish oral tradition by which culture is passed from one generation to another and it is this tradition, among others, that Joyce will critique in the novel. He does not appear to share Yeats's love of native myth and legend – for him these are at best dubious means to guide the Irish on their journey to independence (p. 195).

Joyce continues to experiment with narrative throughout the *Portrait*, mainly using free and indirect style to convey the state of Stephen's consciousness at different stages of his development. As a child, for instance, he is preoccupied with sensory experience, as in his description of wetting the bed (p. 3). By the end of the novel, the free and indirect discourse – which, to remind ourselves, is the merging of the narrator's and character's voices – gives way to Stephen's own voice as he makes entries in his diary. Another aspect of the narrative is that we often find ourselves in the middle of a situation or a conversation for which there is no context. An example is where Stephen is gazing at some birds and musing on the nature of symbols. Suddenly we are plunged into a series of comments about a play and then we are in a library (pp. 245–6).

Such abrupt changes of scene are disorientating but beneath the apparently random movement of the narrative are numerous connections. In this instance we could begin by pointing out that the birds are connected to Stephen's ambition to 'fly' Ireland as well as to his surname, Dedalus, a variation of Daedalus, who as the father of Icarus in the Greek myth devised a set of wings for human flight. Flying involves height and so it's no surprise to find Stephen on the balcony of a theatre. The play on which he looks down represents the narrow, provincial culture he wishes to escape but it is also related to the episode of the Whitsuntide play (pp. 76–91). Then, since Stephen proposes to create a new literary culture, it is logical that we should next find him in the library.

Yet another aspect of the narrative is the extensive use of quotation. The many and frequent references to theological treatises, literary works, histories and so on represent a respect for an intellectual tradition that helps bind the novel together. We have already encountered this tactic in Eliot's *The Waste Land* (1922), but these references are also a continual reminder that the Irish speak a borrowed language. To that extent we are to regard them as form of imprisonment, established ways of perceiving and thinking from which Stephen must liberate himself. However it is not possible to break completely with the past, as is clear from Stephen's views about art, which are mostly based on religion.

Stephen models his idea of art on what Saint Thomas Aquinas (1225–74) says about beauty, whose constituents are wholeness, harmony and radiance (p. 229). These constituents correspond to the three stages of apprehending an artwork. First, we separate it off from the objects which surround it, that is wholeness. Second, we analyse its form and feel the rhythm of its structure, that is harmony. Third, we appreciate the work for what it is and that is radiance (p. 231). Despite Stephen's commitment to Aquinas's philosophy he believes it suffers from two problems. The first is that it rejects the body and the second is that it potentially makes art a mere symbol for a meaning that lies beyond it: God's providence, Christ's mercy and so on.

Since Stephen feels that art should embrace the whole of human experience and not be merely symbolic of a supernatural reality, he feels compelled to move beyond Aquinas's position, to find a new means of expression (p. 227). In artistic terms this means, in the first instance, not shying away from describing dirt, filth and rubbish. Hence the *Portrait*'s numerous references to ordure and excrement. We can also sense here an attack on the nineteenth century novel: how could it claim to be realistic if it excluded such things?

Stephen's savouring of words, their contours, sound and arrangement is reminiscent of the Aesthetic Movement in the 1880s and 1890s (see his wonderful description of a single phrase as both treasure and a beautiful cloudy day, p. 180),* but it is also Joyce's attempt to rid art of its symbolic character, an impossible undertaking. To the extent that literature refers to things in the world it is always going to be symbolic of them. Stephen's very name is symbolic, and the literature he hopes to create will become symbolic of the new consciousness of his people (see p. 276).

Although Joyce wanted to rid himself of a religious *conception* of art he retained a religious *organisation* of it. His impulse to confer significance on every aspect of human activity derives from his Catholic education. The church calendar means that each day has its own special meaning, aligned to key figures of faith (see p. 159). It is no surprise, then, to find a similar detailed ordering of life in Joyce's masterpiece, *Ulysses*. The novel is divided into eighteen episodes, each one of which corresponds to a part of Homer's *Odyssey*, which tells of Ulysses's adventures on his return home from the Trojan war. The eighteenth episode, for example, which consists of Molly Bloom's soliloquy, relates to Penelope, Ulysses's wife. The complex and conflicting feelings Molly has for her husband are contrasted with Penelope's determined and single-minded fidelity to hers. Joyce's use of Homer underlines the

* See Part Two: 'A Cultural Overview' for more on the Aesthetic Movement.

claim that art always has a symbolic dimension. The wanderings of Leopold Bloom are not simply his own, for they stand for those of Ulysses too.

It is as well to remember this point when we consider Stephen's assertion that all art is either static or kinetic (*Ulysses*, p. 222). Art that is static appeals to the intellect and requires that we contemplate it. Art that is kinetic appeals to our appetites and requires that we satisfy them. This distinction is the basis for distinguishing between good and bad art but it has the disadvantage of implying that the very best art stands apart from the rest of society and serves no useful purpose. If we are right in saying that art, by its very nature, always has some relation to reality, then Stephen's distinction begins to look decidedly untenable.

In any case, Stephen's view of art, like Aschenbach's, is bound up with a vision of another. As he is walking along the beach Stephen is struck by the sight of a girl staring out to sea, a scene that has parallels with the Nausicaä episode in *Ulysses*. Her image passes into his soul and she becomes both an object of contemplation, and an object of desire (*Portrait*, p. 186). She unites in her person the static and kinetic aspects of art, the spiritual and the physical that tore Aschenbach apart. It is a reminder that part of modernist art is about making connections, between body and soul, between seemingly fragmented parts of a work – and even between works themselves.

Notes

1   M. H. Abrams, *A Glossary of Literary Terms* (Boston, MA: Heinle and Heinle, 1999), p. 299.

2   James Joyce, *Ulysses* with an Introduction by Declan Kiberd (Harmondsworth: Penguin, 1992), p. 63.

3   Gustave Flaubert, *Madame Bovary* translated with an Introduction by Geoffrey Wall (Harmondsworth: Penguin, 2003), p. 123.

4   Pericles Lewis, *The Cambridge Introduction to Modernism* (Cambridge: Cambridge University Press, 2007), p. 34.

5   Thomas Mann, *Death in Venice and Other Tales* translated by Joachim Neugroschel (Harmondsworth: Penguin, 1998), p. 359.

6   Franz Kafka, *Metamorphosis and Other Stories* translated with an Introduction by Michael Hoffman (Harmondsworth: Penguin, 2007), p. 87.

7   Franz Kafka, *The Trial* translated with an Introduction by Idris Parry (Harmondsworth: Penguin 2000), pp. 71, 89, 99.

8   See James Joyce, *A Portrait of the Artist as a Young Man* edited with an Introduction and notes by Seamus Deane (Harmondsworth: Penguin, 2000).

The Modernist Novel in England: Saki, Woolf and Lawrence

When we think of the modernist novel we tend to think of James Joyce (1882–1941), Virginia Woolf (1882–1941) or even of the American William Faulkner (1897–1962) because they are all exemplars of the stream of consciousness technique. In *The Sound and the Fury* (1929), for example, Faulkner charts the decline of the American South through several eyes, most notably those of Benjy Compson, a thirty-three year old 'idiot'.

The stream of consciousness technique is usually held to be the defining characteristic of the modernist novel, the clear mark of its difference from the nineteenth century realist novel. While there is some truth in this account we should not forget that a concern with subjective experience is also present in nineteenth century writers such as Charles Dickens (1812–70), Fyodor Dostoevsky (1821–81) and, of course, Henry James (1843–1916). This would suggest that modernist authors did not break with their predecessors so much as develop and extend their interest in rendering inner life.

The point is that if we define the modernist novel solely in terms of the stream of consciousness technique then we end up with a very limited view of it. Our focus, indeed, would still be on 'character'. We may acquire a more sophisticated understanding of the term, but we would nevertheless remain within the parameters of traditional criticism of the novel. Hence we would be in danger of overlooking the modernist novelist's interest in symbol, in the nature of fiction, in the organising power of art and in the nature of language, how 'it ceases to be what we see through and becomes what we see'.[1]

Another important issue for modernist novels concerns narrative, or how stories are told. In Ford Madox Ford's *The Good Soldier* (1915) the narrator, John Dowell, tells the story of Florence, his wife and her affair with Edward Ashburnham (the good soldier of the title). Florence kills herself when she discovers that Edward is falling in love with his young ward, Nancy Rufford. However, Dowell does not relate these or other events in the order in which they happened but rather as he remembers them, leaving the reader to reconstruct their sequence.

Ford (1873–1939) was interested in 'the impression, not the corrected chronicle',[2] in how we piece together a story which may or may not reflect what actually happened. Dowell's failure to tell a straight story is symptomatic 'of his inability to know and be himself'.[3] His fumbling attempts at narrative undermine the novelist's traditional claim both to imitate life and to provide an insight into human character. This implies that narrator and reader inhabit different worlds and that the nineteenth century ambition of the novel as creating a shared vision, a community of like-minded souls, is finally abandoned.

The Modernist Novel and Time

The clock rules all aspects of modern life. What time to rise, what time to leave the house, what time to start work, what time to finish, what time to come home, what time to eat, what time to sleep. For the modernists time divided up the day and each day was the same as every other, except for Sundays when time came to a standstill before resuming again on Monday. This was time as repetition, not time as growth.

They felt the burden of this 'empty' time and sought to give it meaning and direction. They explored the relation of the present to the past, they examined the difference between subjective and objective time and their work often contained little epiphanies, momentary manifestations of an order that transcended mundane existence.

Joyce's 'mythical method', the paralleling of characters and events in *The Odyssey* with those in *Ulysses*, is one means of exploring the relation between past and present. Joyce's Homeric references can be seen in at least two ways. The first is satirical: Bloom cannot possibly be compared to Odysseus. He has not fought in any battles, he does not have legendary cunning, he stays in one place, Dublin, and he is only away from home a few hours. Odysseus fought at Troy, has a wily intelligence, travels far and wide and his separation from his wife lasts many years. However, the Homeric references also serve to confer heroic status on Bloom and suggest that modern life too has an epic quality. The novel supports both these interpretations. The classical past is either a measure of how far we have fallen away from it or else it is a reminder of our capacity for greatness. Either way it suggests the past is still an active force in the present.

A writer who examines the relation between subjective and objective time is Marcel Proust (1871–1922). In contrast to Joyce, who locates his characters very firmly in 'real' time and space,* Proust seems unconcerned about details of where and when. His seven volume, semi-autobiographical *À la recherche du temps perdu* (1922–31) contains many themes, including art and homosexuality, but the main one is memory.

Proust distinguishes between a voluntary and an involuntary memory. The first is the one we use in everyday life while the second, dormant but powerful, can be reawakened by a sight, a sound, a smell that instantly transports us back to the past. The most famous example is the taste of madeleine (a tiny sponge cake) dipped in tea which reminds the narrator of the ones he used to eat at his aunt's house when a boy. The subjective, remembered past seems more tangible, more real, than the actual but somehow insubstantial present. We never escape the past, Proust seems to be saying, it lies all around, waiting to reclaim us.

The epiphany is another way in which modernist authors give meaning to time. When drafting *A Portrait of the Artist as a Young Man*, Joyce defined epiphany as 'a sudden spiritual manifestation' adding that it was 'the most delicate and evanescent [fleeting] of

* Joyce used a 1904 street directory to ensure accuracy when describing his locations.

moments'.[4] An example from the novel is the scene where Stephen sees a girl staring out to sea. He compares her to an angel who, in an instant, throws open to him all life's possibilities.[5]

A less glorious version of epiphany characterises the stories in Joyce's *Dubliners* (1907). Far from being spiritually uplifting, the epiphanies in these tales are moments where characters realise the death of their dreams, the futility of their hopes and the impossibility of their desires. In 'Araby' the narrator understands that his love for Mangan's sister will come to nothing while in 'A Little Cloud' Little Chandler accepts that he will never be a poet.

Woolf subscribes to Joyce's more buoyant view of epiphany. In *To the Lighthouse* (1927) characters can suddenly become aware of the existence of a higher reality: 'And suddenly the meaning which, for no reason at all descends on people, making them symbolical, making them representative … Then after an instant, the symbolical outline which transcended the real figures, [sinks] down again'.[6] Art is the means by which we sense 'the coherence of things' (p. 114) and *To the Lighthouse* is very much concerned with the nature of art and the problems involved in creating it.

The Waves (1931), Woolf's most accomplished novel, contains a similar epiphany. Sitting with his friends, Louis receives 'a hint at some other order, and better, which makes a reason everlastingly', an order that can piece together a 'shattered mind'.[7] Woolf's epiphanies are related to a character's sense of self. At a very basic level, characters are fragmented, but the fleeting vision of the connectedness of things restores their sense of wholeness, albeit briefly. *The Waves*, a profoundly poetic meditation on human identity, love and friendship, pushes this idea further and asks whether at the moment we are 'most disparate', we are also most 'integrated' (p. 57).

Henri Bergson and Time

Joyce, Proust and Woolf all address, in one way or another, the problem of time in modern society. A classic expression of the problem was provided by the French philosopher Henri Bergson (1859–1941). In *Time and Free Will* (1910) he distinguished between mechanical time and duration. The former is measured out in hours, minutes and seconds while the latter is marked by memory and those visionary or mystical moments where we seem to stand outside time altogether. Which, of course, is another description of epiphany.

Bergson later developed a theory of identity which necessitated a slight modification to his notion of duration. This now becomes 'the continuous progress of the past which grows into the future ... grows without ceasing, so there is no limit to its preservation'.[8] Bergson's basic claim is that as we cannot know the whole of this past – it is simply too vast – we extract from it only what is useful for fulfilling our needs and desires. The consequence of not knowing the past is that we do not really know ourselves or understand the forces that shape us.

Moreover, even if we could know the past we are still faced with a further problem: the addition, each moment, of something new to our personality. Hence, claims Bergson, we are in a continual state of becoming and, because there is no end to that process, there can be no self-knowledge in any meaningful sense of the term. What Bergson seems to be saying, then, is that our identity cannot unfold through time. The past is hidden from us, the present adds to us and the future eludes us. We never arrive at the final point where we can say 'this is me.'

He is also making a point about how we regard the world around us. The attitude that we apply to the past, taking from it what is useful, is the same attitude that we apply to 'the nature of the real', with the result that 'we become unable to perceive the true evolution, the radical becoming' (p. 12). We therefore need to understand that the practical approach to life has its limitations and that we also need to attune ourselves to the internal process of continuous creation. Birkin voices a similar sentiment in D. H. Lawrence's *Women in Love* (1920), '"you must leave your surroundings sketchy, unfinished, so that you are never contained, never confined, never dominated from the outside"'.[9]

Like modernist novelists, Bergson was responding to the new experience of time in contemporary society. Before the industrial revolution time followed the cycle of the seasons. New plants came forth in spring, flowered in summer, ripened in autumn and died in winter. As humans moved from the country to the city, their experience of time changed. It was no longer linked to the seasons, but to the machine. It became mechanical, repetitive and even dictatorial. This was particularly the case in the factory, where the Time and Motion Study stipulated how workers should move and the amount they should produce in a given time.

Part of the modernist project, therefore, was to give a human meaning to time. Bergson's notion of duration was his way of giving emphasis to the qualities of memory, vision and creativity and there are at least three ways in which his ideas complement the development of the novel. First his conception of the dynamic, multi-faceted nature of our inner life finds expression in the stream of consciousness technique. Second, his claim that our identity is always in process finds a parallel in the portrayal of characters in the modernist novel as sketchy, unfinished and incomplete. Third, and we have already made this point, Bergson's moment of vision corresponds to the modernist epiphany.

So far we have argued that to define the modernist novel solely in terms of the stream of consciousness technique is to limit our understanding of it. We therefore mentioned some other aspects of the novel in which authors were interested, principally narrative and time. These are largely the property of the canonical modernists, however. What about other authors writing at the same time? Just because they do not participate in the formal experiments associated with 'high' modernism does not mean that their work fails to engage with modernity or show an interest in its art. Indeed, it is possible to be both modern and traditional at the same time. The short story writer Hector Hugh Munro (1870–1916), more familiarly known as Saki,* is a case in point. The frequent mention of open doors and windows in his work perfectly captures the sense of being on the threshold of a new age.

---

* *Saki* is often thought to be a reference to the cupbearer in the *Rubáiyát of Omar Khayyam* (1859), a poem mentioned disparagingly by the eponymous character in 'Reginald on Christmas Presents' (1910). In addition it is the name of a primate, a small, long-tailed monkey from South America that is a central figure in 'The Remoulding of Groby Lington' (1911). It is also a Japanese beverage. Munro's pen name is itself modernist because it has multiple meanings, demands to be interpreted, is linked to a literary work and is incorporated in a self-conscious fashion into at least two of his stories.

Saki: An Unregarded Modernist?

Before modernism there was Edwardianism, a sort of dress rehearsal before the main event. Edwardianism was a reaction to the stuffiness of the Victorian world. The term Edwardian covers the years 1900–14.* It was during this period that Saki wrote his short stories, the first appearing in 1904 and the last in 1914. In addition to his short stories, he also wrote political sketches, a history of Russia, a play and two novels. Saki was killed in the trenches by a sniper bullet in 1916. His last words were 'Put that bloody light out.'

The Edwardian period was characterised by excitement and a new sense of freedom, but it lacked direction. How were writers and artists to respond to the loss of Victorian certainties concerning God, the social structure and England's place in the world? These were the sorts of issue addressed by writers from Arnold Bennett (1867–1931) to H. G. Wells (1866–1946). Although Joseph Conrad (1857–1924) was already beginning to experiment with the novel's form, most fiction of the period was concerned, in one way or another, with national values as embodied in the countryside and the upper class house. Both feature strongly in Saki's stories, for example, 'Tobermory' (1911), the tale of a talking cat who unnerves the country house guests by revealing what they secretly think of one another. If one of the definitions of 'magic realism' is the presentation of supernatural events in naturalistic prose, then Saki is a pioneer in the field.

It is with Saki as a modernist, though, that we are concerned, and this quality manifests itself in a number of ways. One is the frequent mention of train journeys. 'The Disappearance of Crispina Umberleigh' (1916), for instance starts: 'In a first class carriage of a train speeding Balkanward across the flat, green Hungarian plain, two Britons sat in friendly, fitful converse.'[10] The train is a symbol of modernity first because it is integral to commuting, itself a sign of the increasing separation between private and public spheres, and second because it is

---

* Although the term refers strictly to the dates of Edward VII's reign (1901–10), the more usual sense is as given above.

associated with travel, with the restlessness and indeed rootlessness of contemporary life.

Another aspect of modernity which features in Saki's work is advertising. 'Filboid Studge, the Story of a Mouse that Helped' (1911) teasingly examines the psychology of marketing. A struggling artist manages to promote a previously failed breakfast cereal by a using a picture of the damned in hell with the caption 'They cannot buy it now' (p. 69) written underneath. Beyond the story's obvious humour, and indeed cynicism, is a sense of an emerging consumer culture and the effect this will have on language – how it will become a tool of selling and be diminished as a result.

We should note that the short story appears as a popular genre in the late nineteenth century, the same time as widespread advertising. The two genres are similar because of their focus on a single incident, their artifice and their intensity. Both use a variety of techniques to make an impact on their audience. Saki delights by his humour, for example, 'Susan Mebberley was a charming woman, but she was also an aunt' ('Adrian', 1911, p. 54); he wins our admiration with the inventiveness of his comparisons: 'The wine lists had been consulted, by some with the blank embarrassment of a schoolboy suddenly called on to locate a Minor Prophet in the tangled hinterland of the Old Testament' ('The Chaplet', 1911, p. 57); but he also disturbs by his lightness of tone in the face of potential tragedy. In 'The Quest' (1911), a mother loses her baby and is understandably distraught. Clovis, a character who often features in the stories, asks 'Do you mean that it's dead, or stampeded, or that you staked it at cards and lost it that way?' (p. 60).

The influence of Oscar Wilde (1854–1900) is evident in such quips. Wilde was reacting against Victorian seriousness and sentimentality; so too was Saki. All the same, we are being asked in this story to admire flippancy in the face of distress, and that is something that should make us pause, as too should that word 'it' for the baby. In general, children in Saki's stories are not victims. They are more likely to be perpetrators. Saki's conception of childhood is quite different from Dickens's. They are not lost or innocent, they are sinister, scheming and even sadistic. In

'The Penance' (1916), for instance, three children kidnap a two year old and discuss ways of killing her.

The point to emphasise, however, is the affinity between advertising and the short story. Both, being short, deal with impact rather than recitation. To that extent they are part of the modernist disintegration of narrative. The growth of a character and the complicated plot belong to a more leisurely age. When there are so many things competing for attention in contemporary society what counts is the dramatic incident not the slow unfolding of events. The anecdote, not the chronicle is the medium of modern experience.

It is useful to recall here what we said above about time, namely that before the industrial revolution it was based on the seasons but after it was based on the machine. The seasons allow for growth but the machine does not. With the machine there is no change, only repetition. Might we link this to a theme in modern literature, that of 'nothing happens'? It runs through Woolf, Joyce, Kafka and Beckett. The sameness of the machine, which gives modern society its character, helps create a desire for excitement, for something to interrupt the monotonous beat of modern life.

In a very small way, the advert and the short story do just that, but they do so at a price: not only narrative contraction, but also ethical diminution. In their place we have symbol, irony, ambiguity and subversion. There is nothing wrong with these qualities but when they become the norm then society becomes the poorer. The advert and the short story, albeit in a small way, promote style over substance. They deploy their various techniques to a similar end, the intense effect, with little regard for the wider consequences of their approach. The similarities between advertising and the short story, which we have barely sketched here, underline one of the arguments of this book: that no matter how modernist arts sought to distance themselves from the popular forms of mass society, they remained closely related – at the level of form if not of content.

We have mentioned in previous chapters that the values of scientific management helped shape the modern sensibility, but Saki amusingly subverts the idea that there is a correct way of doing everything in 'The

Schartz-Metterklume Method' (1914). Lady Carlotta has missed her train and is mistaken for Miss Hope, a governess. Lady Carlotta decides it will be fun to pretend to be a governess and teaches the children history using the above-named Method. It involves getting the children to act out an episode from the past rather than read about it in a book. The result is pandemonium and she is dismissed from her post just as the real Miss Hope arrives. The term Schartz-Metterklume is made up and is quite meaningless. Saki seems to be saying that we should not be impressed by such grand-sounding names as they signify nothing. Moreover, while the idea of method implies order, the implementation of the Schartz-Metterklume version leads to nothing but chaos.

Saki doesn't just mock management fads. He also adopts a highly satirical attitude to modern art. In 'The Recessional' (1911) he pokes fun at the *New Age Magazine* (1907–22), which was concerned with the definition and development of modern art, by having a character produce a rival magazine, *The New Infancy*, whose express purpose is to make the New Age seem 'elderly and hidebound' (p. 103). Modernist poetry is also ridiculed. It is regarded as so lacking in technical accomplishment that anyone could do it (at least by Clovis). To prove it he writes what he thinks is a rather good poem in the modernist style. '"Is it all going to be in blank verse?"' (p. 105) asks his friend Bertie wearily after hearing the opening lines. Clovis, however, is not to be deterred. He reads his description of the dawn. Bertie says that it's not a good description of the dawn, but it is a good account of 'an extensive jewel robbery' (p. 106). Saki uses humour to make the point that, by aiming at high art, modernists lose touch with reality. The only way readers can even begin to understand their highly wrought prose or poetry is with the aid of 'explanatory footnotes' (p. 105). It's almost uncanny the way Saki anticipates the scholarly apparatus of T. S. Eliot's *The Waste Land* (1922).

Although he encourages us to laugh at some of its pretensions, Saki is no enemy of modernist art. Indeed, to read some of his stories you would think he was a modernist himself. That may overstate the case, but he does use quotations (pp. 45, 63) and, more importantly, he does play with narrative conventions. In 'The Story Teller' (1914), for instance, an aunt* tries to quieten her nephews and nieces on a train journey with a story about a little girl who was very good. She is saved from a mad bull by 'a number of rescuers who admire her moral character' (p. 193). The children ask some uncomfortable questions about the story, such as would the girl's companions have saved her if she hadn't been good.

A bachelor in the same carriage, whose peace has been disrupted by the children, also tells them a story. It is about a girl who was 'horribly good' (p. 194). The children latch onto that word 'horribly'. The girl wins many medals for her virtue which she hangs round her neck. Unfortunately they make a lot of noise when she walks, which attracts the attention of a wolf, which eats her. Saki is here undermining the idea that stories should have a moral message and he also suggests that there is no correlation between goodness and what happens to us in the world.

The bachelor tells the story to keep the children quiet, which implies that the function of art is to silence us, to keep us quiet, so that we do not bother those who rule over us. The storyteller is sometimes presented as a controlling figure who can make us believe things that aren't real. Such is the case in 'The Open Window' (1914), where the fifteen year old Vera convinces Framton Nuttel, a man of an extremely nervous disposition, that his hostess' husband and two brothers are all dead but that she can't accept the fact and leaves the French windows open, hoping that they will one day return. When Framton sees the family crossing the field, he flees in terror. We are asked to be wary of the storyteller even as he – or in this case, she – entertains us.

Stories, as Emma found in Flaubert's *Madame Bovary* (1857), help us to escape from the dullness of our lives. One of the many themes of modernist literature is the monotony of existence. It is the subject of Saki's story 'The Mappined Life' (1914). The title captures the main idea, that our lives are drawn up for us. We are not just closed in, we are 'mapped-in'. The story opens with an aunt noting that the Mappin

* Saki sometimes defines characters by their function or their relation to others. It is part of the established technique of comic reduction, but it also fits with the modernist characteristic of anonymity.

terraces at the Zoological Gardens allow visitors to have the illusion of seeing the animals in their natural setting. Her niece quickly points out everything the environment lacks to make it natural: climate, correct habitat, predators and so on. The criticism that one character makes of another's observations or literary efforts is a frequent motif in Saki and serves to remind us of his self-consciousness about the art of narrative.

The niece says that we invent fictions to make our lives seem more important than they really are, a theme picked up in 'The Seventh Pullet' (1914), where Gorworth tells his friend to make up stories about himself so that he appears interesting to his fellow commuters. He becomes so addicted to spinning his yarns that when his wife dies he can only think of what a good story it will make. The tales we tell don't just offer a respite from dull routine, they may also reduce reality by turning it into an excuse for fiction. Life can only be justified if it is turned into art. This attitude recalls the Aesthetic Movement* at the end of the nineteenth century, but it also shapes some modernist notions of art, principally that its value resides purely in its formal organisation rather than in its relation to existence.

Stories offer an escape from life, but what really prevents us from living a full life is our lack of initiative. So says the niece in 'The Mappined Life', and Eliot makes a similar point in *The Waste Land*.[11] For Saki, 'real existence' seems to imply, in part, an acceptance of our animal instincts. In 'The Stalled Ox' (1914) an ox breaks into a garden and eventually a sitting room. In 'The Bull' (1916), Laurence is tossed by a bull. There are painters at the centre of both stories and Saki appears to be saying not just that animal vitality can never be captured on canvas but that it is dangerous and likely to erupt at any time.

The theme is treated lightly in the two stories mentioned but there are darker manifestations of it in 'Gabriel-Ernest' (1910) and 'The Music on the Hill' (1911). Gabriel-Ernest is a boy who becomes a wolf and eats a child. Before his transformation he is described as being like 'some wild Faun of Pagan myth' (p. 22). In 'The Music on the Hill' this

---

* The basic tenets of the Aesthetic Movement were the cultivation of beauty and art for art's sake. The movement flourished during the 1880s and Oscar Wilde (1854–1900) was its most high profile proponent. See Part Two: ' A Cultural Overview'.

figure becomes Pan himself. 'The worship of Pan has never died out' (p. 72) says Mortimer to his wife Sylvia. They have recently moved to the country and she finds in the landscape 'a stealthy linking of the joy of life with the terror of unseen things' (ibid.). She encounters a statue of Pan and foolishly removes the grapes that had been left there as an offering. The god takes his revenge by having her killed by a stag while he plays his pipe and watches.

There is a clear connection between this aspect of Saki's work and Freud. Gabriel-Ernest is a symbol of the Freudian view of the child. He is driven by instinct, and this instinct, whether of sex or violence, is always on the verge of eruption. We found a similar view in Thomas Mann's *Death in Venice* (1912, see Part Three: 'The Origins of the Modernist Novel'). Saki may strain against social convention but he is also aware that it is the only thing that stands between us and confusion. His characters are sophisticated if a little eccentric. They dine, they go to the theatre, they have pleasant gatherings at country houses, but at any moment, an ox could break into the living room.

Saki, then, writes about aspects of modernity, satirises features of modernist art and also exhibits some of the self-consciousness of the modernist artist in his play with narrative conventions. In some ways he is a more radical modernist than either Joyce or Eliot because he affirms nothing. We could almost say that he is postmodern because he dissolves truth, tradition and ethics in his all-pervasive irony. Modernist artists may critique these terms but ultimately many still cling to them, whereas postmodernists are utterly sceptical of them. So too, it appears, is Saki, and whereas writers from Flaubert to Joyce place great importance on a relation with another, however troubled that may be, Saki does not. This may be due to the constraints of the short story form but there is no doubt that his characters see others only as an audience before whom they perform. In this too, Saki looks forward to postmodernism, particularly that aspect of it that stresses the plasticity of identity.

Virginia Woolf and the Changing Human Character

In 1924 Virginia Woolf gave a talk to the Cambridge Heretics Society entitled 'Character in Fiction' which became the basis of her famous essay 'Mr Bennett and Mrs Brown'. She begins by quoting Arnold Bennett's claim that the foundation of good fiction is to create character and nothing else, then asks what is meant by 'character'. The question is crucial because she maintains that 'on or about December 1910 human character changed'.[12] This was the date of the first Post-Impressionist exhibition in London.*

The exhibition caused a great deal of controversy. Huntly Carter, a reviewer in *The New Age*, praised the paintings because they were complete forms of self-expression.[13] Others condemned them as crude, vulgar and more fitting for the pavement than the gallery. At stake in these exchanges was not the value of self-expression per se, but the best means to convey it. Should painters develop their own style, or should they adhere to established conventions?

That, then, is the immediate context for Woolf's famous remark. There were others, however, for we should remember that 1910 saw a number of changes, among them the death of Edward VII and the coronation of George V;† the passing of David Lloyd George's The People's Budget, which laid the foundation of the welfare state; and the first short flight in a jet engine plane. All these events and more added to the sense that people were living in a radically new age.

---

* Impressionists painted everyday scenes. They wanted to capture the truth of the moment. They did so by using short, broken brush-strokes that showed the play of light and shadow and colour and how that affected perception of the scene. Post-Impressionists, by contrast, wanted to express how they felt about what they painted or to reveal a spiritual vision. The difference between the two types of painting was summed up by Desmond MacCarthy (1877–1952) who wrote the introduction to the exhibition catalogue. He said that the Impressionists wanted to record 'hitherto unrecognised aspects of objects', particularly colour and light, but the Post-Impressionists wanted to 'express emotions which the objects themselves evoked'.

† The Georgian age (1910–36) carried the liberal spirit of Edward's reign even further. Its prevailing note, according to Woolf's essay, was 'the sound of breaking and falling, crashing and destruction' (p. 246). Those who want to know more about that period should read Frank Swinnerton's *The Georgian Literary Scene 1910–1935* (London: Hutchinson, 1935). The book is a reminder that modernism was only one part of a much larger literary scene.

Woolf explains her remark about the change in human character by way of an anecdote. She caught a train and in her carriage were a man and an elderly woman, whom she decides to call 'Mrs Brown'.* She recounts their conversation: it appears that 'Mrs Brown' is bullied into some arrangement, but the story 'ends without any point' (p. 238). Woolf's 'point', though, is to make us think about the definition of 'character'. The meaning changes according to the writer's age, temperament and country.

Woolf also looks at how her predecessors approached the question of character. She imagines how Bennett would describe Mrs Brown. He would give details of the carriage, the train journey and Mrs Brown's appearance but, by concentrating only on the externals, he would not give the reader any sense of Mrs Brown herself. To do that, Woolf says, the writer must try to capture what he or she believes is common to us all: our 'overhearing scraps of talk that fill [us] with amazement', our being 'bewildered by the complexity of [our] feelings' and our sense that 'in the course of one day, thousands of ideas [course] through our brains, thousands of emotions [meet], [collide] and [disappear] in astonishing disorder' (p. 248). Her description recalls the sixteenth century essayist Michel de Montaigne's claim that 'We are entirely made up of bits and pieces, woven together so diversely and so shapelessly that each one of them pulls its own way every moment',[14] a reminder, yet again, that some of the most celebrated modernist notions are not without precedent.

Woolf gives a more succinct account of what she means in a later essay, 'Modern Fiction' (1925). At every moment, she says, the mind receives 'myriad of impressions, trivial, fantastic, evanescent or engraved with the sharpness of steel' and the impressions come 'from all sides'.[15] Woolf's use of the term 'impression' is significant, not just because it refers to Impressionism in painting but also because it recalls Walter Pater's famous 'Conclusion' to his *The Renaissance: Studies in Art and Poetry* (1873).

---

* It is interesting to note that Woolf, like Saki, makes much of incidents on trains.

Pater (1839–94), whose views underpinned the Aesthetic Movement, argued that we live in a blizzard of impressions. Our attention is captured for a moment and then is seized by something else. His observation is partly a response to the experience of city life. There are so many sights and sounds we have to process in the urban environment that our senses feel continually under siege. Baudelaire, remember, defined modernity as 'the transient, the fleeting and the contingent'* and Pater would seem to agree, claiming that the dynamic nature of contemporary society means that we 'regard all things and principles of things as inconstant modes of fashion'.[16] The observation makes its way into literature: 'There is no stability in the world' says Bernard in *The Waves*, and Rhoda echoes him: 'nothing persists. One moment does not lead to another' (pp. 88, 97).

Baudelaire also remarked that modern art had in part to be based on the moment. Impressionism is an example of such an art. Painters such as Claude Monet (1840–1926) sought to convey a scene in all its immediacy. The very term 'impression', however, implies the artists were giving their own personal view of their subject. Pater suggests that we can never escape our impressions for they are 'ringed round ... by that thick wall of personality' (p. 151) which prevents us from reaching out to others or them reaching out to us. We exist, so to speak, in the prison of our impressions.

What, then, is the nature of this self that so exists? It is nothing but the sum of our impressions at a particular moment. As they change, so too does the self. We are, says Pater, 'perpetually weaving and unweaving ourselves' (p. 152), an observation echoed by Bernard in *The Waves*: 'I am made and remade continually' (p. 100). Since everything is ephemeral, the best we can hope for is to make the most of our moments as they pass. Art helps us to do that. It prolongs the instant, it keeps perception fresh and it makes us appreciate beauty before it vanishes forever. Above all, art prevents us from forming habits. Routine dulls our senses, lets dust gather on the soul, but poetry, painting and music prompt us to look – and look again – lest we miss the diamond in the dirt.

---

* See Part Three: 'Modernist Poetry: French Origins, English Settings'.

Woolf is rooted in the traditions of French Impressionism and English Aestheticism. Both these movements show that human character had begun to change long before she said it did. Woolf shares many of Pater's ideas, in particular the notion that how we perceive shapes what we perceive. In *To the Lighthouse* Woolf contrasts the way Mr and Mrs Ramsay see the world. He divides reality into subjects and objects: the subject perceives a world of objects that are quite separate from himself. His philosophical work is all on this theme (p. 28); the theme that we are able to give an objective account of reality.

Mrs Ramsay is the opposite. She abolishes the distinction between subject and object: 'one leant to things ... felt they expressed one, became one' (p. 70). Impressions pour in on Mrs Ramsay, making her wonder how to make sense of them all: 'How then did it work out, all this?' (p. 29). The suggestion is that we *cannot* make sense of all our impressions. They are added to, contradicted, fade and are forgotten. They are, in Pater's words, 'continually vanishing away' (p. 152). However, Woolf, like Pater, seeks to make the most of the passing moment. Louis, in *The Waves*, strives 'to fix the moment in one effort of supreme endeavour' (p. 28).

Pater's claim that we are cut off from each other is reflected in Woolf. Her characters seem isolated from one another. Mrs Ramsay, for example, in *To the Lighthouse*, believes that it is impossible for husband and wife ever to know one another: 'She would never know him. He would never know her. Human relations were all like that ...' (p. 101). Pater also implies that self-knowledge is not possible. Our identity, built on the shifting sands of our impressions, changes every moment. Once again, we find a similar view in Woolf: Mrs Ramsay's self is 'a wedge-shaped core of darkness' and beneath that 'it is all dark, it is all spreading, it is unfathomably deep' (p. 69).

It is worth noting the metaphor of water in that quotation. Water is one of Woolf's most persistent symbols. It has many meanings including time, writing, happiness, ordinary life, the feminine, the flow of perception, the self, passion and chaos, and even Woolf's childhood holidays in Cornwall. The significance of water is reflected in the titles of *To the Lighthouse* and *The Waves*, and, of course, Woolf committed suicide by drowning. Water is also a symbol of community. Despite what we said above, there is in Woolf a sense that characters are not separate from one another. Mrs Ramsay muses on 'that community of feeling with other people ... it was all one stream' (p. 123) and in *The Waves* Bernard says that 'we melt into each other with phrases. We are edged with mist' (p. 10). Later, he declares 'we are not single, we are one' (p. 50).

This is one explanation of why the characters in Woolf's fiction all sound more or less the same. The tone, the rhythm of their sentences, the images they use are all very similar. In the previous chapter we argued that the stream of consciousness technique was a manifestation of internal freedom and individual expression. Woolf herself says as much when she criticises Bennett for his failure to give any sense of Mrs Brown's unique identity. Yet in her fiction it is difficult to tell her characters apart; one interior voice sounds much like another.

What are we to make of this? Does the sameness of each character's stream of consciousness suggest that inner, as well as outer life, is being standardised? That is certainly an interesting argument if only because it lends further support to one of the claims of this book, namely that modernist art is complicit in some of the developments of the early twentieth century, particularly the process of dehumanisation evident in the factory and in the growth of bureaucracy. Against that, however, we could argue that the characters in Woolf's fiction sound so alike because they are all speaking with one voice: hers.

Art as the expression of the self is Lily's fundamental belief. She struggles 'against terrific odds' to say '"this is what I see, this is what I see"', to hold 'her vision to her breast' while 'a thousand forces did their best to pluck it from her' (*To the Lighthouse*, p. 24). Why, though, should anyone want to rob Lily of her way of seeing? There are at least two answers. One is that modern society was becoming increasingly uniform and therefore the individual must be made to conform; the other is that women were effectively second class citizens. It wasn't until 1928, one year after *To the Lighthouse* was published, that they all got the vote.

Lily faces various obstacles to becoming an artist. She has to look after her father, 'keeping house for [him] off the Brompton Road' (p. 24). Then there are her own feelings of inadequacy (ibid.) which are accentuated when Charles Tansley tells her that women can't write or paint (p. 54). Mr Ramsay's view of the arts, that they 'are a decoration on top of human life, they do not express it' (p. 49) further diminishes her sense of vocation. It is not just men who deride Lily's ambition, however. Mrs Ramsay herself does not take Lily's painting very seriously (p. 21). No wonder Lily feels that her painting is a waste of time and that it will 'never be seen, never be hung even' (p. 173).

Lily's thoughts about art are central to the novel. The nature of art, indeed, is one of its themes, as it is in other modernist works. This is because, as we have said, various factors, such as the rise of mass culture, combined to undermine some of art's traditional functions. The idea that art should represent things, for example, gives way to the idea that it records our impressions of things. Its value, in other words, no longer resides in how accurately it reflects society but in how intense or truthful are the artist's impressions of that society. How accurately, though, does the artist convey the experience of impressions that last only moment, and how does he or she organise this flow of impressions so that they do not simply succeed one another but have some kind of structure?

These are the problems that preoccupy Lily. They centre on her painting of Mrs Ramsay, a work which takes her the duration of the book. Mrs Ramsay, incidentally, dies about half way through the narrative. We learn of her death in one sentence (p. 140). The woman who had seemed to be at the centre of the novel is suddenly no longer there. Sometimes death takes people like that, without warning, and that's what happened to Woolf's mother, upon whom Mrs Ramsay is based. The report of her death is also a landmark in modern literature because it is so brief in comparison to the treatment of death in the nineteenth century novel, particularly when it involved children.

To return to Lily: she wants to paint 'a scene that was vanishing even as she looked' (p. 121). How, though, can she fix the passing moment? By bringing together the solid and the fluid, by joining that which endures with that which is ephemeral. This is a problem of form because it involves the reconciliation of two opposites. Hence Lily's constant worry about the shape and structure of her painting: 'If there, in that corner, it was bright, here, in this, she felt the need of darkness' (p. 59).

The purpose of form is to bring order to life. Otherwise it remains 'aimless', 'chaotic' and 'unreal' (p. 160). Art is about finding a balance, creating a contrast, making a connection between its various components. By so organising its various elements, art enables us to see 'the coherence in things' (p. 114), if only momentarily. It is this coherence that ensures the survival of those moments of vision.

We said earlier that gender was an issue in art. Lily feels her work is dismissed because she is a woman, but the fact that she *is* one is also important to her art. Women, claims Woolf, perceive, feel and think differently to men and this needs to be reflected in how they express themselves. A man's sentence is rigid and highly structured whereas a woman's is more open and flowing. A man's sentence denotes what is, a woman's what may be.

What Lily seeks to do in her painting is unite male and female – something that, according to Mrs Ramsay, can never happen in life. Lily 'saw the colour burning on a framework of steel; the light of a butterfly's wing lying upon the arches of a cathedral' (p. 54, and see p. 186). These different elements correspond to the principles of masculine and feminine. The 'masculine intelligence is like iron girders, spanning the swaying fabric, upholding the world' (p. 115), while the female intelligence resolves itself into the impressions of things (p. 29). Woolf seems to suggest that in order to express ourselves completely we need to balance the male and female elements in us all. More broadly, her distinction between the butterfly wing and the arch of a cathedral recalls Baudelaire's hope for a modern art based on the transient and the eternal, the fleeting and the immoveable. When Lily finally draws 'a line there, in the centre' (p. 226) of her painting, that hope is realised.

Extended Commentary: Lawrence, *Women in Love* (1920)

At first sight it seems strange to include D. H. Lawrence (1885–1930) in a chapter on the modernist novel. After all, he wrote in a fairly realistic manner and contributed little to the formal development of the genre. In some ways, though, he was the most radical modernist of all. Many artists have questioned contemporary civilisation, but none more fiercely than Lawrence, and what they regarded as possible answers – for example the redemptive powers of tradition, or the energising properties of the machine* – he rejected outright. For Lawrence, they were part of the problem, not the solution, and the search for that solution would take him all over the globe.

The main characters in *Women in Love* are Rupert Birkin, Ursula and Gudrun Brangwen and Gerald Crich. Birkin and Ursula form one couple, Gerald and Gudrun another. The novel traces the differences between and the development of their respective relationships. *Women in Love* starts with a critique of marriage. By contrast, the nineteenth century novel usually ends with a celebration of it. Another difference is that, generally, the nineteenth century novel draws all the narrative threads together. The final chapter often gives an account of the fate of the characters, rewarding or punishing them according to their actions during the course of the story. This is not, however, what happens in *Women in Love*. The novel ends in the middle of an argument about love and relationships. There is no closure – the conversation between Ursula and Birkin could continue indefinitely. Thus although Lawrence may write mainly in the style of the nineteenth century novel, that is realism, he dispenses with some of its conventions. Some, not all, for the

---

* *The Founding and Manifesto of Futurism* (1909) demanded a break with the past and its academic culture and urged readers to embrace technology, dynamism and power. In language it advocated the destruction of punctuation and grammar in the name of the 'free word'. In painting, it advocated the representation of movement and speed. The movement's founder, Filippo Tommas Marinetti (1876–1944), glorified war and was associated with Italian fascism.

characters do what some of their nineteenth century counterparts did; namely leave England in search of a better life elsewhere.*

If Lawrence does not overtly experiment with form he certainly engages with it. He shared Eliot's vision that contemporary civilisation was a 'waste land' where nothing can grow. The individual had disappeared into the crowd (p. 32); society had shrunk to the couple 'in its own little house, watching its own little interests and stewing in its own little privacy' (p. 366) and, most damaging of all in Lawrence's eyes, its ruling principles were mechanism and materialism. The former refers to the nature of work and the latter to the growing spread of consumerism.

When Gerald takes over the mine from his father he rejects the old paternalism and runs it along scientific lines. Lawrence describes this change as 'the substitution of the mechanical principle for the organic' (p. 239). In very basic terms, this means treating the colliers not as men but as units of production. 'The sufferings and feelings of individuals did not matter in the least ... What mattered was the pure instrumentality of the individual. As of a man as of a knife: does it cut well? Nothing else mattered' (p. 230).

Because the mechanical principle now rules our lives we can no longer grow and develop. Birkin complains that he can't 'blossom'. The flower of his self is 'either blighted in the blood or has got the smother fly, or it isn't nourished' (p. 130). His particular condition affects everyone. All suffer from arrested growth, and we respond to this by buying things to make up for our loss of being. Even Birkin, who earlier pours scorn on Gerald's desire to have 'a motor car' and an 'up-to-date-house' (p. 54), goes shopping with Ursula. They purchase a chair but it provokes an argument, with Birkin protesting that possessions bully you and turn you 'into a generalisation' (p. 371).

If you are a generalisation you are not real, indeed Birkin makes precisely that point when he declares that there are no people, only 'simulacra' (p. 131). Lawrence thought people weren't 'real' because

---

*There were at least three conventional ways of ending a nineteenth century novel, particularly those which dealt with the 'condition of England' question: marriage, inheritance or emigration.

they had lost touch with what he calls the 'circumambient universe'.[17] We care for how we appear to others, not for how we connect with the cosmos. Man, says Birkin, lives for the sake of that Brocken spectre,* 'the reflection of himself in the human opinion' (p. 54).

There are two other ways in which we are not real, or rather not rounded individuals. First, we value the mind and the will too highly, and second we do not value the body and the life of the instincts enough. Birkin attacks his former lover Hermione who, incidentally, was based on Lady Ottoline Morrell, wife of the Liberal member of Parliament, Philip Morrell and also the philosopher Bertrand Russell's mistress. 'You haven't got any real body' Birkin says to her, 'any dark sensual life of the body. You have no sensuality. You have only your will and your conceit of consciousness, and your lust for power, to *know*' (p. 41).

One of the most disturbing scenes in the book is Gerald forcing his sensitive Arab mare to remain at a level crossing while a train passes noisily. The horse is terrified but Gerald holds her there, his spurs bloodying her sides (p. 114). In a later episode, Gudrun dances before a herd of cattle who watch her 'as if hypnotised' (p. 172). Both these actions symbolise, in very broad terms, the repression of the sexual instinct.

The repression of this instinct leaves both characters incomplete. Hence Birkin is irritated by Gerald's 'fatal halfness' (p. 214) while Gudrun always seeks the approval of others to compensate for her lack of being (p. 170). Gerald validates his selfhood by dominating others. As a boy, he 'longed to go with the soldiers to shoot [the striking miners]' and as a man he applies the new principles of scientific management to the colliery, so that the miners 'were reduced to mere mechanical instruments' (pp. 233, 238).

What, then, can be done? One suggestion is to escape from people altogether. Birkin does this temporarily when he wanders into a valley and lies down, naked, on the grass and flowers. 'Nothing else would do, nothing else would satisfy, except this coolness and subtlety of

---

* The Brocken mountain is the highest of the Harz range in Germany. 'Spectre' refers to the occasional play of light whereby the shadow of the observer is projected onto cloud or mist.

vegetation travelling into one's blood ... how fulfilled he was, how happy' (p. 110). Another suggestion, far more extreme, is to annihilate humanity. If 'every human being perished tomorrow', Birkin says, 'the reality would be untouched'. Indeed, 'it would be better' for the 'real tree of life' would then be rid of rotten humanity which won't fall off the tree when ripe but hangs on until it is 'infested with little worms and dry rot' (pp. 130–1).

There remain at least two further courses of action: art and love. The one explored most fully in the novel is love. Birkin objects to the word because it has been 'vulgarised' (p. 134). He is a modernist to the extent that he wants to 'let the old meanings go' (ibid.). Birkin searches for an experience that is different to the romantic conception of love and which requires a new language. He describes himself and Ursula as 'two single beings' in equilibrium, 'constellated together like two stars' (p. 207). His choice of words shows that he wants to integrate his relationship with the surrounding universe, to become part of the creative continuum.

This is evident in the language used to describe Ursula's growth in the novel. At first she believes that her 'active living was suspended, but underneath, in the darkness, something was coming to pass. If only she could break through her integuments' (p. 7). A little later we are told her life is 'like a shoot that is growing steadily, but which has not yet come above ground' (p. 51). Further on we learn that Ursula 'had fallen strange and dim out of the sheath of the material life, as a berry falls from the only world it has ever known' (p. 148). After she and Birkin make love Ursula is 'as beautiful as a new marvellous flower opened at his knees' (p. 325) and towards the end of the novel she is described as 'dilated and brilliant, like a flower in the morning sun' (p. 423).

The metaphor of the seed coming into flower contrasts with Birkin's image of humanity hanging on a bush but not dropping off when ripe, becoming instead little 'balls of bitter dust' (p. 130). The act of lovemaking is of supreme importance for it transforms the consciousness of self, which separates man from the cosmos, into an experience of being at one with it. 'It was a perfect passing away for both of them, and at the same time the most intolerable accession into being' as they are drawn into 'the deepest life-force, the darkest, deepest, strangest life-force of the human body, at the back and the base of the loins' (p. 326).

Lawrence also uses a religious idiom to convey the extent and depth of Birkin's and Ursula's intimacy. Ursula, for example, is prompted to think of the book of Genesis, for Birkin appears to her as 'one of the sons of God ... looking down on her and seeing she was fair' (p. 324). Birkin too resorts to sacred terminology when he describes the 'wonder of existing not as oneself but in a consummation of my being and her being in a new one, a new paradisal unit regained from the duality' (p. 385). Lawrence's use of natural and religious imagery suggests that he is not really a modernist because he is reaching back to romanticism and English spiritualism for a solution to contemporary problems. There is some truth in that claim but the picture is more complicated than that.

Lawrence, like Woolf, was well aware that human character had changed. He was as much concerned as she was with the notion of selfhood. Indeed the central question in *The Rainbow* (1915), which is the prequel to *Women In Love*, is 'How to become oneself, how to know the question and answer of oneself, when one was merely an unfixed something nothing'.[18] However, Lawrence differed from Woolf in one important respect. She accepted the new notion of self and sought a new style in which to render it; Lawrence certainly did not accept the new notion of the self and vigorously criticised it. He conceived of selfhood not as the expression of an isolated individual but as the unique manifestation of the life force. The purpose of art, therefore, was to show how humans could once again become part of the creative principle underlying all things.

There are frequent references to art in *Women in Love*, showing once again how its nature is a key theme of modernist writing. Gerald is puzzled by a sculpture of a negro woman. 'Why is it art?' he asks. 'Because it conveys a complete truth' Birkin replies, in this instance a truth about sensuousness (p. 80). This is one of the best examples, in novels of the period, of how artists looked to the 'primitive' in order to revitalise the attenuated instincts of modern man. Art is also a way of bridging the gap between self and not self, as Birkin explains to

Hermione. Copying a drawing of Chinese geese, he learns 'what centres they live from, what they feel and perceive' (p. 91).

Gudrun's art is quite different. Her sculptures are always of 'small things' and this reflects her habit of watching people 'with objective curiosity', seeing 'each one as a complete figure ... a finished creation' (pp. 38, 12). In contrast to the hard outline of Gudrun's sculptures we have those of Rodin and Michelangelo who 'leave a piece of raw rock unfinished to [their] figure' (p. 371). Birkin applies this directly to life, telling Ursula, '"you must leave your surroundings sketchy, unfinished, so that you are never contained, never confined, never dominated from the outside"' (ibid.). We should remember here that the novel itself is unfinished, the conversation on which it concludes could go on.

Women in Love is a rich, absorbing work. It distances itself from the nineteenth century novel but it does not embrace modernist experimentation, at least in terms of form. It breaks with some traditions at the same time as it is rooted in others, for example romanticism. It aims to do what Lawrence said art should do: restore our connection with the 'circumambient universe' and reveal things in their different associations. As we can see from the constantly evolving bond of Birkin and Ursula, relationships are not fixed. By restoring our connection with the circumambient universe, by revealing things in their different relationships, we come to a different understanding of our feelings, our morality and ourselves.

This union does not last, however – in the end, Birkin does not find this as fulfilling as he had hoped, telling Ursula that in order to be completely happy he needs 'eternal union with a man too' (p. 499).

Notes

1   John Fletcher and Malcolm Bradbury, 'The Introverted Novel' in Malcolm Bradbury and James McFarlane (eds), *Modernism: A Guide to European Literature 1890–1930* (Harmondsworth: Penguin, 1976), pp. 394–415, p. 401.

2   Ford Madox Ford, *Critical Writings* edited by Frank MacShane (Lincoln: University of Nebraska Press, 1964), p. 41.

3   David Trotter, 'The Modernist Novel' in Michael Levenson (ed.), *The Cambridge Companion to Modernism* (Cambridge: Cambridge University Press, 1999), pp. 70–99, p. 71.

4   James Joyce, *Occasional, Critical and Political Writing* edited with an Introduction and Notes by Kevin Barry (Oxford: Oxford University Press, 2000), p. 102.

5   James Joyce, *A Portrait of the Artist as a Young Man* edited with an Introduction and notes by Seamus Deane (Harmondsworth: Penguin, 2000), p. 186.

6   Virginia Woolf, *To The Lighthouse* edited by Stella McNichol and with an Introduction and Notes by Hermione Lee (Harmondsworth: Penguin, 1992), p. 80.

7   Virginia Woolf, *The Waves* edited and with an Introduction by Kate Flint (Harmondsworth: Penguin, 2000), p. 28.

8   Henri Bergson, *Creative Evolution* (New York: Random House, 1944), p. 8.

9   D. H. Lawrence, *Women in Love* edited and with an Introduction by David Bradshaw (Oxford: Oxford University Press, 1998), p. 371.

10   Saki, *The Best of Saki* (London: Picador, 1976), p. 220. All references to Saki are to this edition.

11   See T. S. Eliot, *The Complete Poems and Plays of T. S. Eliot* (London: Faber, 1978), p. 74.

12   Virginia Woolf, 'Mr Bennett and Mrs Brown' in S. P. Rosenbaum (ed.), *A Bloomsbury Group Reader* (Oxford: Blackwell, 1993), pp. 233–49, p. 235.

13   Huntly Carter, 'The Post-Savages', *The New Age*, 8:6 (1910), pp. 140–2.

14   Michel de Montaigne, *The Complete Essays* translated by M. A. Screech (Harmondsworth: Penguin, 1991), p. 380.

15   Virginia Woolf, 'Modern Fiction' in Andrew McNeillie (ed.), *The Essays of Virginia Woolf*, Volume 4 (London: Hogarth, 1994), pp. 157–65, p. 160.

16   Walter Pater, *The Renaissance: Studies in Art and Poetry* with an Introduction by A. Philips (Oxford: Oxford University Press, 1986), p. 150.

17   D. H. Lawrence, *Study of Thomas Hardy and Other Essays* (Cambridge: Cambridge University Press, 2002), p. 116.

18   D. H. Lawrence, *The Rainbow* edited by Mark Kinkead-Weekes and with an Introduction and Notes by Anne Fernihough (Harmondsworth: Penguin, 1995) p. 264.

The European Stage and Theatrical Thinkers: Ibsen, Strindberg, Pirandello, Artaud and Brecht

Most discussions of literary modernism tend to focus on poetry or the stream of consciousness novel. But questions about the nature of art, a self-consciousness about genre and an interest in experimentation were also a feature of theatre from the late nineteenth to the mid twentieth centuries. Perhaps one reason for the omission of drama from some accounts of modernism is that, according to Christopher Innes, on the stage 'art could neither assert itself as an autonomous activity, independent of external experience, nor aspire to pure form. In sharp contrast to the modernist drive in poetry or painting, imitation was always present, being the essential basis of acting.'[1]

An alternative explanation may be that the modernism in theatre was a rather muted affair because a consciousness of artifice has always been a part of theatrical history, even before Jaques, in Shakespeare's *As You Like It* (1599), first declared that:

> All the world's a stage,
> And all the men and women merely players:
> They have their exits and their entrances;
> And one man in his time plays many parts (II.vii.140–3)

Actors in ancient Greece used masks, they spoke in verse and the chorus sang and danced, all of which served to show that theatre was a highly stylised affair, not a realistic representation of life.

Naturalism

Yet another reason why modernism in the theatre has often gone unremarked is that just as artists were beginning to take more of an interest in the nature of art than in the nature of the world, dramatists were moving in the opposite direction. While poets such as Mallarmé (1842–98) were espousing Symbolism, novelists such as Emile Zola (1840–1902) were expounding the doctrine of naturalism, which he defined as 'the return to nature and man, direct observation, exact anatomy [and] the acceptance and depiction of what is'.[2]

Zola contrasts naturalism with the two main traditions in French theatre, tragedy and romance. Tragedy, which was usually set in the classical world, was dominated by Aristotle's three unities – confining the action, time and place of the drama – and it focused on the mind of the hero. It gave way, in the eighteenth century, to romantic drama which was set in the Middle Ages and had lots of action.

Zola praises romantic drama because its emphasis on action, 'its mixture of laughter and tears, [and] its research into accuracy of costume and setting'[3] pave the way for naturalism. However, he also criticises it because is set in a distant time and the characters 'are no longer living people but sentiments' (p. 363). Consequently romanticism has nothing to say to contemporary society.

Naturalism, on the other hand, does. It deals not with 'metaphysical man' but with 'physiological man' (p. 367). It deals, in other words, not with the soul but with real people, particularly with how they are shaped by their environment. This means that naturalistic plays must portray life as it is lived now, not as it was lived in the past.

To that end, it should be based on real life stories, set in real life places such as factories and mines, with characters wearing real life costumes and speaking in real life voices, not a 'theatre voice' (p. 370). Moreover, since the dramatist is conducting an experiment to see how characters are determined by their surroundings he or she must, like a scientist, be strictly impersonal. He or she must not give his or her vision of things, just show them as they are.

Naturalism is the art form of the modern age. It reflects its spirit of enquiry, analysis, method and experimental science. This makes it very different to, say, Symbolism or Expressionism, both of which seek to escape the world, not to study it. The basic doctrine of naturalism, that art should show how society works in order, ultimately, to improve it, is also quite different to the conventional view of modernist art; that it stands apart from the rest of society and that therein lies its value.

Symbolism, Naturalism, Melodrama and the Well-Made Play

If we had to choose a practitioner of naturalistic theatre, then the Norwegian playwright Henrik Ibsen (1828–1906), would be a good candidate. His plays deal with a range of social issues from syphilis to women's rights and they are all written in a clear, comprehensible manner. He also seems to echo Zola's own words when he writes that he transports 'facts' to the stage but does not draw any conclusions from them. 'My calling is to question, not to answer' he writes.[4]

But Ibsen also saw himself as a poet and, to that extent, his plays are part of the modernist fascination with symbolism. His early play *Peer Gynt* (1867), for example, is deeply symbolic of the Norwegian character; it also moves effortlessly from the conscious to the unconscious and makes free with notions of time and space.

Symbolism and naturalism co-exist in all Ibsen's plays. First one predominates, then the other. The interplay between them reflects the swing of the pendulum in European theatre between what we might also call a poetic and a political conception of the theatre. While both are distinct, they each entail new forms of staging, showing that theatre too is at the heart of the modernist 'crisis of representation'.

Both poetic and political drama developed in reaction to melodrama and the well-made play, both of which flourished in the nineteenth century. The stock characters of melodrama were a hero, heroine and villain. The plots were sensational and the morality simple: good always triumphed over evil. The well-made play was so called because of the clever way the plot was put together. Eugène Scribe (1791–1861) is often regarded as one of its best exponents. He designed his plays around the revelation of a secret. The organisation of the action was more important to him than the exploration of character. He believed that the purpose of theatre was not to educate or correct but to amuse and relax, and for that people needed fiction not truth.

Ibsen, *An Enemy of the People* (1882)

The action of this play revolves around Dr Thomas Stockmann, who discovers that the town's new baths are polluted. His solution is to re-lay the whole water system. At first he receives some support but when the town's various political and commercial organisations realise the cost, they conspire first to discredit and then to silence him. Gradually, Stockmann's supporters fall away, but he refuses to give up the fight, declaring at the end that 'the strongest man in the world is he who stands most alone.'[5]

An Enemy of the People is an almost perfect illustration of Zola's naturalistic stage. The story is based on two real life incidents. The first is that of a medical officer who reported an outbreak of cholera at the spa town of Teiplitz in the 1830s. As a result, the season was ruined and the angry residents stoned the doctor's house. The second is based on a chemist named Harald Thaulow who was prevented from speaking at a meeting when he tried to criticise a charity organisation for its neglect of the poor.

In addition, Ibsen's dialogue sounds more like 'common speech' than a literary creation. Finally, there is no real resolution to the conflict between public duty and private interest that the play presents. Although we are encouraged to side with Stockmann he becomes an increasingly unsympathetic character as the play progresses. His desire to clean up the baths is, in the end, less a matter of civic responsibility than self-aggrandisement. As early as Act Three he declares he is just doing his duty, his 'job as a citizen' while at the same time anticipating that the people of the town will be so grateful they will probably organise a 'banquet' or a 'torchlight procession' for him (p. 177).

It is clear that *An Enemy of the People* is a naturalistic play and to the extent that naturalism is one aspect of modernism, that makes it a modernist play too. Are there any other ways in which this play can be described as modernist? In terms of theme and form it seems to belong more to the nineteenth than the twentieth century. The opposition between the individual and society and the realistic presentation of the action were tropes that could be found in the Victorian novel if not on the Victorian stage, where sensation and sentiment were the norm.

Despite that, *An Enemy of the People* ultimately points forward rather than backward. To begin with its main characters – a doctor, a teacher, a journalist and a property owner – are from the professional classes whereas, by and large, the main figures in eighteenth and nineteenth century literature were drawn from the gentry. Some of them, such as the Mayor, 'A Worker', 'Another Worker', are referred to by their function; others by their status: 'First Citizen', 'Second Citizen', 'Third Citizen' and so on. Finally we have characters who have neither status nor function. 'First Man', 'Second Man', 'Third Man', 'Fourth Man' and 'The Drunk Man'.

We find the same sort of labelling in H. G. Wells's *The Time Machine* (1895), a novel which displays a modernist fascination with machines and their potential. Here there is 'The Time Traveller', 'The Psychologist', 'The Provincial Mayor' and 'The Medical Man'. If we compare this presentation of characters with those we find in, for example, Restoration comedies and the eighteenth century and even some nineteenth century novels we find one significant difference. In the earlier works, characters are named after their personal or moral qualities. In George Etherege's *The Man of Mode* (1676), for example, there is a character called Sir Fopling Flutter, a name which perfectly captures his love of fashion, while in Henry Fielding's *Tom Jones* (1749) we have characters such as Squire Allworthy and Mr Thwackum, appellations which are self-explanatory. But in Ibsen and Wells characters are named after their function or their position in the social order. This tells us that as we move into the modern world the idea of the individual becomes less important and role he or she fulfils more so.

If we can accept that then we can see why Stockmann's fight against the authorities is also an assertion of his self-hood. It is a form of protest, one among many in modern art, against the anonymity that mass society imposes on its members. The irony is that, by not naming some of the characters, *An Enemy of the People* contributes to that anonymity at the same time as it criticises it. Even more ironically, the person who insists most on his individuality, Stockmann, is the one who can never remember the name of the family's maid: 'What the devil's her name. You know, the maid' (p. 139).

John Carey has argued that 'the principle around which modernist literature and culture fashioned themselves was the exclusion of the masses, the defeat of their power, the removal of their literacy and the denial of their humanity.'[6] On that criterion alone, *An Enemy of the People* qualifies as an example of modernist literature. At first Stockmann believes that once presented with the facts about the baths, the public will support him. 'Do you know what I have behind me?' he asks Catherine, his wife. 'Is that a good thing?' she enquires. 'Of course it's a good thing' he retorts. 'The solid majority ... How splendid to feel that one stands shoulder to shoulder with one's fellow citizens in brotherly concord' (p. 151).

As this 'solid majority' is manipulated by vested interests to oppose Stockmann, however, his opinion changes. They are a more dangerous 'enemy of truth and freedom' (p. 192) than politicians. 'The solid, liberal, bloody – majority – they're the ones we have to fear' (ibid.). They cling to outmoded truths and stifle the minority who wish to forge ahead and establish new ones. We couldn't have a clearer expression of Carey's thesis than Stockmann's cry that 'the masses, the mob, this damned majority – they're the thing that's poisoning the sources of our spiritual life and contaminating the ground we are walking on!' (p. 194).

This indicates another way in which *An Enemy of the People* can be considered a modernist work: its use of symbolism. The spa's polluted waters, like any symbol, have a number of meanings. First they stand for political corruption, for how the affairs of the town 'have fallen into the hands of a small clique of bureaucrats' (p. 144). Then they signify the various interests in the town who 'swing this way and that, and spend so much time looking at every side of the question that they never make a move in any direction' (p. 149). A third meaning is that the polluted waters stand for the entire community. 'This whole community's got to be cleansed and decontaminated ... All these skimpers and compromisers have got to be thrown out' (p. 165).

This sentiment, incidentally, reflects the view of some moderns, such as the father of scientific management, Frederick Winslow Taylor, that there should be a complete break with the past and an entirely new way of doing things – an attitude that finds an echo in some modernist views of literature (see Part Two: 'A Cultural Overview'). It was Ezra Pound (1885–1972), remember, who said 'make it new'. The polluted water also stands for the poisoning of 'all our spiritual resource' and for the fact that 'the whole of our vaunted social system is founded upon a cesspit of lies' (p. 190).

We could mention further interpretation, for example how the state of the baths also reflects something rotten in Stockmann himself (his lack of restraint, his failure to consider anyone else's feelings), but the point is the same. *An Enemy of the People* has a symbolic as well as a naturalistic character and both represent different aspects of modernism. As always, though, we need to be careful. Ibsen loads the symbol of polluted waters with many meanings, including the idea that industry is destroying nature. But his use of symbols differs from that of, say, Mallarmé, who used them as a gateway to a more spiritual realm. In general, Ibsen's symbols point more towards earth than to heaven.

Strindberg, *The Father* (1887)

The Swedish playwright Johan August Strindberg (1849–1912) dealt mainly with psychological states, whereas Ibsen dealt mainly with social problems. This is apparent in their respective views of naturalism. For Ibsen, it was essentially a way of portraying society as accurately as possible, but for Strindberg 'naturalism was not a dramatic method like that of photography [but one] which seeks out those points in life where the great conflicts occur, which rejoices in seeing what cannot be seen every day.'[7] The focus on the mind, how it is affected by conflict, and on what cannot normally be seen, ultimately necessitates a move away from the sort of naturalistic forms of representation that we find in Ibsen.

Despite their differences, Strindberg recognised an affinity with Ibsen. In *The Father*, one of his early plays, the character of the Doctor refers to Ibsen's *Ghosts* (1881): 'When I sat in the theatre the other evening and heard Mrs Alving orating over her dead husband, I thought to myself: "What a damned shame the fellow's dead and can't defend himself!"'[8]

At that point in the play Mrs Alving is telling Pastor Manders about her husband's infidelities, including one with the housemaid. Strindberg seems to latch onto this part of the play because it touches on a major preoccupation of his work, the nature of the male–female relationship. It is one of the themes that will become prominent in Expressionist drama, of which Strindberg is regarded as a precursor.

The best example in his *oeuvre* is *The Dance of Death* (1900), a two part play in which a couple find ways to endlessly torment each other, even drawing a visitor into their games. It was a big influence on Edward Albee's play, *Who's Afraid of Virginia Woolf?* (1963), and the theme is already evident in *The Father*. The plot is very simple. The Captain's wife, Laura, makes her husband doubt that he is the father of their child, Bertha. This is due to two issues: how best to manage the family finances, and disagreement about how to bring up their daughter. Neither, however, really explain or justify the depth of Laura's malevolence towards her husband.

In Strindberg's universe men and women struggle for power, but without any real reason. Is it because, as the Captain says, they are descended from two 'different species of ape'? (p. 61). Or is it because nature's fundamental law is 'to eat or be eaten'? (p. 71). Either way it means that, as the nurse puts it, 'they torment the life out of each other' (p. 41).*

---

* If we move outside the play, we can find several reasons for the tortuous relationship between the Captain and Laura. One is Strindberg's own relations with women. He was, for example, married three times, none of them happily. From Darwin he drew the idea that life was a battle for survival and that civilisation had weakened men, making them vulnerable to women's weapons of emotional

The war between men and women is one aspect of their relationship. Another is the Oedipus complex which, incidentally, loosely underpins a number of modernist works from Kafka's *The Castle* (1926) to Aldous Huxley's *Brave New World* (1932). Sigmund Freud's (1858–1939) famous theory refers to boys. Put simply he argues that the infant wants to kill his father so that he can sleep with his mother. The relationship between Laura and the Captain is a bit like that between mother and son. 'Weep, my child', says Laura. 'Your mother is here to comfort you' (p. 60). 'I loved you as my child' she says a little further on and then shudders with disgust when she admits 'the mother became the mistress' (ibid.).

In Freud's version of the Oedipus complex, the son fears the father will punish him, symbolically castrate him, because of his 'desire' for the mother. But, in Strindberg's play, the Captain is 'castrated' by the nurse. She removes the gun – a symbol of the penis – from his hand and manipulates him into a straitjacket. 'Caught, cropped and cozened' cries the Captain when he realises what has happened (p. 72). The nurse completes what Laura had begun when she caused him to doubt that he was Bertha's father.

The mother, then, not the father is the one with power in Strindberg's version of the Oedipus complex. Laura breaks the Captain's will – 'the backbone of the mind' according to the Doctor – and when that is impaired, 'the mind crumbles' (p. 38). The Captain's mental state disintegrates as he becomes obsessed with whether Bertha is or is not his child. He is reduced from being a father to being a child. At the end of the play he asks to rest his head on the nurse's bosom, and with a cry collapses onto her lap.

---

manipulation and 'spiritual murder'. Strindberg had also read Otto Weininger's highly misogynistic *Sex and Character* (1903) which claimed, among other things, that women were driven by sexual desire and only by denying them fulfilment could men lift them to a higher plane. Strindberg's views of women were another mark of his difference from Ibsen, who in plays such as *A Doll's House* (1881), championed their rights. Strindberg was a virulent opponent of women's rights because he thought such reforms would only lead them to increase their power over men.

The Father and Modernism

The Father isn't just the disturbing story of a power struggle to the death. It also reflects at least two aspects of modernism: first, the experience of doubt and second, the position of women. There is an argument for saying that the modern age began with the French mathematician and philosopher René Descartes (1596–1650) because he rejected accepted ideas and knowledge in order to build truth on a firm foundation. His method was to doubt everything. The only thing which could not be doubted was that he himself existed and it was on that basis that he built his system of knowledge.

Similarly, in the nineteenth century, Friedrich Nietzsche announced that it was necessary to be sceptical of all inherited concepts, and we can read the Captain's doubts about his paternity as one expression of that scepticism; for to doubt fatherhood is to doubt the authority of the past, to refuse to take tradition on trust. To be modern is therefore to realise that 'one never knows, one only believes' (p. 69). But such doubt carries with it uncertainty and insecurity, and even the possibility of mental illness, as illustrated in the Captain's breakdown. He experiences, in an extreme form, the same sense of loss and disorientation as the narrator of T. S. Eliot's *The Waste Land* (1922) and, like him, ransacks classical culture for a sense of continuity and consolation but, unlike the narrator of *The Waste Land*, the Captain can find no 'fragments to shore against his ruin' (see Part Three: 'Modernist Poetry: America, Ireland and England'). Descartes's dream, of truths of which we can be absolutely sure, lies in ruins.

The battle between the Captain and Laura over their daughter's future partly reflects the debate about female emancipation. All over Europe women were demanding the right to vote, to enter the professions, to have access to birth control and so on. The position of women in Sweden gradually improved during the nineteenth century. For example they were allowed to attend school, they received an equal share of inheritance with male heirs and unmarried women were able to enter the professions – the country had its first woman dentist in 1861 – though they had to wait until 1918 before they got the vote. What made the question of female emancipation so contentious was that it intensified men's anxieties about their own status in the modern world. The factory system made them a cog in the machine while the industrialised slaughter of the First World War made traditional notions of courage and honour seem almost obsolete.

Since Strindberg is frequently accused of being anti-feminist, it is worth pointing out that the Captain does not want 'to play the pimp and educate [Bertha] just simply for marriage' (p. 31). Rather, he wants her to become a teacher so that she will be able to support herself. Laura would like Bertha to become a painter. The choice between these two professions is in part a dramatisation of what's at stake in modernism itself. The teacher passes on traditional values but the painter is someone who breaks with them in order to say something new. Bertha's mother-in-law, however, would like her to be a spiritualist, her governess a Methodist, and her nurse a Baptist. This represents another battle that is being fought in modernism – that between science, the Captain's particular interest, and religion, in the broadest sense of the term. Bertha, in fact, becomes a symbol for the future: what direction it will take; what character it will have.

Strindberg, *Miss Julie* (1888)

Another of Strindberg's plays which both reflects and indeed shapes the modernist revolution is *Miss Julie*. Again it centres on the conflict between a woman and a man, the eponymous heroine and her father's servant, Jean. He seduces her and then pushes her to commit suicide; but it is equally the case that Miss Julie manipulates the situation so that Jean behaves in the way that she wants.

At the beginning of the play, for example, she expresses a desire to kill herself. She describes a dream in which she is at the top of a pillar. She longs to fall, but lacks the courage. Yet 'I know I shall find no peace till I come down, no rest till I come down, down to the ground. And if I could get down, I should want to burrow my way deep into the earth.'[9] She uses Jean to help achieve that aim. 'You know what I ought to will myself to do, but I can't. Will me to Jean, order me!' (p. 145).

Miss Julie and Modernism

Miss Julie contributes to the modernist revolution in a number of ways. It is frank about bodily functions – 'oh she's got her monthly coming on' (p. 111); it shows an interest in the primitive, that is in ritual, violence and sacrifice (pp. 122, 139); and it promotes the idea that humans have no core identity, they simply invent themselves over and over again. 'I have no self' declares Miss Julie (p. 145) while Jean fashions himself out of novels, plays and hearing the 'gentry talk' (p. 120).

It is Strindberg's 'Preface' to the play, however, which is probably of most interest to students of modernism. He starts by attacking the current state of theatre. It is dominated, he says, by farces and musicals designed to appeal to a mass and largely uncritical audience. What is needed therefore, is a new type of 'psychological drama' (p. 103), of which *Miss Julie* is to be the exemplar. Strindberg's hostility to popular theatre is unmistakeable: it portrays the world 'as though it were peopled by lunatics with an insatiable passion for dancing' (p. 93). His attitude is typical of some modernists, such as E. M. Forster, who despised the institutions of mass culture.

Strindberg, though, casts this division in gender terms. He sees contemporary audiences as having largely female characteristics because they are dominated by feeling. They therefore 'accept the illusion [of what is happening on stage], and react to the suggestion of the author' (p. 91). The new drama will require an audience to reflect, analyse and investigate what is happening on stage. It will, in effect, be a 'masculine' audience because its response to a play will be based on reason not emotion. Strindberg's views on women demonstrate a peculiar feature of modernism: that those who were progressive in art could be conservative in politics.

Strindberg does not propose a new theme for his 'psychological drama'. On the contrary, 'the problem of social ascent or decline, of higher or lower, better or worse, man or woman, is, has been and will be of permanent interest' (p. 92). What he proposes instead is a new form for it; one, for example, that moves beyond the conventions of tragedy since they appeal to our feelings at the expense of our judgement.

Indeed, Strindberg looks forward to a time when 'we shall have become so developed and enlightened that we shall be able to observe with indifference the harsh, cynical and heartless drama that life presents' (ibid.). The idea that being able to look upon suffering with 'indifference' is a sign of 'enlightenment' and heightened 'development' is certainly an unusual take on what we mean by those terms. Strindberg's attitude here is reminiscent of Zola's view of naturalism: that it should be removed, detached, objective.

It is when Strindberg starts to talk about the changes he would like to make to theatre that we notice an apparent inconsistency in his views. He criticised the contemporary audience for its acceptance of illusion yet his intention to have only one set, to abolish the interval and to use décor 'borrowed from the impressionist painters' is done with the aim of 'further[ing] illusion' (p. 101).* How are we to account for this discrepancy? Here we need to remember Strindberg's distinction between two types of drama.

The first is popular and requires no effort from the audience while the second, which is less popular, does. The first type of play offers an illusion which the viewer simply accepts while the second asks that the viewer participate in the creation of the illusion by foregoing the interval, which always breaks the spell, and by building up the set for themselves. As Strindberg puts it: 'The fact that the one does not see the whole room and all the furniture leaves room for surmise ... the audience's imagination is set in motion and completes its own picture' (p. 101). The answer to the problem of Strindberg's apparent inconsistency over the matter of illusion in the theatre, then, is that he seems to be talking about two different types: one which bears little relation to life and which the audience simply accept, and the other which reflects life and which the audience help to create.

---

* See the Extended Commentary below for discussion of Brecht's corresponding 'alienation effect'.

At the same time that he is trying to make theatre more authentic, however, Strindberg is also drawing attention to its artifice. He identifies the three arts which properly belong to the drama – monologue, mime and ballet – and incorporates them all into *Miss Julie*. While we may regard the monologue as being realistic – Strindberg's contemporaries did not – it is much harder to see the other two arts in that light. The mixture of authenticity and artifice in Strindberg's theatre is similar to the mixture of naturalism and symbolism in Ibsen.

Indeed, we could use the same terms for Strindberg himself. The set for *Miss Julie*, a kitchen, is both naturalistic and symbolic. The naturalism is there in such detail as the two shelves with utensils of copper, iron and pewter while the symbolism is apparent in the lilacs on the table, which have a number of meanings. They refer to the story of Pan and Syringa, in which he chases her and to escape she turns herself into a lilac bush. The myth has parallels with the relationship between Miss Julie and Jean. Lilacs are also associated with love and pride, both of which have a bearing on the play.

The mixture of naturalism and symbolism is a way of portraying the complexity of 'psychological drama' more effectively than conventional means of representation. Just as James Joyce uses the stream of consciousness technique to convey the reality of inner life so Strindberg uses a combination of naturalism and symbolism to show the workings of the mind we don't normally see. Also, just as Joyce returns to classical mythology to give his narrative unity so too does Strindberg revive elements of classical drama to help structure his story.

Strindberg and Character

The key focus of Strindberg's discussion of psychological drama is 'character'. Aristotle, in his *Poetics* (350 BC) said that character was the second most important element in drama. The first was plot. He also stipulated that character should embody a moral quality. This view survived, in a modified form, right up to the nineteenth century where character was seen, in Strindberg's words, as 'the immutability of the soul' (p. 94), that is, a person dominated by a single trait: miserliness, drunkenness, courage and so on.

Strindberg wanted to move beyond this conception of character to one which takes account of the many layers which make up a person. Hence his characters are 'agglomerations of past and present cultures, scraps from books and newspapers, fragments of humanity, torn shreds of once fine clothing that has become rags' (p. 95). This view of character can be found, in different forms, in Joyce, Woolf and Lawrence. It also receives dramatic expression in *The Waste Land* where the narrator ransacks past and present, 'shoring fragments against his ruin'.

The patchwork nature of the modern character is evident in Miss Julie herself. She is motivated by a number of factors, including the traits she has inherited from her mother, her susceptibility to suggestion, the onset of her period, the smell of flowers and the festive atmosphere of the midsummer celebrations. How, though, can the dramatist convey these different motives on stage?

Dialogue is one answer. The contemporary fashion, Strindberg tells us, is for characters to ask 'stupid questions in order evoke some witty retort' (p. 98). By contrast, he allowed dialogue to follow the irregular course of characters' minds, to wander, 'providing itself in the opening scenes with matter which is later taken up, worked upon, repeated, expanded and added to, like the theme in a musical composition' (p. 99).

Another answer is to remove footlights, which not only make actors look fat in the face but also 'annihilate all subtle expressions in the lower half of the face' (p. 102). Strindberg also recommended that actors not wear make-up as this tends to sit on the face 'like a mask' (p. 103). Strindberg advocated these changes because he saw the face as being far more expressive of character than words or gestures. Strindberg's focus on character, particularly on the mind, place him firmly in the modernist camp, as do his experiments in representation.

Strindberg, *A Dream Play* (1902) and Expressionism

If Ibsen is important to modernist theatre, Strindberg is essential. It is he, rather than Ibsen, who develops its expressive possibilities. As mentioned earlier, he influenced expressionist drama, particularly in his portrayal of relationships. The Oedipal conflict, for example, is the subject of Arnolt Bronnen's *Vatermord* (1920). The father is a sadistic bully and the mother tries to seduce her son. As she faces him, naked, the father enters and the son stabs him to death.

The basic tenet of Expressionism, which was a movement in painting before it was a type of theatre, was that artists should use shapes and colours to express how they felt about the world. On the whole they regarded it as a prison or place of corruption. They did not seek to portray the world for that would only intensify their sense of confinement and decay. Rather they sought to transcend it, either by returning to primitive art, which represented an instinctive and therefore innocent form of expression, or by developing an art of pure form containing shapes and patterns, suggestive of higher realms and deeper truths than could be found in the world around them.

Many of these themes and more can be found in Strindberg's *A Dream Play* (1902). The god Indra sends his daughter down to earth to find if the 'complaints and wailings [of mankind] are well-founded'.[10] The world is seen as a prison, and Indra's daughter feels trapped: 'My thoughts can no longer fly. Clay on my wings; earth on my feet' (p. 237). The world is also corrupt to the extent that those who commit crimes, who oppress the poor, not only go 'unpunished', they sit in a casino and 'eat eight courses with wine' (p. 232).

'Right-minded' people add to the corruption because of the way they treat anyone who wants to make things better: 'all the improvers end in prison or the madhouse. Who puts them in prison? All right thinking people' (p. 233). Poetry is seen as a way of transcending the world. It is 'not reality', declares Indra's daughter, 'it is greater than reality' (p. 237).

Many of the characters also spend much of their time waiting, a theme which will receive its most famous expression in Samuel Beckett's

Waiting for Godot (1955), to be discussed in the next chapter. The debate between the Dean of Philosophy, the Dean of Theology and the Dean of Medicine approximates to that characteristic division of modernity, identified by the philosopher Immanuel Kant (1724–1804), between science, morality and aesthetics. Each is a separate sphere of knowledge with its own criteria of truth. Simplifying greatly, Kant argues that what happens in science can never be the basis for our moral actions, and our moral actions can never be the basis for our aesthetic judgements, and so on. Kant's 'division of the faculties' may also help us to understand more fully the doctrine of art for art's sake, though that is not something we can pursue here.

A Dream Play is perhaps most influential for the manner in which it rejects naturalistic representation. As Strindberg says in his 'Author's Note', 'everything can happen, everything is possible and probable' (p. 175). Hence we see Indra's daughter appearing on a cloud, a castle rising out of the ground and a lime tree becoming a coat stand. We also have rapid changes of scene and characters who 'split, double, multiply, evaporate, condense, disperse, assemble' (ibid.).

Strindberg takes this approach partly because 'psychological drama' needs a new form; partly because the conventional means of representing reality do not fully capture its deep truths; and partly because Strindberg wants to express how he feels about a world in which 'the twin halves of the heart are wrenched asunder / And one is torn as between raging horses / Of contradictions, irresolution, discord' (p. 254).

Pirandello, *Six Characters in Search of An Author* (1921)

Luigi Pirandello (1867–1936) is sometimes overlooked in histories of modernism.* Perhaps commentators are embarrassed by the fact that, in 1924, he joined the Fascist Party. Its leader, Benito Mussolini (1883–

---

* For example there is no mention of Pirandello in Peter Gay's monumental *Modernism: The Lure of Heresy* (2007), nor in Peter Nicholls's intellectually sophisticated *Modernism: A Literary Guide* (second edition 2009). We might expect to find a reference to him in Michael Levenson (ed.), *The Cambridge Companion to Modernism* (1999) but there too we are disappointed. It's the same story in Philip Tew and Alex Murray (eds), *The Modernism Handbook* (2009).

1945), even attended the opening production of one of Pirandello's plays, *Festival of our Lord of the Ship* in 1925. However, this embarrassment does not prevent these same commentators from discussing the work of other writers who flirted with fascism, for example Ezra Pound and W. B. Yeats, so why Pirandello is so often ignored is something of a mystery.

His *Six Characters in Search of An Author* is indisputably a modernist work. It integrates questions about the nature of drama and the relation between the stage and the world into the action of the play. The plot is as follows. As a producer and his cast are rehearsing a play, they are interrupted by six Characters all wearing masks. The Characters are Father, Mother, Stepdaughter, Son, Madame Pace, and Boy and Girl, who do not speak. The Father and Stepdaughter ask the producer if he will stage their story, at the heart of which is a scene in which he tries to seduce her, though he did not know she was his stepdaughter at the time.

The theme of incest is widespread in modernist literature (see also Part Three: 'The British Stage and Theatrical Thinkers'). Pirandello also seems to share some aspects of Strindberg's view of character: 'each of us is several different people' declares the Father, 'and all these people live inside us.'[11] It is precisely this idea, that we have many selves, that is expressed in the stream of consciousness technique that we find in some modernist novels (see Part Three: 'The Origins of the Modernist Novel').

Later, though, the Father seems to contradict himself for he claims that characters have a definite identity compared to 'real people'. The Producer, asserts the Father, will constantly change: 'whatever you touch and believe in and that seems real for you today, is going to be – like the reality of yesterday – an illusion tomorrow' (p. 64). The Characters, however, do not change, a fact symbolised by their masks. They must live the same reality again and again because 'it is already determined, like this, forever, that's what's so terrible. We are an eternal reality' (ibid.). Actors who play the Father will come and go, but the Father will always remain the same.

A clue as to how we may be able to reconcile these apparently contradictory statements by the Father, that he is made up of different selves but yet has a definite identity compared to the Producer and his cast, lies in the characters' objections to the actors who will play them. No matter how well they perform their roles, the cast will never be able to convey all aspects of the Characters. 'However much they want to be the same as us, they're not' says the Father (p. 53).

What he fails to appreciate, however, is that each actor interprets a Character differently. One actor will emphasise one part of the Character's self, another actor another part. All the selves of the Character will therefore appear, but one at a time, not altogether. He or she will be revealed chronologically rather than simultaneously, and that is how a Character can have both several selves and a definite identity.

Nevertheless, the Characters do worry about how they are portrayed. The Stepdaughter complains that the leading actress does not 'burst out laughing' as she did when the Father said 'good afternoon' to her 'in that way' (p. 51). Her anxiety is yet another aspect of that crisis of representation that lies at the heart of modernism. The Stepdaughter wants the Producer to perform the play from her point of view. 'I want you to show my drama. Mine!' (p. 55).

This remark is a reminder that the individual voice is made to blend with all the other voices by the institutions of mass media. It is they who produce that organ known as 'public opinion' whose purpose is to provide support for prevailing orthodoxies. Art is one of the few places where the individual may be heard. Heard, but not necessarily understood. Here, once again, we touch on that notorious characteristic of modern art: its difficulty.

Complexity, intricacy and allusiveness reflect the extremes the artist must go to in order to sound distinct in a society dominated by the blandishments of the popular press. If his or her art proves too hard to understand, however, then how can the artist hope to have his or her individuality recognised? One answer is to form small coteries of like-minded individuals who give each other mutual support and validate each others' views.

The Producer touches on these issues in his reply to the Stepdaughter. He points out that the play is not just her drama, 'it's drama for other people as well' (p. 56). This can be interpreted as a reaction against the excesses of expressionist theatre, which can seem more like private nightmares than public performances. In Oskar Kokoschka's *Murderer, Hope of Women* (1907), for instance, which is only a few pages long, a man brands a woman with an iron, she stabs him and he is placed alive in a coffin while she screams at him through a grille. It caused a riot when it was first performed.

In a play, says the Producer, 'everything needs to be balanced and in harmony' (p. 56). This seems to be more a romantic than modern view of art since it stresses smoothness rather than the jagged edges of Cubism or jazz. However, as we saw with *The Waste Land*, it is possible to see an underlying unity beneath the broken surface.

Six Characters in Search of an Author is a dazzling piece of theatre that relentlessly plays with the idea of illusion and reality until we can barely tell which is which. It opens with a stage-hand building the set. This simple action alone draws our attention to how the illusion of 'real life' is created on stage. In this and other ways Pirandello challenges the assumptions of naturalism. He shows that it is not a reflection of real life but a construct. He also calls into question the ideas of Expressionism. If the debate between the Characters and the Producer tells us anything it is that we do not have a real self to express. Instead we have multiple selves that cannot be resolved into one, except perhaps in art.

Do the Characters and the Producer reveal any other aspect of modernism, apart from the problematic nature of identity in the early twentieth century? The answer is yes: to the extent that the Characters are doomed to repeat themselves, they symbolise the idea that we cannot break with the past. This is further illustrated by the Producer, who chooses to stage the Characters' story rather than the new play he is rehearsing. *Six Characters in Search of an Author* is very much part of the modernist dilemma of whether to reject the past or to utilise it. The Characters' story is ultimately a tragic one: the Boy and Girl die, suggesting that here is one part of the past that should be discarded – but the implication is that it can't, and must be endured.

The Characters also represent the notion of artistic autonomy. 'When a character is born he immediately assumes an independence even of his own author … and acquires a meaning that his author never dreamed of giving him' (p. 65). This doctrine also breaks with Expressionism. It is potentially democratic because it frees the reader from having to rely on the author's view of the work, but it is also intimidating because the reader requires a great deal of cultural capital to access the work, and in this sense it acts as a precursor to modern critical 'reader response' theory, which promotes the role of the reader and their response to a work in creating its meaning. The result, ultimately, is to make art an object of study rather a shaping presence in the culture.

Antonin Artaud (1896–1948)

While some people were writing plays others were thinking about drama and how best to experiment with the form. Strindberg wanted to develop a new 'psychological' theatre, but the French actor, director and dramatic theorist Antonin Artaud was hostile to the idea. He associated it with 'an economic, utilitarian and technological state'.[12] Psychology, he argued, brought 'the unknown down to a level with the known [and] has caused [a] fearful loss of energy' (p. 58). By making everything known, psychology complemented the modern bureaucratic state's desire for information about its citizens.

Everything must be made visible so that it can be controlled. The same principle was at work in the factory where the time and motion man observed workers to ensure they were carrying out their tasks efficiently (see Part Two: 'A Cultural Overview').

Why should 'psychology' cause a loss of energy? Perhaps because the constant exercise of one faculty, not necessarily in work but in general social life, leaves it exhausted. Work could be tiring, though, for a different reason. Its repetitive nature dulled the senses leading to a state of lethargy. Here we may have an answer to a question posed in Part Three: 'The Origins of the Modernist Novel', namely why do so many of Kafka's characters conduct their business from bed? Because the monotonous nature of modern work, whether in the factory or the office, lowers energy levels.

Artaud wanted a theatre that appealed to the 'whole man', not just the mind. He called it the 'theatre of cruelty'. This term has often been misunderstood. It 'has nothing to do with the cruelties we practise on one another', Artaud writes, rather it compels us to recognise that 'we are not free and the sky can still fall on our heads' (p. 60). This simply means that we are subject to natural laws, which gives us a kinship with everything that exists. The aim of the theatre of cruelty is to remind us of our connection with the rest of creation so that we can take our place within it.

How do we establish the theatre of cruelty, and what would it look like? The first thing, says Artaud, is to abandon the script: 'Dialogue does not belong to the stage but to books' (p. 27). Words address the intellect and ignore the senses. Artaud believes that making speech the dominant medium of theatre 'means turning our backs on the physical requirements of the stage and rebelling against its potential' (p. 52).

Artaud looks outside Europe for a model of drama. He finds it in the Balinese theatre. Its themes, 'the soul as prey to the spectres and phantoms of the other world' (p. 39), are conveyed through body language, costume and ritual gesture. Watching a performance reawakens the rapture that should be the proper experience of theatre. It gives us an emotional understanding of our relationship with a reality far greater than the one studied by science.

To achieve this effect, every aspect of the production has to be clearly defined. Each movement has 'to obey a very precise, musical indication … a deliberate accuracy directs everything' (p. 40). This characteristic of Balinese theatre corresponds to another aspect of Artaud's definition of cruelty, 'a kind of strict control' (p. 80). In this context, the 'submission to necessity' (ibid.) means abiding by the conventions of performance in order to fulfil the aims of the production.

There seems to be an irony here: Artaud wants to use theatre as a means of challenging the stark utilitarianism of modern society, and yet his insistence on discipline, on performance as 'systematic depersonalisation' (p. 40) is consistent with the techniques of scientific management which treat humans as so many units of 'horse power'.[13] The irony, though, is only apparent. For the kind of impersonality to which Artaud refers is not that of a human reduced to a machine but the experience of belonging to something greater than ourselves, whatever that may be. In that respect, Artaud is like D. H. Lawrence, who wanted to restore our relation to the 'circumambient universe' (see Part Three: 'The Modernist Novel in England').[14] Only then can we come fully into being.

Like any self-respecting modernist, Artaud wrote a manifesto. As he favoured the poetic idiom, his ideas are inclined to be somewhat cloudy. We could spend a long time pondering sentences such as this one: Theatre, 'because it requires spatial expression (the only real one in fact) allows the sum total of the magic means in the arts and words to be organically active like an exorcism' (p. 68). New concepts, though, do require new forms of expression and while it can be a struggle to understand them, it is usually worth the effort.

Artaud begins by reiterating his general principle that the theatre of cruelty will not use speech to communicate but movement, attitude, gesture, music and dancing. Where words are used they will be sung or chanted. The costumes will evoke ancient rituals and ceremonies and the props will include puppets, masks and 'objects of strange proportion' (p. 75). There will be no clear distinction between the stage and the auditorium, allowing the actors to connect more easily with the spectators. Performances will be based on real life events, 'facts or known works' (p. 76). These will distil our dreams, good and bad, thereby reviving our inner life.

Artaud's vision of theatre never materialised. It is interesting, however, not only for the challenges it poses to our thinking about drama but also because of its relation to modernism. The criticism of contemporary culture, in particular its 'longstanding habit of seeking diversions' (p. 64), the return to myth, the attraction to primitive energy, the desire to innovate, the need to give life significance and the belief in the power of art to redeem the modern world are all themes we have encountered before.

However, what makes Artaud stand out from other artists is that his experiment with the form of theatre was not intended to distance the masses but to include them. 'If the masses do not frequent literary masterpieces', he writes, 'this is because the masterpieces are literary, that is to say, set in forms no longer answering the needs of the times' (p. 56). The theatre of cruelty was meant to do just that. Sadly, Artaud went mad and spent the last years of his life in and out of psychiatric institutions. What an irony for someone who opposed psychological theatre.

Extended Commentary: Brecht, *Mother Courage and her Children* (1939)

Bertolt Brecht (1898–1956) is regarded as one of the great innovators of modern drama. His experiments were intended to help audiences not only to understand society but also to change it for the better. The aim of epic theatre, as Brecht called it, was to develop techniques that would 'portray social processes as seen in their causal relationships'.[15]

Brecht distinguished epic theatre from dramatic theatre. The first difference is that dramatic theatre uses plot, and epic theatre uses narrative. The plot, in traditional plays, awakened the audience's curiosity and made them want to know what happens next. It also encouraged them to emotionally identify with the principal characters. By contrast, the scenes in epic theatre do not build to a climax nor do the actors encourage audience identification by becoming the part they play.

Brecht's model for epic theatre is 'an incident such as can be seen at any street corner: an eyewitness demonstrating to a collection of people how a traffic accident took place' (p. 85). The demonstrator acts the behaviour of driver or victim, or both 'in such a way that the bystanders are able to form an opinion about the accident' (ibid.). The demonstrator does not create the illusion of the crash, nor are the bystanders meant to enjoy the drama of it. Instead the demonstrator relays only those elements which will help them understand why the accident happened.

Similarly, in the theatre, the audience must not get caught up in the action but examine how it arose, and what consequences could follow from it. The actors help them to do this by 'sketching' a character rather than 'being' one. This is part of Brecht's famous 'alienation effect' which is intended to subdue the audience's emotion while stimulating their intellect. Other examples of the alienation effect, all of which are found in *Mother Courage and her Children*, include: setting the action in historically distant periods and geographically remote places; banners announcing what will happen in each scene, hence removing the element of surprise; and songs which not only sum up the theme of a scene but also invite the actor to step out of role and address the audience.

Another difference between dramatic and epic theatre is that in the former the audience are passive while in the latter they are active. This difference in response is due to dramatic theatre presenting audiences with an illusion which requires no effort on their part to accept while epic theatre is constantly provoking them to think about what they see. The other major differences between the two types of theatre are that in the dramatic man is seen as a fixed point but in epic theatre he is seen in process; and in dramatic theatre thought determines actions while, in epic, environment determines thought.

Mother Courage and her Children is an example of Brecht's epic theatre. It tells the story of how Anna Frieling, the Mother Courage of the title, fights to keep her business – selling goods from her cart – going during the Polish–Swedish war (1622–29), a fight that results in the death of her three children. The play could be described as a traditional tragedy except for three things. First, Mother Courage is a lowly figure rather than an aristocrat, second, she is largely responsible for her own fate and third, the genre of tragedy had more or less died by the time Brecht wrote the play. If Brecht evokes the tragic form by the deaths of Mother Courage's children, it is only to show that we have outgrown it.*

The first way in which *Mother Courage* is an example of epic theatre is in its organisation. There are no acts, as in traditional plays, only

---

* *Mother Courage* could be considered as a rewriting of Euripides's *Medea* (431 BC) which tells the story of a woman who kills her children in order to take revenge on Jason, the husband who abandoned her.

scenes. Moreover, the scenes are self-contained; they do not follow on from one another. Scene three, for example, takes place three years after scene two, and scene five takes place two years after scene four. This break in temporal continuity helps prevent 'the engendering of illusion' ('The Street Scene', p. 86) which Brecht saw as such a blight on theatre.

Though the play jumps about in time, however, each scene is closely related to every other in terms of both action and theme. There are twelve scenes in the play. All have reference to the war, and the first eight show Mother Courage engaged in haggling or bargaining. There is, in other words, a great deal of repetition throughout the play. This accords with Brecht's model for epic theatre. The street demonstrator's performance is, he says, 'essentially repetitive' (p. 86). The purpose of repetition is to get the audience to look at the same action from different angles.

A good example is the two scenes where one of Mother Courage's children, Eilif, kills some peasants and takes their stock. The first time he is hailed as a hero, but the second time he is taken away to be shot. 'Tell her it wasn't any different', he says in a final message to his mother, 'tell her it was the same thing.'[16] It's not, however, quite the same because the first time he did it in war, the second time in peace. Brecht is asking the audience to think about whether an action can be good or bad in itself or whether it always depends on the circumstances. Encouraging the audience to think about these matters is another mark of epic theatre.

Mother Courage and her Children also exemplifies the aspect of epic theatre that involves the notion that man is not fixed but in process. The chaplain, for example, is forced to take refuge with Mother Courage when the Catholics break into Protestant territory. At first he complains that his talents and abilities 'are being abused ... by manual labour' (p. 57) but he later asserts that 'since I came down in the world I've become a better person, I couldn't preach to anyone now' (p. 66). This shows that he can change.

What about Mother Courage herself? Does she change during the course of the play? She is as concerned for her business at the beginning as she is at the end. She wants to provide for herself and her children, and she believes that war stimulates trade. On this matter, however, the sergeant asks her a pertinent question: 'Want to live off the war but keep yourself and your family out of it, eh?' (p. 13). His point is that Mother Courage cannot hope to profit from the conflict without in some way being affected by it.

Of course, he is right. For the great irony of the play is that it is by attending to her business that she loses her children. Swiss Cheese, for example, is shot while his mother hesitates over whether she can afford to put her cart up for security in order to get the money to pay his ransom. Mother Courage does not develop during the course of the play, she simply loses those she loves.

Her not changing, though, is precisely the point. The audience understand what Mother Courage does not: namely, that as long as she adheres to her belief that war is good for business she will only suffer further privation and heartache. She supports the system that destroys her life. Here we see another aspect of epic theatre, that people's ideas are shaped by the circumstances in which they find themselves. Mother Courage would not think the way she does if she lived in a different environment. This brings us back to the purpose of epic theatre, in particular the alienation effect, which is to make the familiar strange so that we can look at it critically and alter it for the better if necessary.

In what ways, then, is Brecht a modernist? First and foremost he is an innovator, but his theatrical experiments are not mere formal exercises, they are geared to social change. Brecht's art had a political immediacy – *Mother Courage and her Children*, it should be remembered, was finished in 1939, the year the Second World War began, and this gives many of the remarks about war in the play a sense of real urgency. This makes him different to those modernists such as Woolf who were more interested in aesthetics than politics. Having said that, though, both Brecht and Woolf were engaged in the wider modernist project of making us see the world differently.

His alienation effect is a kind of refined naturalism. Ibsen gave us the appearance of things, Brecht makes us look into their reality, and he had little use for symbols. He wanted to inspire audiences to start a revolution, but he failed. Western society, with all its inequalities, remains much as it was when he was writing. There have been some changes, people are generally better off, but the fundamental power structures remain in place. Of Brecht it can be said that he changed the theatre, but not the world.

Notes

1   Christopher Innes, 'Modernism in Drama' in Michael Levenson (ed.), *The Cambridge Companion to Modernism* (Cambridge: Cambridge University Press, 1999), pp. 130–56. p. 130.

2   Emile Zola, 'Naturalism on the Stage' in Vassiliki Kolocotroni, Jane Goldman and Olga Taxidou (eds), *Modernism: An Anthology of Sources and Documents* (Edinburgh: Edinburgh University Press, 1998), pp. 170–3; p. 173.

3   Zola, 'Naturalism in the Theatre' in Eric Bentley (ed.), *The Theory of the Modern Stage* (Harmondsworth: Penguin, 1992), pp. 351–72, p. 355.

4   William Archer, 'Henrik Ibsen: Philosopher or Poet' (1905) in Kolocotroni et al., *Modernism: An Anthology of Sources and Documents*, pp. 145–7, p. 145.

5   Ibsen, *Plays: 2 A Doll's House, An Enemy of the People, Hedda Gabler* translated and introduced by Michael Meyer (London: Methuen, 1993), p. 222.

6   John Carey, *The Intellectuals and the Masses: Pride and Prejudice among the Literary Intelligentsia 1880–1939* (London: Faber, 1992), p. 21.

7   Strindberg, Preface to *Miss Julie* in *Plays One: The Father, Miss Julie, The Ghost Sonata* translated and introduced by Michael Meyer (London: Methuen, 1994), p. 93.

8   Strindberg, *The Father* in *Plays One*, p. 55.

9   Strindberg, *Miss Julie* in *Plays One*, p. 116.

10   Strindberg, *Plays Two: The Dance of Death, A Dream Play, The Stronger* translated and introduced by Michael Meyer (London: Methuen, 1993), p. 185.

11   Luigi Pirandello, *Six Characters in Search of an Author* translated by John Linstrum with Commentary and Notes by Joseph Farrell (London: Methuen, 2004), p. 29.

12   Antonin Artaud, *The Theatre and its Double* translated by Victor Corti (London: John Calder, 1985), p. 81.

13   See Frederic Winslow Taylor, *The Principles of Scientific Management* (New York: Harper Row, 1911). Full text available at www.eldritchpress.org/fwt/t2.html from where this quotation is taken.

14   D. H. Lawrence, *Study of Thomas Hardy and Other Essays* (Cambridge: Cambridge University Press, 2002), p. 116.

15   Bertolt Brecht, 'The Street Scene: A Basic Model for an Epic Theatre' in Eric Bentley (ed.), *The Theory of the Modern Stage*, pp. 85–96, p. 85.

16   Brecht, *Mother Courage and her Children* translated by John Willett, with Commentary and Notes by Hugh Rorrison (London: Methuen, 1983), p. 69.

The British Stage and Theatrical Thinkers: Wilde, Shaw, Coward and Beckett

The English painter and dramatist Wyndham Lewis's short play *The Enemy of the Stars* (1914) is as outrageous as any expressionist drama for its assault on reason and the senses. It contains only two scenes, the first of which is set in a circus ring. There are two characters. The first is named Manish, a Hindu term for God of the Mind, and is an 'immense collapse of chronic philosophy [who] bulges all over with simple fire of life.'[1] At first he is alone. Suddenly a 'human bull' rushes into the ring before disappearing into the earth. The second character is called Gamin, an Irish term for traveller, and is a 'bourgeois' with a 'criminal instinct'. Nothing really happens in the scene, the two characters simply strike a pose. That of Manish implies that the mind must give way to the body while that of Gamin implies an aversion to the 'statue mirage of Liberty in the great desert'.

The second scene builds on this theme of the mind having to submit to the body. It is set near a hut at the entrance to a mine. Nearby there is wheelwright's yard and a canal. Everything is bathed in a red light. Once again there are two characters: Arghol, who represents the mind and the freedom of the artist, and Hanp, who represents the body and the mediocre mass of humanity. Despite trying to stay aloof from Hanp, Arghol is eventually drawn into conflict with him. They fight and Hanp eventually murders Arghol while he sleeps. The moral is that the artist can never transcend the world no matter how much he or she tries.

The Enemy of the Stars is obsessive and distorted. It is written in continuous prose rather than dialogue and the elaborate, moody scenery overwhelms the characters who are, in any case, little more than abstractions. It is entirely untypical of British drama of the period, which compared to the bold and experimental theatre taking place on the continent, seems, at first glance, unexciting. On the whole, playwrights here did not go in for the kind of formal experimentation or theorising about theatre that we find in Ibsen, Strindberg, Pirandello, Artaud or Brecht (see previous chapter). In general, we can characterise the British theatre from the late nineteenth to the mid twentieth centuries as modernist content fitted into traditionalist forms. It is also dominated by Irish writers: Oscar Wilde, George Bernard Shaw and Samuel Beckett. We turn to Wilde first.

Wilde, *Lady Windermere's Fan* (1892) and Modernism

In general terms, Oscar Wilde (1854–1900) can be described as modernist because he shows an awareness of change and how it affects his society. More specifically he, like other modernist artists, distances himself from Victorian values but, unlike them, he cannot quite break from them.

The story of *Lady Windermere's Fan* is quickly summarised. Lady Windermere has been told that her husband, Lord Windermere, may be involved with another woman, one Mrs Erlynne. Mrs Erlynne is, in fact, Lady Windermere's mother, whom she believes is dead, and who caused a scandal by deserting her daughter when she was a baby. She has promised not to reveal her true identity if Lord Windermere re-establishes her in society by inviting her to Lady Windermere's birthday party.

Convinced this is an attempt to shame her, Lady Windermere flees to Lord Darlington, who loves her and whose advances she had previously rejected. She is saved from potential disgrace by her mother's intervention. At the end, Lord and Lady Windermere are happily reunited while Mrs Erlynne, who keeps her secret, marries Lord Augustus and they go to live abroad.

Lady Windermere's Fan is, if not a modernist play, a play that engages with modernity. The word 'modern' occurs at least seven times and the play contains possibly the first reference in English literature to tinned food.[2] More generally, *Lady Windermere's Fan* registers one of the decisive movements of modernity, the final stage in the transformation of a culture based on Christian ethics to one based on commercial expediency. Lady Windermere herself remarks on this. 'Nowadays people seem to look on life as a speculation. It is not a speculation. It is a sacrament' (p. 8). Her mother also remarks on this change, but from the opposite point of view: 'In modern life margin is everything' (p. 35), by which she means the profit margin. Mrs Erlynne also rejects the idea of repentance: 'what consoles one nowadays is not repentance, but pleasure' (p. 58), a remark that hints at the attractions of the consumer society.

The modernity of *Lady Windermere's Fan* is also apparent in its critique of the high literature of the Victorian period. One characteristic of that literature was its seriousness. Mrs Erlynne complains that 'London is too full of serious people' and when Lady Windermere asks why Lord Darlington talks so 'trivially about life' he replies that it 'is far too important ever to talk seriously about' (pp. 11, 54). The modern age prefers wit to gravitas. It is also marked by an irreverent attitude towards age. The Victorian patriarch was a highly respected figure but, in this play, age is a figure of fun: 'The youth of the present day are quite monstrous. They have absolutely no respect for dyed hair' (p. 46).

Wilde is also sceptical about those great Victorian institutions marriage and the family. Lord Augustus, for example, cannot remember how many times he has been married, while Lady Plymdale adds that the world 'has grown suspicious of anything that looks like a happy married life' (p. 25). Where a Victorian novel, melodrama or even another of Wilde's plays would end with the revelation of a secret or a family connection, Lady Windermere never learns that the woman who helped her is her mother.

Apart from the substitution of wit for seriousness, however, these are all minor differences between the *fin de siècle* and high Victorianism. A more substantial one is the attitude to morality, particularly the fallen woman, that recurrent figure of nineteenth century fiction. The play's attitude to morality is summed up in Mrs Erlynne's comment 'manners before morals' (p. 55). Lord Darlington makes a more serious point when he remarks that 'good people do a great deal of harm in the world' (p. 9). It is for that reason that he does not, like a stern Victorian novelist, divide people into good and bad, but into either 'charming or tedious'. In the end, both he and Mrs Erlynne value a person more for their social graces than their ethical principles, for their wit rather than their seriousness.

Mrs Erlynne is quite unlike the fallen woman of Victorian fiction, who having been seduced as a young maiden or taken a lover as a married woman, is driven out of respectable society and forced to fend for herself. Overcome with the effort, and with shame, she usually takes her own life. In *Lady Windermere's Fan*, however, Mrs Erlynne is brought back into society. Lord Windermere, even if he does not approve of her, appreciates, at least at first, that she has suffered for her mistakes. The real break with Victorian convention, however, comes when Mrs Erlynne herself describes what it is like to be 'despised, mocked, abandoned, sneered at' (p. 42). In the literature prior to *Lady Windermere's Fan*, the fallen woman rarely spoke for herself unless it was to proclaim her shame.

Does the play, then, overturn Victorian values? No: it may mock them, but it remains in thrall to them. *Lady Windermere's Fan* follows the classic pattern of many nineteenth century works which see the hero or heroine move from a state of ignorance to a state of knowledge. At the beginning of the play, for instance, Lady Windermere states that women who have erred 'should never be forgiven' (p. 9) but by the end she has learnt that: 'There is the same world for all of us, and good and evil, sin and innocence go through it hand in hand' (p. 63).

Although the play can't quite shake off the Victorian frame of mind, it is nevertheless profoundly modernist to the extent that it poses the problem of the self. Nowhere is this more clear than in the opposition between artifice and authenticity. Lady Windermere accuses Lord Darlington of 'affectation' (p. 10), implying that she is genuine and true to herself, but when she is called to act in accordance with her beliefs, she cries 'I am afraid of being myself' (p. 31). She prefers a 'false existence' (p. 30) to a life of integrity. Being herself is much harder than Lady Windermere thought, and how to be yourself is one of the central questions of modernist literature.

The play is also modernist in its 'difficulty' at the level of theme, if not of form. How can a character like Lord Darlington say he does not divide people into good and bad yet claim Lady Windermere is 'the only good woman I have ever met in my life' (p. 47)? The play both dispenses with the notion of the good and espouses it. It is the same with artifice. Characters demand authenticity yet delight in affectation. By posing questions that become ever more complex as the action proceeds, *Lady Windermere's Fan* anticipates the complexity, irony and ambiguity that is characteristic of modernist literature.

The play also flirts with symbolism. Lord Windermere gives his wife a fan for her birthday. Fans were not just cooling instruments, they were also forms of communication, usually of an amorous kind. A fan placed near the heart, for example, meant 'you have won my love'. There are numerous references to Lady Windermere's fan throughout the play. She says that she is going to use it to strike Mrs Erlynne but in fact accidentally drops it when she sees her – an action which, in the coded language of fans, means 'we will be friends', and so it proves.

At one point Lord Darlington has the fan and Lady Windermere asks for it back, an exchange which symbolises her thinking about giving herself to him but, in the end, deciding not to. It is the fan which threatens to betray her presence at Lord Darlington's and in the exchange between him and Lord Windermere it takes on a sexual significance. Finally Lady Windermere gives the fan to Mrs Erlynne who has taken 'a great fancy' (p. 61) to it. Lord Windermere gave it to his wife as a token of love; it now goes to her mother with whom he was suspected of having a liaison. The fan symbolises, in short, Lord Windermere's repressed longings for Mrs Erlynne.

We could say more, but the point has been made. The fan may not offer access to a higher reality but it does have myriad meanings, which is one of the characteristics of the modernist symbol. The title, *Lady Windermere's Fan*, tells us the that the play is about the fan. The fan, in turn, symbolises the play because, like the play, it has numerous meanings. The meanings of the play – artifice, authenticity, wit, seriousness, manners, morality and so on – are never synthesised into a coherent statement and neither are those of the fan. This is an early example of the modernist notion that a work of art is as much, if not more, about itself than the world.

We can perhaps interpret Mrs Erlynne's removal of the fan abroad as a rejection of the chaotic plurality of language and as a desire for more direct forms of communication. Modernity, though, will be characterised by both. Its art will be rich in meaning but the workplace, where we find the most direct forms of communication (see Part Two: 'A Cultural Overview') will reduce humans to instruments in pursuit of ever greater efficiency.

Shaw, *Widowers' Houses* (1892) and Modernism

Widowers' Houses was George Bernard Shaw's first play. He would later call it one of his worst. However, it caused a sensation when it was first performed, as did many modernist works. At the premiere of Igor Stravinsky's *The Rite of Spring* (Paris, 29 May 1913), for instance, the audience traded punches over 'this grotesque caricature' of ballet.[3] *Widowers' Houses* did not provoke such outrage but Shaw (1856–1950) was hooted when he made a speech after the show and the play was hardly out of the news for the next fortnight.

What was the cause of this reaction? 'Real life' is the short answer.[4] The stage, Shaw complained, was 'artificially simple and well understood by the masses; but it is very stale; its feeling is conventional; it is totally unsuggestive of thought because all its conclusions are foregone; and it is constantly in conflict with the real knowledge which the separate members of the audience from their own daily occupations' (p. 176). Shaw, who was greatly influenced by Henrik Ibsen (1828–1906, see Part Three: 'The European Stage and Theatrical Thinkers'), not only wanted to reform play-writing, he also wanted to transform the institutions of theatre.

In particular, he wanted an independent playhouse for the promotion of new works, to abolish the official censor and to publish plays as literature. The ambition to write a new kind of drama, to create a space for innovation and to raise the status of the script all support the view of Shaw as a proto-modernist, as does his contempt for the average theatre goer, who finds 'the higher drama ... as perplexing as the game of chess is to a man who has barely enough capacity to understand skittles'.[5]

Shaw wanted to use British theatre to portray the problems of British society. In *Widowers' Houses* the problem is slum landlords. Sartorius has made his money from buying and renting property to the poor. When Dr Trench, his prospective son-in-law, hears about this he is shocked, but is even more shocked to learn that the annuity he receives derives from Sartorius's badly maintained houses. The play concludes with Trench agreeing to a financial speculation on the basis of those properties and marrying Sartorius's daughter, Blanche.

Is *Widowers' Houses* a modernist work? The fact that it has a professional as one of the main characters certainly qualifies it as work of modernity, but that does not necessarily make it modernist. The play does have themes that we find in other modernist literature, incest for example.* It is implied when Blanche throws her arms round her father's neck and says 'I don't want to marry: I only want to stay with you and be happy as we have always been. I hate the thought of being married. I don't want to leave you.'[6] Also, the brutal way in which Blanche treats the parlour-maid shows that conflict between the classes which Marx said would characterise modernity (see Part Two: 'A Cultural Overview').

However, we can also find in *Widower's Houses* nineteenth century themes such as that of the self-made family marrying into the aristocracy. In some ways, the play is a bit like the 'condition of England' novels of the mid Victorian period because it exposes social evils with the aim of pricking the nation's conscience, or at least that part of it which goes to the theatre. There is, though, a big difference.

* See also Part Three: 'The European Stage and Theatrical Thinkers'. Other works that deal with the theme of incest during this period include Ernst Barlach (1870–1938), *Der Tote Tag* (The Dead Day, 1913) and William Faulkner (1897–1962), *Absalom, Absalom* (1936).

In a nineteenth century novel the evil would most likely be rooted out and justice done but, in *Widowers' Houses*, it is even more firmly established. The delightfully named Lickcheese, a former rent-collector for Sartorius, comes up with the plan of improving properties so that, when they are cleared away to make room for new developments, landlords will receive compensation as well as money from the sale.

The failure to expose and punish those who put personal profit before the well being of their tenants suggests that *Widowers' Houses* belongs more to twentieth century than nineteenth century literature. Moreover, the success of Lickcheese's scheme dramatises the fact that making money lies at the heart of modern culture. It is as 'a man of business' that Sartorius views the public arena. 'We live in a progressive age, and humanitarian ideas must be taken into account' (p. 89), but only so long as they do not interfere with his profit making schemes. If *Lady Windermere's Fan* is about the moral education of Lady Windermere, *Widowers' Houses* is about the financial education of Dr Trench. 'I'm afraid Dr. Trench', says Sartorius, 'that you are a very young hand at business ... May I ask you to suspend your judgement until we have had a little quiet discussion of this sentimental notion of yours?' (p. 70). Money, Trench learns, comes before morality.

He learns his lesson well: 'I recognise the uselessness of putting the moral point of view to you' says Trench's friend Cokane, 'but you must feel the cogency of Mr Lickcheese's business statement' (p. 90). Trench does, but he makes one last effort to behave ethically, declaring 'I won't have the relations between Miss Sartorius and myself made a part of the bargain' (p. 93), although it is no use. If he doesn't marry her, then he will not benefit from the scheme. It is too good an opportunity to miss. Modern man, in Lickcheese's phrase, has become a 'calculating machine' (p. 92). This makes for a shocking ending, but then it is the job of modern art to shock.

The novelist E. M. Forster (1879–1970), a member of the Bloomsbury Group,* famously said 'only connect'. *Widowers' Houses* does just

---

* The name given to a group of friends, who met at 46 Gordon Square, Bloomsbury. Famous names included Virginia Woolf and the economist John Maynard Keynes. They were in revolt against the Victorian period and believed that the enjoyment of beautiful things was one of the great pleasures in life.

that. It shows how the rich exploit the poor and how the rest are complicit in the process but do not wish to know of their involvement. Blanche sums up this attitude when she says 'I don't want to know about them [the poor]' (p. 87). Her wish to remain ignorant about the source of her father's wealth symbolises the tendency of some modernist artists to withdraw from society into the self. They feel more comfortable showing the workings of the mind than the workings of the world.

What we see or don't see is not just a matter of choice, it also depends on the state of the language which conditions our perception of the world. This is another theme of *Widowers' Houses*. It asks us to look at 'tact' and 'plain-speaking'. The word 'tact' is used in the very first speech and occurs many times in the play, whereas the term 'plain speaking' occurs only once (p. 62). Clearly, Shaw is asking us to think about what 'tact' means. Tact can be defined as 'an intuitive sense of what is fitting or right, adroitness in doing or saying the proper thing' and that is largely how the term is used in the play. Cokane is always urging other characters, particularly Trench, to be tactful. When Sartorius asks Trench to write to his aunt, Lady Roxdale, to confirm that she would be happy for him to marry Blanche, Trench delegates the task to Cokane. Sartorius enters and helps in the composition of the letter.

In allowing others to speak for him, the episode symbolises how Trench surrenders his integrity, but it has a further meaning. To draw attention to the writing process – which words to use, how to phrase a particularly delicate point – shows the kind of artistic self-consciousness that we associate with modernism. Of course Shaw is not a modernist in the sense of, say, Pirandello or Brecht, but this little scene with its emphasis on how something is said – not 'picked up' but 'had the privilege of becoming acquainted with' (p. 49) – prefigures the modernist preoccupation with form.

Cokane also helps Lickcheese with his business correspondence: 'I've no literary style and that's the truth; so Mr Cokane kindly puts it into my letters and draft prospectuses and advertisements and the like' (p. 88). One of the things we have argued in this book is that some modernist literature expresses, in a different form, values that can be found in the workplace. The imagist poem, for example, was modelled on the machine. What we have in *Widowers' Houses* is clear evidence of the alliance between literature and business.

Cokane uses his literary style, his tact, not to tell the truth about Lickcheese's scheme, but to gloss over what it actually involves. He did the same thing in his letter to Trench's aunt, not giving her a straightforward account of her nephew's meeting with Blanche but one which would be sure to win her consent to the match. As he said at the time, 'everything depends on the way the matter is put to Lady Roxdale. But as to that, you may rely on me' (p. 48).

'Tact', in short, is a 'tactic' of evasion, it is not simply good manners. It is a way of disguising reality, of hiding it from view. What this tells us is that the 'perceptual revolution' of modernism is not always about finding new ways to see a new reality, it can also be a way of ensuring that we do not see reality for what it is: in this case a system of economic exploitation of the poor.

Thinkers and Experimenters

While some people were writing plays others were thinking about drama and how best to experiment with the form. The thinkers considered in this section, E. Gordon Craig and W. B. Yeats, have similar views. In general, they react against the idea that theatre should hold, in Hamlet's words, 'the mirror up to nature'. Craig says that it is impossible to copy nature, all we can do is 'suggest some of her beautiful and living ways'.[7] He and Yeats seek to take theatre back to its roots and to revive the arts of dance, gesture, costume and symbol. They do this because they want theatre to address the whole person rather than, as naturalism does, the mind alone.

E. Gordon Craig (1872–1966)

E. Gordon Craig was the son of the famous nineteenth century actress, Ellen Terry (1847–1928) and the architect, stage designer and theatre director Edward William Godwin (1833–86). With that background, it's not surprising he worked in the theatre, first as an actor with Sir Henry Irving (1838–1905) at the Lyceum,* and second as a stage designer. It is for the latter that he is best known.

Craig set out his ideas in a short pamphlet called 'The Art of Theatre' (1905) which was later incorporated into a book that bore the same name. It is in the form of a conversation between a stage-director and a play-goer. The stage-director, who is the voice of Craig, complains that a play is no longer 'a balance of actions, words, dance and scene, but it is either all words or all scene' (p. 116). Consequently, the director looks forward to a time when theatre doesn't have to 'rely upon having a play to perform' but can 'perform pieces of its own art' instead (p. 117). This art consists of 'action, words, line, colour and rhythm' (p. 113), none, with the possible exception of action, being more important than the others. The reason action may be more valuable is that it is the source from which theatre sprang. The earliest performances did not involve words, argues the stage-director, but movement and dance, a fact too often forgotten in modern theatre.

The person who will bring the different elements of the art of theatre into a unity, and who will eventually be a more dominant force than the playwright, is the stage-director. He will be skilled in all the arts of theatre from lighting to acting and it will be his job to tell all those involved in the production of a play exactly what they must do. There is to be no room for individual initiative, each person must 'follow orders' as if they were sailors on a 'ship' and the stage-director were the 'captain' (p. 131).

The stage-director begins his work by reading a play and getting rid of all the stage directions so that he can more easily attune himself to the play's 'colour, tone, movement and rhythm' (p. 119). Once he has chosen colours that are 'in harmony with the spirit of the play' (p. 124), he creates a pattern into which he weaves objects mentioned in the play.

The actors must be part of the pattern and follow the stage-director's

---

* Irving was the most famous actor of the last third of the nineteenth century. He was noted for his Shakespearean roles and for his management of the Lyceum with Ellen Terry, who was often his leading lady and, it was rumoured, his lover.

instructions absolutely. An actor 'must move and speak as part and parcel of the design. He must move across our sight in a certain way, passing to a certain point, in a certain light, his head at a certain angle' (p. 130). The play-goer asks if the stage-director isn't treating actors like puppets, and he doesn't disagree. In fact later in his career Craig stated that 'There is only one actor – nay one man [*sic*] who has the soul of the dramatic poet, and who has ever served as the true and loyal interpreter of the poet. This is the marionette.'[8] The stage-director justifies his need for total control over every aspect of the production by saying that this is the only way theatre will become 'a creative art' instead of merely 'an interpretative craft' (p. 136).

Can we describe Craig as a modernist? He was an innovator, he didn't imitate nature, and he was deeply interested in theatrical form. Arthur Symons (1865–1945) said that Craig worked in 'squares and straight lines' in order to evoke a higher reality.[9] He saw him, in other words, as a symbolist. However, Craig's work also anticipates Frederic Winslow Taylor's *The Principles of Scientific Management* which appeared in 1911, the same year, coincidentally, as Craig's book, *The Art of Theatre*.

The basic principle of Craig's theatre, the division of labour, is exactly the same as that of Taylor's factory. Each person has a part he or she must play properly if the whole is to be a success. Craig describes his theatre as 'a masterpiece of mechanism' (p. 135) and Taylor uses the same term for a factory and for scientific management itself. The stage-director and the scientific manager both insist on 'discipline' in the carrying out of tasks, the one reduces actors to puppets, the other reduces workers to machines.

Finally, we can see that the theatre is like a factory to the extent that the stage-director has an overview of everything that is happening on stage just as the scientific manager, situated in his panoptican,* has an overview of all the workers in his charge. If Craig is a modernist, he is so in more senses than one.

---

* Designed as a prison by the eighteenth century philosopher Jeremy Bentham, in a panopticon inmates were arranged in open cells that were all visible from a central hub. The system was also used in factories in the late nineteenth and early twentieth centuries.

W. B. Yeats (1865–1939)

Yeats wanted to create 'an unpopular theatre and an audience like a secret society where admission is by favour and never too many'.[10] Here is a perfect expression of the modernist artist's desire to withdraw from the wider culture to create an art that would be appreciated by the discerning few. Yeats was reacting to the prevailing view that theatre should be an imitation of life, and in this too, he shows himself to be a modernist, for one facet of modernism is a retreat from naturalism.

Yeats complained about a number of features of contemporary theatre: the caricatures of comedy, the predictable plots of domestic dramas and, in particular, the audience demand for stories about the upper class. All these plays portrayed only the external form of life, not its inner structure. To redress that balance, Yeats called for anti-theatre, one 'that can appease all within us' (p. 337). Ideally he sought a form of performance that would blend both what he called the 'subjective' and the 'objective' parts of experience. However, that required a revolution in theatre.

The first step was to abandon the kind of plays Yeats had been criticising. In their place he proposed dramas based on Irish mythology, particularly the exploits of Cuchulain.* Some modernist writers, such as James Joyce and T. S. Eliot, used myth to make sense of modern life, to give it shape, meaning and significance. Yeats was doing something slightly different, though. Where they sought to integrate myth and modernity, he used Irish folklore as a means of expressing a national identity whose values were opposed to those of contemporary society.

The second step was to create a theatre that worked by suggestion, not statement, and the form of communication that did that best was dance. Through 'complexity of rhythm, colour and gesture' it reminded

---

* Cuchulain (pronounced 'cuHOOlin') is the central figure in a series of ancient stories known as the Ulster Cycle. He was originally called Setanta but changed his name when he killed a guard dog belonging to a man called Culann. By way of reparation, Setanta offered to take the place of the dog, which protected the pass into Ulster, until a replacement could be reared. The name 'Cú Chulainn', to give the proper spelling, means hound of Culann. Cuchulain was a mighty warrior known for his terrifying battle frenzy. One of his most famous exploits was his single-handed defence of Ulster against Queen Medb of Connacht.

the audience of 'dearly loved things' (p. 335). Dance, for Yeats, is also a form of prophecy, although he is not very clear about what he means by this. Basically, physical movement puts us in touch with the unconscious, from which future change will come.

Yeats's *Four Plays for Dancers* (1921) was an attempt to realise this type of theatre. He was influenced, in writing them, by the Noh musical drama of Japan. These short, highly ritualistic plays are performed four or five at a time to display a complete life cycle. They cover such traditional subjects as the gods, battles, morality, a psychological piece and a 'play of women'. The action is highly codified, with four categories of performer: the *shite* or doer, the *waki*, his counterpart, the *kyōgen*, who perform during the interludes between the plays, and the *hayashi* or instrumentalists. The actors, usually male, wear masks and heavily decorated costumes. The most commonly used prop is a fan. One of the most striking features of the actors is that they will not always sing or chant in character. Occasionally, they will sing from the point of view of another character. This is quite different to the Western style where the actor is encouraged to identify with his or her part.

Yeats's interest in Noh drama is another example of a tendency we find in modernism – to look outside Europe for artistic inspiration – and the fact that he places so much emphasis on music is a reminder of its importance in the period as a model for literature. Yeats believed that a concerto does not reflect reality, it has its own reality: intricate, impersonal and self-validating. Most of all, Noh drama offered Yeats a model of how the subjective and objective might be integrated.

The division between mind and body was felt acutely during this period when humans were treated like machines in factories. Art was a way of bringing the two together. Finally, Noh drama with its ritual enactment of old stories answered the question of how dance could be a form of prophecy, because it showed that the future was the same as the past: the old truths, the old values, the old virtues, though we may sometimes forget them, will endure forever. Modernism was not always about making it new. Sometimes it was about remembering the old.

Noel Coward and Modernism

Noel Coward (1899–1973) is not regarded as a modernist. He is famous as a writer of light comedy and patriotic drama, but while he may not have challenged the theatrical establishment, or experimented with dramatic form, his work is not wholly devoid of modernist traits.

They are evident in his first successful play, *The Vortex* (1924) whose major theme, incest, crops up in a number of writers from Woolf to Huxley. Nicky, the central character, is upset that his mother, Florence, takes young lovers and ignores him. The final scene, where he confronts her in her bedroom, is similar to the scene in which Hamlet confronts his mother in her closet. In each case there is jealousy, a threat of violence, a demand that the mother accept her guilt and a strong erotic charge. 'You are not to have any more lovers' he screams at her, 'you're going to be my mother for once.'[11] 'I love you', he declares (p. 54), at which point, say the stage directions, '*He falls on his knees and buries his face in her lap*', where he remains until the curtain falls, with his mother stroking his hair.

Taking young lovers is Florence's way of staving off age. She inhabits a world where there is pressure to be young and where an omnipresent sense of an impending but unspecified disaster means nothing matters. Everyone is 'hectic and nervy' (p. 25) complains Nicky. 'There's no peace anywhere', he says later, 'nothing but the ceaseless din of trying to be amused' (p. 59). The play, in short, captures the emptiness of modern life, the sense of spiritual desolation that T. S. Eliot delineated in *The Waste Land* (1922). He turned to myth and religion as a way of reviving civilisation, but Coward's characters frantically seek distraction in sex, drugs and endless partying. Like Conrad's Kurtz and Mann's Aschenbach (see Part Three: 'The Origins of the Modernist Novel), they have looked into the abyss. Not so deeply perhaps, but enough to know that, as Nicky puts it, 'we swirl about in a vortex of beastliness' (p. 60).

The many references to theatre in the play also suggest Coward may be more of a modernist than we at first think. One of the main characters, Helen, says she does not want to go and see the new play because one of the cast 'always over-acts' (p. 10) but this precisely how characters behave in *The Vortex*, as is evident in the way they speak to one another: 'too divine', 'too tiresome', 'perfectly marvellous', 'most frightful', 'thank you a *thousand* times' and so on. Helen's comment, in other words, applies to the play in which she herself is a character. In this and other ways, Coward shows precisely the sort of self-consciousness about his medium that is characteristic of modernist artists.

Private Lives (1933) is a bridge between Oscar Wilde and Samuel Beckett (1906–89), in that Coward's wit looks back to Wilde while his sense of the emptiness of existence looks forward to Beckett. One of the themes of *Lady Windermere's Fan* is the state of modern marriage and that is also the subject of *Private Lives*. However, the relationship between the protagonists, Elyot and Amanda, is ultimately more like Strindberg than Wilde, in that Strindberg's theme is the battleground of marriage (see Part Three: 'The European Stage'). Elyot and Amanda were married and then divorced. They re-marry but on their respective honeymoons they discover they are in adjoining rooms in the same hotel. They decide to desert their new partners and go to Paris where, despite being in love, they torment each other and have physical fights. In Amanda's words: 'Selfishness, cruelty, hatred, possessiveness, petty jealousy. All those qualities came out in us just because we loved each other.'[12]

The language, though, is far more Wilde than Strindberg. There's even an echo of Lord Darlington's remark that 'life is too important to be taken seriously' in Amanda's 'Don't be angry, it's all much too serious to be angry about' (p. 80) and Elyot's 'You mustn't be serious my dear one, it's just what they want' (p. 56). The difference between Wilde and Coward is that Wilde at least appeared to affirm certain values – goodness, decency and love – even though he was also scathingly witty at their expense.

There is no such affirmation in Coward. As in *The Vortex*, we are presented with a bleak view of modern civilisation. Technological progress is a source of anxiety. It forces us to be either specialists, but then we miss 'all the other things going on', or else to be 'ordinary observers', in which case it is all 'too much' (p. 51). There is no God and no sure foundation for morality. Human beings are capable of anything. As Amanda famously says:

> I think very few people are completely normal really, deep down in their private lives. It all depends on a combination of circumstances. If all the various cosmic thingummies fuse at the same moment, and the right spark is struck, there's no knowing what one mightn't do. (pp. 16–17)

As for love, that is simply a matter of chemicals. When Amanda refuses Elyot's advances she remarks 'You can't bear the thought that there are certain moments when our chemical, what d' you call 'ems don't fuse properly' (p. 53).

Like other modernists Coward is well aware that the world has changed and that we need new ways of making sense of reality. Elyot recognises that he and Amanda have behaved badly by abandoning their new partners but the old moral codes no longer apply: 'it's the true values of the situation that are really important' (p. 47). Since 'the situation' will change, however, so too will values. Reality, in other words, seems new at every moment. Hence we can neither appeal to tradition nor develop forms for the future. We must live in an eternal present, as do Vladimir and Estragon in Beckett's *Waiting for Godot* (1955, see below) because they can hardly ever remember what they did yesterday.

Humour seems to be the best way to deal with this profound disorientation. 'Has it ever struck you', says Elyot to Victor, Amanda's new husband, 'that flippancy might cover a real embarrassment? [and since] We have no prescribed etiquette to fall back upon I shall continue to be flippant' (p. 71). Humour, however, is more than just compensation for the disappearance of established forms of social intercourse, it is primarily a defiant gesture made to a meaningless universe. 'Laugh at everything' says Elyot, 'Let's blow trumpets and squeakers, and enjoy the party as much as we can, like very small, quite idiotic school children' (p. 57). It's not a joyful laughter, however; it's one that borders on hysteria.

Coward's sense that life lacks meaning, that our traditional framework for making sense of the world has gone, and that relationships are a struggle for power between people who want to leave each other but can't, means that he looks forward to Beckett as well as back to Wilde. The opening of *Private Lives* is a conversation between Elyot and his new wife Sybil. Many of the things they say to one another are repeated in the next conversation between Amanda and Victor. The repetition of a conversation – and indeed situation – is a structuring device in both *Waiting for Godot* and *Endgame* (1958). It would be ironic indeed if Coward, the conventional dramatist, turned out to have influenced one of the great experimenters with the form.

Extended Commentary: Beckett, *Waiting For Godot* (1955)

Samuel Beckett (1906–89) was, like Wilde, Shaw and Yeats, an Irishman. He was a friend of James Joyce and also his assistant, helping him with research on both *Ulysses* (1922) and *Finnegans Wake* (1939). Beckett lived most of his life in Paris and wrote primarily in French. The original title of *Waiting for Godot* was *En attendant Godot* and it was first performed in Paris in 1953. The English language version was first performed in London in 1955. The play shows two tramps, Estragon and Vladimir, finding ways to pass the time while they wait for the mysterious Godot, who never appears. Audiences were baffled because, as Vivian Mercier, the drama critic of the *Irish Times* wrote in his review of the production, 'nothing happens, twice'.[13]

This, in itself, is enough to tell us that we are dealing with a modernist work. We do not, for example, find much action in Joyce, Woolf or Kafka. However, these are all novelists; Beckett is a playwright and action is the lifeblood of drama. Aristotle, in his *Poetics* (350 BC), defines tragedy as 'a mimesis of a complete, that is a whole action [and by] "whole" I mean with a beginning, middle and an end'.[14] The imitation of an action was essential if tragedy was to be cathartic, that is, for it to arouse, channel and expel feelings of pity and fear, and since *Waiting for Godot* has no action, it also has no catharsis.

Beckett's break with the classical tradition seems complete when he gives us, in Vladimir and Estragon, characters who neither suffer a reversal in fortune nor move from a state of ignorance to a state of knowledge, qualities which Aristotle said were a necessary part of tragedy. Yet Beckett does not relinquish all of Aristotle's rules. He keeps, for example, the idea that 'action' should occur in one place and where Aristotle stipulates that the 'action' should last no more than twenty-four hours,* Beckett cheekily makes his tramps wait thirty-six hours for Godot.

It is clear, then, that Beckett rejects most, but not all of the Aristotelian tradition. He has a similar relationship with Shakespearean drama. Beckett is self-reflexive about theatre in the same way that Shakespeare is when he has Jacques declare in *As You Like It* that 'all the world's a stage'. Vladimir and Estragon, for example, 'play' at being Pozzo and Lucky (a master and his slave who appear briefly in each act). The fact that Shakespeare explores the nature of his medium – where does the stage end and the world begin? – shows that artistic self-consciousness is not confined to the modernist era.

If Beckett continues with one Shakespeare tradition, however, he disrupts another – the soliloquy. One of the most notorious passages in *Waiting for Godot* is Lucky's long speech. Pozzo makes Lucky 'think'[15] as a way of thanking Estragon and Vladimir for their company. The speech is pure stream of consciousness. It has, for instance, no punctuation. Lucky's outpouring is the very opposite of the Shakespearean soliloquy. Beckett does not use it to reveal the character's mind, or to celebrate the power of self-expression, but to lay bare the wreckage of the Christian and the Enlightenment traditions: God does not exist, we cannot know anything, all effort is useless and so we can do nothing but 'waste and pine' (p. 36). This is the tragic view of modernity. We may be

---

* Aristotle does not mean that the play itself should last for twenty-four hours, just that the action depicted in the play should not extend over weeks, months and years. This is partly a matter of credibility but it is also one of effect: the shorter the time in which the action occurs, the greater its intensity.

able to live with the idea that 'God is dead' but not with the notion that whatever we do makes no difference. Such an attitude flies in the face of the modernist belief in progress.

The clown is a minor figure in Shakespeare. We laugh at his antics and his malapropisms,* but Beckett puts the clown centre stage. What's more, Vladimir and Estragon are figures of pathos rather than foolishness, representatives of humanity rather than aberrations. In their observations on life, Beckett also seems to have incorporated the cryptic wisdom of Shakespeare's fools: 'We are all born mad. Some remain so' (p. 73).

Vladimir and Estragon also belong to the tradition of music hall. They don't so much speak as perform verbal routines, as when discussing what Godot has to offer them. Here their speech repeats and overlaps, as the characters answer their own questions and provide echoes of each other, for example: 'Estragon: And what did he reply? / Vladimir: That he'd see / Estragon: That he couldn't promise anything / Vladimir: That he'd have to think it over' (p. 11). There is also physical humour. Trousers fall down, boots won't come off and there is a splendidly comic scene where they swap three hats, putting them on and taking them off in rapid succession. The inclusion of elements from the music hall shows that modernist art did not always separate itself from popular culture.

At least part of the modernity of *Waiting for Godot*, then, lies in its complex relation to the dramatic traditions of Aristotle and Shakespeare. The play implies that these traditions, particularly the classical one, have little to teach us and so we must create new ones. However, the new in *Waiting for Godot* can look simply like the absence of the old. There is no plot, no character, no scenery and nothing to delight the senses. Beckett turns his back on naturalism and ritual and yet seems to put nothing in their place. It is as if we have come to the end of tradition and there is nowhere else to go. Consequently we feel forced back on

---

* A malapropism is the mistaken use of one word for another. It is named after Mrs Malaprop, a character in Sheridan's play *The Rivals* (1775), who was fond of using *malapropos* (i.e. inappropriate) statements such as 'Illiterate him, I say, quite from your memory' (meaning 'obliterate') or 'My affluence over my niece is very small' (meaning 'influence').

the past in the same way that Vladimir and Estragon feel forced to return each day to wait for Godot. Godot, in other words, may be the symbol for exhausted traditions to which we obstinately cling.

Waiting for Godot invites a symbolic reading because it is not set in a particular time or place. The stage, apart from a solitary tree, is bare, allowing us to focus more clearly on what it means to be alive. There is no clutter, no distraction, no social problem: just an empty space in which to express the intense, elemental sense of existence. What is conveyed most powerfully is a sense of human insignificance. 'All my lousy life', says Estragon, 'I have crawled around in the mud' (p. 52). 'We've arrived' announces Vladimir when he falls to the ground with Estragon and doesn't get up (p. 74). Man appears to be nothing more than a piece of earth recalling, perhaps, Hamlet's description 'this quintessence of dust'.

The problem with this reading of the play is that it lifts it out of its historical moment and elevates its insights – 'they give birth astride of a grave, the light gleams for an instant and then it's dark once more' (p. 82) – into universal truths. There is nothing wrong with a work of art telling us that life is short and that we are going to die, but we also need to explain the work of art. Martin Esslin, for example has argued that *Waiting for Godot* belongs to the theatre of the absurd. The lack of plot, the absence of motivation, the indeterminate spatial and temporal co-ordinates are ways of expressing 'the senselessness of the human condition'.[16]

Why should the theatre of the absurd appear in the mid twentieth century, though? What is it about that period that calls forth that particular form of expression? The short answer is the Second World War (1939–45). If the First World War (1914–18) called into question the idea of progress in all areas of civilisation, the Second World War seemed to dash any remaining hopes that humanity would improve. Worst of all, our much prized rational faculty had been used to devise methods of mass extermination. If that was what reason did, then it was better not to be reasonable, so artists started to dismantle the rational structures of their art: verse in poetry, perspective in painting and plot in drama.

Waiting for Godot, though, is not just a response to the devastation of war. It is also a comment on modernity in general. We have said many times that modernity breaks with tradition and that can lead to a loss of cultural memory. This is the background to Vladimir and Estragon often being unable to remember their own past: 'Estragon: We came here yesterday / Vladimir: Ah no, there you are mistaken' and 'Vladimir: What did we do yesterday? ... / Estragon: Yes / Vladimir: Why ...' (p. 7).

Because they cannot remember their past, they are doomed to repeat it. Hence their returning each day to wait for Godot. The play is built on repetition. What happens in act one happens in act two, but with a slight variation. In act one for example, Estragon asks Vladimir for something to eat. Vladimir gives him a carrot. In act two Estragon again asks him for something to eat and this time Vladimir gives him a radish. This repetition mirrors the routines of modern life, how it consists of doing the same thing over and over again: getting up, going to work, returning home, getting up, going to work, returning home. The routines give a shape to life but no meaning. The rift with tradition, the mechanised nature of labour and the passing pleasures of mass culture neither sustain the self nor allow it to grow. The individual cannot find meaning outside him- or herself – there is no Godot – it must come from within. That perhaps explains why so many modernist artists are preoccupied with the nature of the self.

Notes

1   See www.unirioja.es/wyndhamlewis/pdf/writing/enemy.pdf for the text of this play. All quotations come from this site.

2   Oscar Wilde, *Lady Windermere's Fan* in *The Importance of Being Earnest and Other Plays* edited with Introduction, Commentary and Notes by Richard Allen Cave (Harmondsworth: Penguin, 2000), p. 15.

3   Modris Eksteins, *Rites of Spring: The Great War and the Birth of the Modern Age* (London: Black Swan, 1990), p. 34.

4   George Bernard Shaw, 'A Dramatic Realist to his Critics' in Eric Bentley (ed.), *The Theory of the Modern Stage* (Harmondsworth: Penguin, 1992), pp. 175–96, p. 176.

5   Shaw, 'Appendix' to 'The Quintessence of Ibsenism' in Bentley (ed.), *The Theory of the Modern Stage*, pp. 197–223, p. 203.

6   Shaw, *Widowers' Houses* in *Plays Unpleasant* with Introduction by David Edgar (Harmondsworth: Penguin, 2000), p. 77.

7   E. Gordon Craig, 'The Art of Theatre' in Bentley (ed.), *The Theory of the Modern Stage*, pp. 113–37, p. 126.

8   Cited in J. M. Walton, *Craig on Theatre* (London: Methuen, 1983), p. 34.

9   Arthur Symons, 'A New Art of the Stage' in Bentley (ed.), *The Theory of the Modern Stage*, pp. 138–47, p. 138.

10 W. B. Yeats, 'A People's Theatre' in Bentley (ed.), *The Theory of the Modern Stage*, pp. 327–38, p. 335.

11 Noel Coward, *The Vortex* (London: Methuen, 2002), p. 54.

12 Coward, *Private Lives* (London: Methuen, 2000), p. 32.

13 Vivian Mercier, *Irish Times*, 18 February 1956, p. 6.

14 D. A. Russell and M. Winterbottom (eds), *Ancient Literary Criticism: The Principal Texts in New Translation* (Oxford: Oxford University Press, 1972), p. 100.

15 Samuel Beckett, *Waiting for Godot* (London: Faber, 2006), p. 35.

16 Martin Esslin, *The Theatre of the Absurd* (Harmondsworth: Penguin, 1980), p. 24.

Part Four
Critical Theories and Debates

Literature, Visual Art and Music

Romanticism had brought with it the notion of the artist, the creator, as having a distinct identity and justification in art. In the late nineteenth century this tendency became increasingly self-conscious, so that artists were content not only to produce works of art, but to use art as a means of expression about the very nature of being an artist. As art sought to separate itself from bourgeois culture it became the subject of art. The exploration of the artist's consciousness was increasingly the object that was the basis of art. At first this tendency was part of the late romantic art for art's sake movement and the concern with aesthetics that that movement drew attention to.* Gradually literature became more directly influenced by music and painting (and later by photography and film). Modern critical approaches have encouraged an interdisciplinary reading of texts along with associated visual arts and music.

Aesthetic Beginnings

Any discussion about modernism and the visual arts and music must begin with an account of the influence of John Ruskin (1819–1900). Ruskin had become the most important art critic by the middle of the

* See the section on the Aesthetic Movement in Part Two: 'A Cultural Overview'.

nineteenth century, especially championing the work of J. M. W. Turner (1775–1851). He then took up the cause of the Pre-Raphaelite painters when they were just setting out on their careers; and it is probable that, without his public support, the Pre-Raphaelite Brotherhood (or PRB) would never have had a chance to establish a reputation. His work, which did much to popularise art at a time when culture seemed to be increasingly materialistic, was based on a desire to preach a doctrine of the social importance of art. Ruskin was appointed as the first Slade Professor of Fine Art at Oxford in 1869, and continued to exert an influence through a steady stream of tracts that ranged widely from the purely artistic to economics and politics – Ruskin believed that 'The art of any country is the exponent of its social and political virtues.'[1] Ruskin was an important influence on the work of Marcel Proust (1871–1922), who translated some of his writings into French (*The Bible of Amiens* and *Sesame and Lilies*). Ruskin's autobiography *Praeterita* (1885–9) anticipates Proust's evocation of things past in his great novel sequence *À la recherche du temps perdu* (1913–27). Ruskin's relation to modernism has been explored in Giovanni Cianci and Peter Nicholls's (eds) *Ruskin and Modernism* (2000), which looks at the extent to which Ruskin was a significant pre-modernist and the way that writers such as Ezra Pound, Ford Madox Ford, T. S. Eliot, Wyndham Lewis and D. H. Lawrence responded to his work and teachings.

Fiction, Visual Art and Music

The novelist Joseph Conrad (1857–1924) was one of the first writers to express this aspiration to compare the art of fiction with that of painting and music. In the 'Preface to *The Nigger of the "Narcissus"*' (1897) he wrote that 'Fiction – if it at all aspires to be art – appeals to temperament. And in truth it must be, like painting, like music, like all art, the appeal of one temperament to all the other innumerable temperaments.' He develops this theme by stressing that it is only by an 'impression conveyed through the senses' that a work of art can communicate, and he rejects the notion that didactic literature can be art.[2] In some sense this would seem to reject that element in realist and naturalist fiction (as found in the work of Charles Dickens [1812–70] and Emile Zola [1840–1902]) that sought to amend abuses through the effect of the written word in a narrative. Conrad was partly influenced by the example of French writers Gustave Flaubert (1821–80) and Guy de Maupassant (1850–93), but he goes much further to suggest that the written word must:

> Strenuously aspire to the plasticity of sculpture, to the colour of painting, and to the magic suggestiveness of music – which is the art of arts. And it is only through complete, unswerving devotion to the perfect blending of form and substance; it is only through an unremitting never-discouraged care for the shape and ring of sentences that an approach can be made to plasticity, to colour, and that the light of magic suggestiveness may be brought to play for an evanescent instant over the commonplace surface of words: of the old, old words, worn thin, defaced by ages of careless usage. (p. 12)

Note in particular the emphasis here on music – the writer of prose in envy of the composer of music – and the significance of the last statement about words. One of the key mottos of modernism was Ezra Pound's 'make it new'; and here Conrad makes a similar plea. While this attitude to art owes something to the art for art's sake movement, Conrad also makes it clear that what he is after is something that is more durable. This attempt by Conrad to distance his credo as an artist from the background of aestheticism was no doubt influenced by the scandal of the trial and imprisonment of Oscar Wilde (see Part Two: 'A Cultural Overview'). The artist for Conrad should labour to make known the 'core of each convincing moment' (p. 13). The focus is on the way in which an effect is achieved; and artistic 'truth' is understood to exist in fragments that the writer links together to form a narrative. Thus Conrad was able to bring to the novel a poetic richness.

This concern with the construction of a work of art as distinct from the social and intellectual context was one of the factors in the development of Formalism. Formalism was a reaction against the romantic view of the artist as the individual creative personality, which had generated an inexact way of understanding literature. Formalist critics, such as those in Russia, sought to find a more scientific basis with which to interpret texts.* Similarly, New Criticism – which dominated English and American critical practice in the middle of the twentieth century (from the 1920s to the 1950s) – sought to locate a work's significance outside knowledge of the author's own life.† The influential Cambridge critic F. R. Leavis was associated with this type of critical analysis; and it is not, perhaps, surprising to learn that he was particularly interested in Conrad's work (see *The Great Tradition*, 1948). Formalism still underpins much Poststructuralist criticism; the notion of the close reading of literary texts was derived from it and is its legacy.§

Following Conrad's example, the new fiction of the early twentieth century took on some of the attributes of poetry and music. The novelist now regarded him- or herself as a dedicated artist, not a mere entertainer. He or she sought to achieve a mastery of style, and as a consequence developed a fascinated preoccupation with 'art' and 'artists': the lives and works of composers, painters, sculptors as well as writers now became the subject of the novel. Novelists attempted to respond to the changes that had brought about new movements in the theatre and in painting and music. The new novelist therefore often chose to write about characters who were themselves either writers or

---

* Russian Formalism was a school of literary criticism that flourished between about 1914 and the mid 1930s. Its principal exponents included Viktor Shklovsky (1893–1984), Yury Tynyanov (1894–1943) and Boris Eikhenbaum (1886–1959). The purpose of Russian Formalism was to make analyses of literary texts free from the influence of philosophy, psychology and cultural historical approaches, by concentrating on purely literary devices.

† The title of the movement was taken from John Crowe Ransom's *The New Criticism* (1941). The term has been associated with T. S. Eliot and William Empson, but is probably better understood in relation to the work of the American critics Robert Penn Warren (1905–89) and Cleanth Brooks (1906–94).

§ Poststructuralism is the term used to denote the general attempt to challenge the notion put forward by Structuralists, who used the example of linguistics, that a text can be known by a study of signs and sign systems. Poststructuralism is associated with the practice of Deconstruction, feminist criticism, psychoanalytic criticism and Marxist criticism, which all make use of 'close reading'.

artists. Instead of rendering the varied panorama of an objectively observed social world, writers concentrated on the creative act and demonstrated skepticism of the way the outward reality of society was presented. As a result, the artist in the late nineteenth century was seen as increasingly at odds with bourgeois society. The artist became the embodiment of the individual opposed to the philistine social structure.

One of the first writers to take the artist as the subject for his fiction was the American-born Henry James (1843–1916), who made his home in Europe from the 1870s. In 1890, he published a novel about the career of an actress, *The Tragic Muse*. This novel prefigured and anticipated James's own attempts to write successful plays during the 1890s. However, it was in short novels such as 'The Lesson of the Master' (1888) and 'The Real Thing' (1893) that he explored what it was to be an artist and the nature of art itself. These works were still essentially 'realist' (Balzac had written about the artist in *Le Chef-d'œuvre inconnu* in 1831) but the refinement demonstrated in these stories of aesthetic discussion can be seen as related to the dissatisfaction that writers were feeling towards the description of the exterior world, as found in the work of the realist and naturalist novelists. George Gissing (1857–1903) was another novelist who chose to write about the business of writing. *New Grub Street* (1891) describes the struggles of Edwin Reardon, a young novelist of great sensitivity and undoubted integrity, but who lacks the necessary robust strength to survive in the literary world of the late nineteenth century. The novel is set against the economic forces determining the late Victorian book industry of the days of the 'Three Decker' novel and the influence of the subscription libraries.* Similar themes of the artist in opposition to an all-powerful philistine culture reappear in John Galsworthy's *The Man of Property* (1906) and E. M. Forster's *The Longest Journey* (1907). Mention should also be made of American writer Theodore Dreiser (1871–1945), who produced a novel on the subject of the artist in *The 'Genius'* (1915).

* The 'Three Decker' (the printing of novels in three separate volumes) was the staple fare of mid to late Victorian publishers, for the material reason that this was the format favoured by the commercial libraries, which exerted a powerful economic control on the book industry. Mudie's Lending Library was perhaps the best known of these subscription libraries, and charged readers a fixed amount per year for the loan of one volume of a novel at a time.

Thomas Mann (1875–1955), the great German novelist, wrote some exquisite short fiction in the first decade of the twentieth century that allowed him to explore themes concerned with his preoccupations as a writer who thought of himself as an artist. The best of these was *Death in Venice* (1912), which is concerned with the dedicated artist's pursuit of beauty and the price that he pays for such a life (see Part Three: 'The Origins of the Modernist Novel'). The artist here is still a writer, but it is significant that the composer Benjamin Britten chose to write music around this story. A related novella, *Tonio Kröger* (1904), deals with the idea that literature is a curse. Tonio Kröger, who is a poet who writes stories for the literary periodicals, has a divided nature, partly derived from his solid bourgeois father from the north of Germany and artistic bohemian mother who comes from the south. The story traces his development from childhood to maturity, from his home town on the Baltic, to his artistic life in Munich, and back on a quest to the north in search of self-knowledge. Finally, he arrives at a dance on the northern coast of Denmark, in which he observes a couple who were once his youthful companions. He comes to realise that his fate is to be outside the bourgeois life that inspires his poetry. In the story *Tristan* (1902) the relationship between music and literature is pursued more openly, if more crudely. The story's title alerts the reader to Wagner's music in *Tristan and Isolde* (1857–9), which was one of the most pre-eminent operas of the nineteenth century, and Mann's story ironically juxtaposes Wagner's doomed romantic couple Tristan and Isolde with their modern counterparts – Herr Spinell (a novelist) and Herr Klöterjahn's wife. The story is rich in musical allusion, with the story's climax enacted in the music that Herr Klöterjahn's wife plays upon the piano at the Swiss sanatorium where the story is set:

> He sat beside her, bent forward, his hands between his knees, his head bowed. She played the beginning with exaggerated and tormenting slowness, with painfully long pauses between single figures. The *Sehnsuchtsmotiv*, roving lost and forlorn like a voice lost in the night, lifted its trembling question. Then silence, a waiting. And lo, an answer: the same timorous, lonely note, only

clearer, only tenderer. Silence again. And then, with that marvelous muted *sforzando*, like mounting passion, the love-motif came in; reared and soared and yearned ecstatically upward to its consummation, sank back, was resolved; the cellos taking up the melody to carry it on with their deep, heavy notes of rapture and despair.[3]

The action does not live up to the passion of the music, and after Gabriele Eckhof (Herr Klöterjahn's wife) has relapsed, Herr Spinell hums the *Sehnsuchtsmotif* (longing theme), before being brought up short by the woman's healthy fat baby son, who laughs with gusto at him; and the novelist walks 'stiffly, yet not without grace; his gait was the hesitating gait of one who would disguise the fact that, inwardly, he is running away' (p. 128). Spinell had earlier romanticised the artistic accomplishments of Gabriele and expressed the view that races with bourgeois traditions would, near the end of their existence, express themselves in some form of art. Later Mann returned to the theme of the artist in *Doctor Faustus* (1947), in which he explores the price the composer Adrian Leverkühn pays for the achievement of his art. The novel was constructed from Mann's reading of German philosopher Friedrich Nietzsche (1844–1900) and his meeting with Arnold Schoenberg (1874–1951), the creator of the atonal revolution.* His conversations with the critical theorist Theodor Adorno were also highly significant.†

D. H. Lawrence's second published novel, *The Trespasser* (1912), is of great interest in relation to this theme of literature and music. The action of the novel occurs not in the usual settings of Lawrence's novels, the countryside around Nottingham and the mining districts, but in south London and the Isle of Wight. It describes a few days in the life of Siegmund, a violinist. He is a married man of thirty-eight who has left

---

* See Part Two: 'A Cultural Overview' for more on Nietzsche.
† Theodor Adorno (1903–69) was a Marxist critical theorist, who had undergone a musical education and had exchanged letters with the composer Alban Berg (1885–1935). He was interested in the atonal revolution initiated by Schoenberg, with its implied criticism of established cultural forms. *The Philosophy of the New Music* appeared in 1949.

his wife and children in order to spend a short holiday with Helena, a cultivated girl with whom he has been having an affair. The couple cannot establish a harmonious relationship, and Siegmund returns to his suburban life and family. The novel illustrates the cultural pre-occupations of the times, and is saturated with musical references, particularly allusions to Wagnerian opera – from which comes the name 'Siegmund' – which link it to the late nineteenth century interest in Wagner which Lawrence's Nottingham circle enjoyed when he attended the University College for teacher training. Wagner's music-dramas were especially admired for providing a fusion of all the arts. *The Trespasser* is of interest because it reflects the preoccupations of the time. Paul Morel, the hero of Lawrence's next novel, *Sons and Lovers* (1913), is an artist in a minor way – at least he achieves a degree of recognition for his paintings – but the pursuit of art is secondary to the development, or growth, of the personality, and Paul is not to be an artist-victim of bourgeois society. At the end of the novel he is a free man, about to leave Nottingham, having released himself from the attachments that bound him to his mother and Miriam and Clara, his former girlfriends. Lawrence's more mature attitude to art is apparent in *Women in Love* (1920), a novel which embodies a discussion about aesthetics (see also the Extended Commentary to Part Three: 'The Modernist Novel in England'). He made a distinction between art that led to the liberation of the feelings, and encouraged more authentic and spontaneous modes of living, and the type of art that was cut off from ordinary living, working out a formal preoccupation with aesthetic concentration. In *Women in Love*, this ideal of liberation through art is endorsed by Gudrun Brangwen and the sculptor Loerke.

There was a continuing concern among modernist writers about the nature of their work in relation to music. James Joyce's early poems, first published in 1907, had the title *Chamber Music*. Virginia Woolf's best known novels – *Mrs Dalloway* (1925), *To the Lighthouse* (1927) and *The Waves* (1931) – exploit the newly won freedom of form to take on the poetic rendering of life in which music provided an example of the way to structure the novel with greater fluidity. For example, the following, from *Mrs Dalloway*, creates an almost musical structure: 'How fresh, how calm, stiller than this of course, the air was in the early morning; like the flap of a wave; the kiss of a wave; chill and sharp.'[4] In these works the narrative becomes poetic and in the case of *To the Lighthouse* the content is concerned with the nature of art and creation. It is not surprising that the text appealed to the composer Michael Tippett (1905–98), who wrote of the novel's 'exquisite and mature art'.[5]

Joyce in particular has taken the novel as far as perhaps it can go into the realms of music. T. S. Eliot famously noted, in the essay '*Ulysses*, Order and Myth' in 1923, that the modern novel needed to find a new way to order the experience of modern life: '[i]n using the myth, in manipulating a continuous parallel between contemporaneity and antiquity, Mr. Joyce is pursuing a method which others must pursue after him.' Eliot argues that it 'is simply a way of controlling, of ordering, of giving a shape and a significance to the immense panorama of futility and anarchy which is contemporary history.'[6] One way in which a new order with which to unify the form of the novel could be achieved was by bringing it closer to musical form. As the critic Walter Allen observed, 'Joyce lived almost entirely in a world of words, and, very often, of words as sounds, divorced, that is, from meaning.'[7] This reliance on the associative value of words as sounds is an example of the way in which modernist writers were blurring the distinctions between the arts. If *Ulysses* (1922) represented a shift in the novel towards the condition of music, it still remained a great comic novel, with a gritty realism comparable perhaps with the naturalist works of Zola. In *Finnegans Wake* (1939), which had been published in fragments through the 1920s and 1930s, Joyce departed from that anchor in descriptive realism. Anthony Burgess's verdict seems to be exact:

> *Finnegans Wake* perhaps had to be written as a horrid warning to musical literary men not to let two irreconcilable arts mate and beget a stillborn hybrid. Certainly, it cannot be repeated … . But, possessing as we do the glorious triumph of *Ulysses* and the glorious failure of *Finnegans Wake*, we can no longer evade a binary view of the art of the novel. The novel can be a plain

representation of human life; it can be a structure which yearns towards the condition of music. Perhaps it is at its greatest when, like *Ulysses*, it is both.[8]

Fusion of All the Arts

The Wagnerian concern for a combination and fusion of artistic activity saw a modernist refinement in two works that have acquired status as key moments of modernist creative action: the collaboration *Parade* in Paris (1917) and in London Edith Sitwell's *Façade* (1922). These works were notable for the cross-fertilisation that their production involved. The background for these developments can be traced to the experiments that were taking place in the late nineteenth century in relation to drama. It was associated with the anti-realist movement that was beginning to appear in Paris at this time, and was close in spirit to the exploratory mood that resulted in the cubist painting of Picasso and Braque, the novels of André Gide and the music of Erik Satie. These attempts towards the establishment of a total theatre tended to emphasise the artificiality of stage performance.* Gordon Craig (1872–1967), in *On the Art of the Theatre* (1911), expounded his ideas on the supremacy of the director, the importance of non-representational décor, and non-naturalistic lighting. These theories were highly controversial but have proved to be very influential, anticipating for instance the ideas of Bertolt Brecht (1898–1956, see Part Three: 'The European Stage and Theatrical Thinkers'). The tendency was to integrate all the arts in one performance.

Parade was an avant-garde ballet that linked the activities of experimental artists in different mediums. It was the result of collaboration between Erik Satie (1866–1925), who wrote the music, and Jean Cocteau (1889–1963), who wrote a one-act scenario. Cocteau, after hearing some of Satie's work, initiated the idea that they work together

---

* Total theatre is the inclusive artistic experience established by the use of non-representational scenes and stage lighting and integrating design with the actors on the stage, to produce a synthesised dramatic form.

on a ballet for Russian Impresario Sergei Diaghilev's (1872–1929) *Ballets Russes*. The ideas for the production soon included the hiring of Pablo Picasso (1881–1973) to design both the set and the costumes; and Léonide Massine (1896–1979), the company's leading dancer, to supply the choreography. The performance was notable for some of Picasso's costumes, which were inspired by Cubism and employed cardboard structures that allowed the dancers very little freedom of movement. Both the background design and the costumes utilised the motif of the skyscraper as the epitome of modern urban life. Cocteau urged Satie to the use of non-musical instruments to make loud noise to enhance the score – these included milk bottles, a fog-horn and a typewriter. The imagery of the skyscraper accompanied by strident jangling noise led to a ballet of harsh juxtaposition encapsulating the clashing discordance of modernity. The poet Guillaume Apollinaire (1880–1918, see Part Four: 'Literature and War') was asked to write the programme notes, and in these he described the work as 'une sorte de surréalisme' (the first recorded use of the term surrealism). While *Parade* was a work without words, it is typical of the modernist moment that some form of verbal explanation or justification (although this can also be seen sometimes as an attempt to tease with explanations that merely add to the bafflement) should attempt to provide an interface between the audience and the performance. Apollinaire's words here gave meaning to what appeared formless.

Façade was based on some experiments that Sitwell had made with matching words to the measures of dance movements, such as waltzes, polkas and foxtrots. The composer William Walton (1902–83) was living with the writer brothers Sacheverell and Osbert Sitwell (1897–1978 and 1892–1969 respectively) at their London house, 2 Carlyle Square, and the resulting work was the product of such close proximity between writers and musicians. The objective had been, as Osbert Sitwell has recorded: 'to exalt the speaking voice to the level of the instruments supporting it, to obtain an absolute balance between the volume of the music and the volume of the sound of the words.' He also highlighted another aim: 'the elimination of the personality of the reciter, and also – though this is of lesser consequence – of the musicians, and the abolition, as a result, of the constricting self-consciousness engendered by it. Towards our purpose, the instrumentalists were secreted behind a curtain.'[9] The work, in its subsequent public performances, attracted the collaboration of artists – Frank Dobson (1923, 1926), Gino Severini (1928) and John Piper (1941). Particularly striking and attracting most of the early outraged criticism was the use of a megaphone (Sengerphone) behind a mask on stage to provide the spoken words – a screen was also employed to hide the human speaker, which was a nod to the non-representational forms of abstract art. The significance of this experimentation was in the way in which the example of the abstract in art was increasingly adopted as a means of modernist performance, as in this case for the declaiming of poetry to an audience.

Music and Poetry

Music was part of Ezra Pound's understanding of poetry. His programme of revitalising poetry was in part based on his research into the troubadours – the wandering poets of medieval France – and he admired and tried to revive the inter-relationship between the two arts that had existed at their time. Pound developed the idea that verse should be composed in 'the sequence of the musical phrase'.[10] He had been profoundly influenced by his reading of Arnold Dolmetsch's book *The Interpretation of the Music of the XVIIth and XVIIIth Centuries* (1915). Dolmetsch (1858–1940) was among the earliest proponents of Early Music; and he made numerous researches into authentic period instruments, making modern reproductions. Pound saw the potential in these activities and how they were related to the interest he had in reviving poetry by returning to regions of the past that had been ignored by nineteenth century developments. Pound was involved in the revival of interest in the work of the early eighteenth century Italian composer Antonio Vivaldi; his companion Olga Rudge, a violinist, was a key figure in the revival of Vivaldi's music in the 1930s. He had written music reviews for *The New Age*; and later championed the young

American composer George Antheil (1900–1959). The first performance of three of Antheil's sonatas – significantly named: 'Airplane Sonata', 'Sonata Sauvage' and 'Mechanism' – in 1923 in Paris created a sensation which was immediately compared to the first performance of Stravinsky's *Sacre du Printemps* (*Rite of Spring*) in 1913. This was typical of the extreme reaction that modernist works could create. Antheil later wrote that:

> My piano was wheeled out … before the huge Léger cubist curtain, and I commenced playing. … Rioting broke out almost immediately. I remember Man Ray punching somebody in the nose in the front row, Marcel Duchamp arguing loudly with somebody in the second. … By this time, people in the galleries were pulling up the seats and dropping them down into the orchestra; the police entered and arrested the Surrealists who, liking the music, were punching everybody who objected.[11]

Pound wrote a notable essay, 'Antheil and the Treatise on Harmony' (1924). It was key for Pound to return to the example provided by music in order to give sense to his poetic structure. In an interview he gave late in life to the renowned Italian poet, novelist and filmmaker, Pier Paolo Pasolini (1922–75), he answered the charge made by critics that his long poem the *Cantos* was made up of pieces chosen at random. He replied that: 'They say they are chosen at random, but that's not the way it is. It's Music. Musical themes that meet each other.'[12] This idea of music, which was derived from the French Symbolists (Mallarmé, Verlaine) and from those late nineteenth century writers (Walter Pater, Arthur Symons, Oscar Wilde and Lionel Johnson), who transmitted these discoveries to an English audience, was pivotal. Pound wanted to develop a kind of poetry that was empowered by music, but he understood that such empowerment was not achieved through marginalising the sense content of words. Rather, he believed that music could enhance sense by alerting the reader, through slowing the movement of the verse down, to the meanings contained in the language.[13]

T. S. Eliot, in his introduction to *Ezra Pound: Selected Poems* (1928), paid attention to 'the importance of *verse as song*'.[14] T. S. Eliot's poems also invite comparison to musical structures. Most obviously, his *Four Quartets* (1936–44) has been read in terms of music. Anthony Burgess claimed that Eliot's quartet poems could only loosely be said to represent the literary equivalent of the musical structures their title suggests.[15] However, he goes on to demonstrate the ways in which *The Waste Land* (1922) can be read in relation to music. It is, he suggests, much more than a literary poem. It is also a collage of musical references. There are some obvious connections to be found in relation to the music of Wagner, which is implied through the quotations and paraphrases of Wagner's verse, particularly *Tristan and Isolde*. As with the literary and contemporary juxtapositions for which the poem is famous, for example the conjoining lines taken from other poets such as Edmund Spenser with the everyday litter floating on the Thames, the effect is to counterpoint utter banality with echoes of past beauty. The life of modernity is caught up in this poetry but then is held at a distance by ironic placement. The sophistication of the modern world allows no simple enjoyment of what might or might not be art – so the narrator sings instead, 'OOOO that Shakespearian Rag – It's so elegant, so intelligent.'[16] It should not be overlooked that Eliot wrote a tribute (1923) to the Music Hall singer, Marie Lloyd (1870–1922), in which he lamented the passing of that form of popular entertainment.

Later modernists such as Basil Bunting (1900–85) have been notable for their insistent concern for the poem as a medium that requires the human voice before it can convey its true quality. In this way words are equated to musical notes. Famously, Bunting declared that:

> Poetry like music, is to be heard. It deals in sound – long sounds and short sounds, heavy beats and light beats, the tone relations of vowels, the relation of consonants to one another which are like instrumental colour in music. Poetry lies dead on the page, until some voice brings it to life, just as music, on the stave, is no more than instruction to the player ... Poetry must be read aloud.[17]

In Bunting's most celebrated poem, *Briggflatts* (1966), it is apparent that the words exist on the page not just as signs indicating meaning but as the texture that provides the poem's unique appeal and meaning. The most satisfactory way to approach this poem is by way of Bunting's own reading.[18]

Cubism, Vorticism: Art and Literature

Modern movements in the visual arts were often closely related to parallel activities in literature. New art movements challenged received opinions about what constituted a picture. As there was no public for this art – apart from the artists themselves and the more advanced critics – it was often necessary to provide some explanation of what the artists were trying to do. This explanation, or defence, was a way in which the artist and the writer became associated in a collaborative activity. For instance, Cubism was initially a term of abuse, but was taken up by a couple of painters who wrote a book called *Du Cubisme* (1912) in explanation of the new aesthetic, and became the adopted name of the movement when the poet Apollinaire published *Les Peintres Cubistes* (1913). Much later the writer Gertrude Stein (1874–1946), who had, under the influence of her art historian and Harvard aesthete brother Leo Stein, moved to the bohemian Left Bank of Paris, was to write a monograph on Picasso (the Steins had been one of Picasso's earliest patrons). In 1909 she had published *Three Lives*, in which she attempted to reconstruct Flaubert's *Trois Contes* in a manner which produced the effect of the ever present of the mind. Malcolm Bradbury has described this method as follows:

> The repetition or recurring was memoryless, and based on a new grammar in which, as in painting, the noun or realistic object is depleted ('A noun is the name of anything, why after a thing is named write about it'), and verbal and adverbial forms predominate. It was a literary version of the method of abstraction, post-naturalist, post-impressionist, moving onward

from Flaubert and Cézanne. And, just as Cézanne was engaged both in creating and de-creating his paintings, in order to convey both the inner energy of subject and the perceptual art of their creation, so in prose Gertrude Stein moved towards a verbal version of estrangement and abstraction.[19]

What is important to notice here is the concern with finding equivalents in literature to the discoveries being made in experimental art. As visual art moved away from representational subjects (which the new art of photography was replacing, especially in areas such as portraiture), the writer felt the challenge to question traditional forms of narrative. Stein experimented with a style that tried to emulate the work of abstract artists, for example, in her poem 'Tender Buttons' (1914).

As we have already seen, Vorticism was a movement that was both literary and artistic. Apart from the work of Wyndham Lewis (1892–1957) and sculptor Henri Gaudier-Brzeska (1891–1915), the photographer Alvin Langdon Coburn (1882–1966) created vortographs, which were photographs that exploded the solid image by placing mirrors in front of the subject. Wyndham Lewis also experimented with literature to see if it could be possible to approximate the verbal construct to the sort of methods of construction being attempted by the continental avant-garde. In the play *The Enemy of the Stars* (1914), Lewis attempts to write in a way that reflects his painting from the same period. The massive satire of *The Apes of God* (1930) is perhaps more conventional, but as Anthony Burgess noted, 'the impression of extreme slowness derives from the careful brushwork'.[20] This slowness is related to the way in which Lewis is concerned with what the eye of the painter sees. Ezra Pound championed the work of Wyndham Lewis and also that of the sculptor Henri Gaudier-Brzeska. Pound's continuing engagement with the visual arts has been usefully charted in Rebecca Beasley's *Ezra Pound and the Visual Culture of Modernism* (2007).

Surrealism: Art, Literature and Film

Surrealism was a movement of visual art as well as literature. It was officially inaugurated in 1924 by the French poet André Breton (1896–1966) in his First Surrealist Manifesto, in which he made an eloquent appeal for the emancipation of imagination from the arbitrary limitations imposed by reason and society. For Breton – who was briefly a psychiatrist during the First World War – the imaginative life embraced the whole world of the unconscious, as revealed by the psychoanalyst Sigmund Freud (see Part Two: 'A Cultural Overview'). 'Surrealism,' he wrote, 'is based on the belief in … the omnipotence of the dream and the disinterested play of thought.' Its aim was 'to resolve the previously contradictory conditions of dream and reality into an absolute reality, a super-reality'; to bring out the odd – and psychologically significant – juxtaposition of normally unrelated images in the mind, and thus convey intense subjective experiences.[21] The poet and the artist had no business with aesthetic standards: their role was to 'detail' the mind, to act as seers interpreting their own subconscious minds. It can be seen in this context that poetry or visual art are equally suitable for notating these discoveries.

This type of 'anti-art' had its nihilistic origins in Dadaism, a movement dedicated to the destruction of all established aesthetic values – including the exclusivity of the poem or the painting as an aesthetic object. Dada was established in Zurich in 1916, and was named by adopting the French child's word for hobby-horse, which had been picked at random by blindly stabbing a French–German dictionary with a paper knife. Dada poems, intoned at the top of the voice, often consisted only of vowels (notice the connection to the experiments made by the Sitwells in *Façade*). Meetings included absurd semi-planned manifestations, the forerunners of 'happenings'.* Kurt Schwitters (1887–1948) made Dada pictures out of 'found

---

* The term 'happening' was first coined in 1957 by Allan Kaprow to describe events, situations or performances which might be considered artworks. However, by the mid sixties, the term was being used more generally to describe any gathering of people for an improvised, informal event.

objects' – tram tickets, shoe-laces and other discarded items. Francis Picabia (1887–1953) carefully delineated meaningless machines. The greatest Dada artist, Marcel Duchamp (1887–1968), exhibited a reproduction of the 'Mona Lisa' decorated with a moustache and an obscene pun, and a urinal entitled *Fountain* and signed R.Mutt. It will be noted that these constructions incorporate object and text. Duchamp's major work was *The Bride Stripped Bare by her Bachelors, Even* (1915 – completed in 1923), which he claimed was only 'finished' when the glass of which it was made was accidentally cracked.

By 1924, Breton was disillusioned with the destructiveness of Dadaism. Its cult of absurdity had reached an extreme. It was Breton who guided Surrealism away from its nihilistic origins. To discover the significant, incongruous objects in the mind, Breton and his co-Surrealist Philippe Soupault (1897–1990) had already experimented with 'automatic writing' in *Les champs magnétiques* (1920) – allowing the hand to transcribe, without any control, 'the real process of the mind', which he compared with psychiatric techniques. It was in connection with this process that Breton first used the word 'Surrealism', a word actually coined by Apollinaire to describe his play *Les Mamelles de Tirésias* (The Breasts of Tiresias) in 1917. The movement was originally a literary one, but artists saw that Surrealist painting could match Surrealist poetry by providing visual rather than verbal images of the subconscious. Max Ernst (1891–1976), a former Dadaist, regarded his *frottage* process – acquiring random images by rubbing pencil on paper spread on any available material – as a visual equivalent of automatic writing. He also combined actual materials with painted figures to exploit 'the chance meeting of distant realities on an unfamiliar plane'.[22] An example of this to be found in his *Two children are threatened by a nightingale* (1924). He also published collage novels.

Salvador Dalí's (1904–89) relationship with and inspiration from the medium of film was explored in a major exhibition at Tate Modern in 2007. The catalogue, edited by Matthew Gale, revealed the persistence of Dalí's fascination with film. In particular his collaboration with Luis Buñel (1900–83) was an essential part of the history of Surrealism. There were two specifically surrealist films made by Dalí and Buñuel,

Un Chien Andalou (An Andalusian Dog) in 1929 and *L'Age d'Or* (The Golden Age) in 1930. The relationship with literature may be strained in this instance but it is well to remember the exploration with narrative and the choice of de Sade as a text. *L'Age d'Or* (1930) was a collaboration that united the visual artist and filmmaker in the act of retelling a literary work (by the eighteenth / nineteenth century French writer the Marquis de Sade).

Harlem Renaissance: Aesthetics, Jazz and Blues

In the 1920s the district of Harlem in New York saw an outpouring of artistic activity among African-Americans; and the wider flowering of black art and literature in the United States has been labelled the Harlem Renaissance. From about the end of the First World War there was a growing need to find expression for the black experience in the densely packed urban spaces of northern American cities such as New York. Black Americans had migrated to the cities from the rural economy of the southern United States, which had been depressed since the South's defeat in the Civil War. There was a consciousness of what was then termed the 'New Negro' which challenged stereotypes and a belief in progressivism. These energies were absorbed by the music of blues and jazz and in the visual arts by modernist experiment. The white writer and photographer Carl Van Vechten (1880–1964) took an interest in this new phenomenon and controversially provided patronage and promoted it. He was especially associated with and supportive of Langston Hughes (1902–67), Richard Wright (1908–60) and Wallace Thurman (1902–34). Van Vechten wrote about literature and music, and his *Vanity Fair* essay 'Negro Blues Singers' (1926) and his novel *Nigger Heaven* (1926) made black culture fashionable. Richard Powell and David A. Bailey's exhibition catalogue, *Rhapsodies in Black: Art of the Harlem Renaissance* (1997), is probably the best place to start for an understanding of the extent of the inter-relationships between art and literature in the formation of the Harlem Renaissance.

Jazz was an important part of the formative expression of the Renaissance. In the work of the painters Aaron Douglas (1899–1979) and Archibald J. Motley (1891–1981) this was adapted into a 'jazz aesthetic'. Douglas's mural *Aspects of Negro Life* (1934) and *The Song of the Towers* (1934) – a painting on the subject of the Great Migration of African-Americans from the South into the North, Midwest and Western states (1910–30) – express this aspect of jazz-inspired rhythm. This is conveyed by the use of repeated semi-abstract shapes and the complex use of colour to link elements in the design and to change those colours at points of intersection. Jacob Lawrence's *The Migration of the Negro Series* (1940–1) was particularly important in codifying the Negro experience. There has been a lot of critical interest in what Martha Nadell has called 'interartistic' texts in recent years.[23] Douglas did a number of illustrations for magazines such as Crisis and Fire!!, but he also illustrated some key Harlem Renaissance texts, including James Weldon Johnson's (1871–1938) *God's Trombones: Seven Negro Sermons in Verse* (1927),[24] and he was an influential designer of book covers too. There was a widely shared interest in visual culture, for example the poet Jean Toomer's (1894–1967) fascination with photography, Nella Larsen's (1891–1964) use of visual tableaux in *Quicksand* (1928) and *Passing* (1929), the proliferation of characters who are aspiring visual artists in the pages of Harlem Renaissance fiction. Finally, the photographer James Van Der Zee (1886–1983) created some of the most iconic images of Harlem in the twenties; and his haunting photographs of the dead resonate with broader literary preoccupations about memory, loss and mourning. Rachel Farebrother's *The Collage Aesthetic in the Harlem Renaissance* (2009) demonstrates the importance of collage in the interaction between visual art and literature during the period.

The Art of the Moving Image

One of the key developments in the arts in the early twentieth century was the birth of the cinema industry. By the end of the nineteenth century photography was a widespread and popular medium. Soon, ways of producing moving images were being explored. The English photographer Eadweard Muybridge (1830–1904) was an important pioneer in the use of cameras to capture images of motion. His pictures of animals and humans in arrested movement were the first to reveal the sequence of what had hitherto been seen only by the naked eye. In particular his images of a horse in motion, taken by a series of cameras alongside a track in 1877 and 1878, proved that the galloping horse is at times completely airborne, with its legs tucked under its belly. This showed that the widespread number of paintings of horses galloping with front and back legs extended were incorrect. His processes included the use of celluloid and led to the popularisation of the idea of the moving image. There was a tension that manifested itself between the reproduction of images of this kind and more traditional forms of art such as poetry. In Thomas Mann's *Tonio Kröger* it is apparent that the artist resents the science of the mechanical image, and its popular proliferation:

> It is against all sense to love life and yet bend all the powers you have to draw it over to your own side, to the side of finesse and melancholy and the whole sickly aristocracy of letters. The kingdom of art increases and that of health and innocence declines on this earth. What there is left of it ought to be carefully preserved; one ought not to tempt people to read poetry who would much rather read books about the instantaneous photography of horses.[25]

This is part of that key debate about modernist art and the public.

However, there is also a side to the poet Vachel Lindsay's (1879–1932) viewpoint that optimistically responded to the opportunities of the new technology of the emergent cinema. In *The Art of the Moving Picture* (1915), an early attempt to theorise the cinematic art, he suggests that 'there is many a babe in the proletariat not over four years old who has received more pictures into its eye than it has had words enter its ear.'[26] This he sees as a positive sign of the great democratic possibilities offered by the motion picture.[27] Significantly, when we consider Lindsay as a maker of a magazine, we see how he envisions the role of the periodical by drawing parallels with the emergent medium of cinema. He chooses to discuss film in terms of photoplay (of course it should be emphasised that his experience is based on the silent cinema). It is also significant that illustration plays an important role in *The Village Magazine* (1910, reprinted with additions in 1920 and 1925), a periodical edited by Lindsay, as a means of imparting understanding. The attraction seems to lie in his conception of 'pure' imagination as a means of communication. This should perhaps be understood in relation to his preaching of an aestheticism to enrich the life of the ordinary American citizen, which he referred to as the 'Gospel of Beauty'. This concept can be traced back through the illustrator and author Aubrey Beardsley (1872–98) to the inspiration of artist-poets such as William Blake (1757–1827). Therefore, the magazine makes use of Lindsay's work as an artist to provide a visual expression of his philosophy.

In the early part of the twentieth century modernist artists were inclined to respond to the potential that they saw in cinema. James Joyce, for instance, was involved in the setting up of a picture house in Dublin, the first cinema in Ireland. The Volta Cinematograph Theatre opened in December 1909, with Joyce briefly as manager, thanks to the backing of businessmen. It has been suggested that this involvement was merely an attempt to raise money rather than an artistic enterprise. Whether this was so or not it should not be overlooked that Joyce understood something of the importance that cinema was going to have in modern society.

The poet H. D. (1886–1961, see Part Three: 'Modernist Poetry – French Origins, English Settings) and the novelist Dorothy Richardson (1873–1957) were both drawn to take serious notice of film as a medium for artistic expression. The magazine *Close-Up*, which was devoted to cinema, published between 1927 and 1933 a series of essays by Richardson that went by the title of 'Continuous Performance'. These essays considered such diverse subjects as: musical accompaniment, captions, slow-motion, popular film, cinemas in the slums, films for children and censorship. There is a relationship between these articles and their concern with charting the developments of cinema and her great sequence of novels *Pilgrimage* (1915–67), which chart the life of Miriam Henderson, a protagonist similar to the author herself.

H. D. was particularly interested in the medium of film and was involved in a complicated three-way relationship with Bryher (Winifred Ellerman, 1894–1983) and Kenneth Macpherson (1903–71) (who was sexually involved with both women), the editor of *Close-Up*. Bryher, with whom H. D. had conducted a lesbian affair, was the financial backer, and with this finance it was possible to start up an independent film company, the POOL Group. One film made by POOL was *Borderline* (1930), which starred H. D. and the African-American singer and actor Paul Robeson (1898–1976) in leading roles. The film is notable for the insight it gives into H. D.'s feminist aesthetic and its use of avant-garde techniques at a time when it was thought that film could combine experimentation with popular appeal. The script was written by H. D. and Macpherson, and concerned the issues of race. H. D. wrote an explanatory pamphlet which was later published in *Close-Up*, to which she also contributed articles.

It will be apparent that modernism was not simply a movement or a period in literature, but part of a dynamic activity that found expression in a range of different artistic disciplines. It will also be clear that many of these activities were attempts to unite the various arts as part of a major project of renovation and the outcome of a change in sensibility. Arts sought to emulate qualities that had traditionally been divided between different disciplines in one or other form. So, poetry attempted to learn from music and was made new by emulating the nature of musical form. Similarly, painting and sculpture provided models by which modernist writers sought to liberate themselves from the habitual assumptions about the genres and forms of the past. Rebecca Beasley has suggested that in constructing a pan-art approach, modernist writers, deliberately or naively, refused to engage with the different traditions by which the arts had separately evolved:

It was in literary modernism's interest to present itself as part of a new aesthetic culture of experiment that pervaded all the arts in a comparable fashion; to acknowledge the reverse, that different arts had different histories and ideologies, even different conceptions of modernism itself, would be to call into question the assumed stylistic analogies that served literary modernism so well.[28]

It is a feature, therefore, of modernism's self-fashioning to find analogies between the different arts. These attempts to expand the range of expression were related to the self-conscious presentation of the writer, musician or painter. In the contemporary fiction of the early twentieth century this was manifested in the numerous ways that artists and writers were depicted as a fit subject for narrative. It was as if in the general fragmentation of culture the arts felt the need to construct an exclusive space reinforced by a total engagement of artistic endeavour.

Notes

1   John Ruskin, 'Lectures on Art' in Richard Aldington (ed.), *The Religion of Beauty: Selections from the Aesthetes* (London: Heinemann, 1950), p. 59.

2   Joseph Conrad, 'Preface to *The Nigger of the "Narcissus"*', *The Nigger of the 'Narcissus'/Typhoon and Other Stories* (Harmondsworth: Penguin, 1983), p. 12.

3   Thomas Mann, *Death in Venice/Tristan/Tonio Kröger* (Harmondsworth: Penguin, 1980), p. 111.

4   Virginia Woolf, *Mrs Dalloway* (Harmondsworth: Penguin, 2005), p. 3.

5   Michael Tippett to Francesca Allinson (1941), *Selected Letters of Michael Tippett*, ed. by Thomas Schuttenhelm (London: Faber & Faber, 2005), p. 80.

6   T. S. Eliot, '*Ulysses*, Order, and Myth', *The Dial*, LXXV (November 1923), p. 480.

7   Walter Allen, *Tradition and Dream: The English and American Novel from the Twenties to Our Time* (London: Phoenix House, 1964), p. 5.

8   Anthony Burgess, *This Man & Music* (New York: Applause, 2001), pp. 148–9.

9   Osbert Sitwell, *Left Hand, Right Hand!* (Harmondsworth: Penguin, 1984), p. 362.

10   Ezra Pound, 'Vers Libre and Arnold Dolmetsch' , *The Egoist*, July 1917, pp. 90–1.

11   George Antheil, *The Bad Boy of Music* (Garden City, NY: Doubleday Doran, 1945), p. 133.

12   Quoted in Michael Coyle, *Ezra Pound, Popular Genres, and the Discourse of Culture* (University Park, PA: Pennsylvania State University Press, 1995), p. 151.

13   An important source of information regarding Pound's involvement with music is R. Murray Schafer (ed.), *Ezra Pound and Music* (New York: New Directions, 1977)

14   T. S. Eliot, 'Introduction', Ezra Pound, *Selected Poems* (London: Faber & Faber, 1959), p. 9.

15   Anthony Burgess, *This Man & Music*, p. 99.

16   T. S. Eliot, *The Waste Land and Other Poems* (London: Faber and Faber, 1981), p. 31, ll. 128–30.

17   Basil Bunting, published in the April (1966) 'Diary' of the North-Eastern Association for the Arts, Newcastle-upon-Tyne. Quoted in Herbert Read, 'Basil Bunting: Music or Meaning?', *Agenda*, 4: 5 & 6 (Autumn 1966), p. 4.

18   See Basil Bunting, *Briggflatts* (Tarset, Northumberland: Bloodaxe, 2009), which includes a CD of Bunting reading his poem.

19   Malcolm Bradbury, *The Modern American Novel* (Oxford: Oxford University Press, 1992), p. 47.

20   Anthony Burgess, *Urgent Copy* (Harmondsworth: Penguin, 1973), p. 108.

21   André Breton, *Manifesto of Surrealism* (1924). See: www.tcf.ua.edu.Classes/Jbutler/T340/SurManifesto/ManifestoOfSurrealism.htm.

22   Peter and Linda Murray, *The Penguin Dictionary of Art and Artists* (Harmondsworth: Penguin, 1979), pp. 435–6.

23   Martha Jane Nadell, *Enter the New Negroes: Images of Race in American Culture* (Cambridge, MA: Harvard University Press, 2004). See also Rachel Farebrother's *The Collage Aesthetic in the Harlem Renaissance* (Farnham: Ashgate, 2009), p. 1.

24   See the catalogue edited by Susan Earle, *Aaron Douglas: African American Modernist* (New Haven, CT: Yale University Press, 2007).

25   Thomas Mann, *Death in Venice/Tristan/Tonio Kröger* (Harmondsworth: Penguin, 1980), pp. 159–60.

26   Vachel Lindsay, *The Art of the Moving Picture* (New York: Macmillan, 1922), p. 186.

27   Myron Lounsbury suggests that Lindsay was 'at heart' a democrat, 'hopeful that the penchant for mechanical reproduction would prove responsive to the human need to know and understand'. Vachel Lindsay, *Progress and Poetry of the Movies*, ed. Myron Lounsbury (London: Scarecrow Press, 1995), p. 20.

28   Rebecca Beasley, 'Literature and the Visual Arts', Peter Brooker and Andrew Thacker (eds), *The Oxford Critical and Cultural History of Modernist Magazines* (Oxford: Oxford University Press, 2009), p. 485.

Modernist Print Culture: Literature, Book History and the Economics of Publishing

One area of modernist studies which has flourished, particularly in recent years, is the study of modernist print culture. Taking its bearings from materialist studies, there has been a major re-examination of the economics of modernist publishing.* Two areas perhaps should be highlighted as having developed our understanding of modernist culture as a whole. Firstly, there is the examination that has been made of the relationships between modernist authors and publishers, and the nature of the text produced by that relationship. Secondly, there has been a growth of interest in the literary periodicals in which many modernist writers first made their appearance in print.

Authors and Publishers

One of the ways in which modernist writers managed to take control of their own publication activities was through establishing independent presses. During the late nineteenth century there was a massive increase in the amount of printed material available for purchase. In Great Britain, the Education Act of 1870 had established the principle of public education and of an educated and literate population, and this

---

* Materialist studies are those that view a text in relation to its production and consumption. This broadly historical approach is informed by Marxist critical theory.

consolidated and extended the growth of the reading public that had been growing since the eighteenth century and provided a largely middle class readership for the realistic novel. The population was also growing and a popular press was encouraging the reading habits of an often newly literate working class audience. This was aided by the fact that reading material could be produced more cheaply by the rotary press and subsidised by commercial advertising.* During the 1870s and 1880s there existed a strong middle class press throughout Europe, represented by the British *Daily Telegraph* and *Daily News*, the French *Le Matin*, the German *Neueste Nachrichten* and the Italian *Il Messaggero*. It was quickly augmented in the 1890s and after by a still more popular and proletarian press, following the example of the Hearst Press in the United States, which had shown how successful such enterprises could be, making their owners extremely wealthy.† Newspapers such as Lord Northcliffe's *Daily Mail* (founded in 1896), the Parisian *Petit Journal*, and the Berlin *Lokal-Anzeiger* were evidence of this expansion.

By 1900 each major European country had some such papers, usually exceeding one million copies in daily circulation and fostering a new type of popular journalism. They were cheaply produced and circulated to generate the maximum number of readers and therefore the largest advertisement revenue, which meant that, like the American *Pearson's Magazine*, the costs were subsidised by the placement of adverts. These publications were commercial in character and were aimed to exploit the new literate and semi-literate public. This created a context in which the publishing industry itself switched to catering for a mass audience, rather than the traditionally perceived literate readership limited largely to the upper and middle classes. As Mark S. Morrisson has convincingly demonstrated, the novel or magazine of the early twentieth century possessed a complicated relationship with 'the explosion of mass market print publications and advertising' which innovations in print-technology and the availability of inexpensive paper at the end of the nineteenth century touched off.[1] Morrisson contends

---

* The rotary press was a method by which the item to be printed could be put onto a cylinder and printed onto a roll of paper. It speeded up the printing process, enabling cheap mass production.
† Orson Welles's classic film *Citizen Kane* (1941) is a fictionalised biopic of Hearst's career.

that interpretations of the avant-garde which depict it as resolutely opposed to the supposed denigrations of mass culture, as suggested in Andreas Huyssen's *After the Great Divide*,[2] fail to note the extent to which certain modernists interacted with and manipulated 'the new institutions of culture of the period to create a prominent public role for their art and literature'. As editors and producers, modernists, far from showing a reaction of anti-commercialism – as has been frequently been suggested – seized upon the relative affordability of the periodical medium as a means of, in Morrisson's words, 'making their voices and their art prominent in the vibrant and exciting new print venues of the public sphere that the commercial culture had helped to create and sustain'.[3]

The inspiration and impetus for all the small presses of the twentieth century can be traced back to William Morris (1834–96) and the founding of The Kelmscott Press in 1891.* Hence, there was an implied emphasis on the unique item, on the beauty of the product, which had its origins in the reaction against the commercialisation of print culture that can be found in the Arts and Crafts Movement. In this case the individual piece selected for publication received the kind of attention that might in medieval times have been reserved for sacred texts. Charles Haslewood Shannon (1863–1937) and Charles Ricketts (1866–1931) were perhaps the most celebrated practitioners of the fine press after Morris, and they also saw the production of magazines and books as a vital part of a communal activity. Their periodical, *The Dial: An Occasional Review* (1889–97), was a suitably lavish production, really an extension of their interest in art and printing. So it is significant that when Ricketts and Shannon wanted to interest 'Michael Field' (Edith Cooper and Katherine Bradley) in their work as printers, it was a copy of *The Dial* which they sent as evidence of their suitability to produce fine books. They wrote (in February 1892):

---

* Morris had combined a career as a decorative artist with that of the creative writer. He also combined an interest in an idealised medievalism with socialist politics, founding both the Society for the Protection of Ancient Buildings (1877) and the Socialist League (1884). These different interests were reflected in the utopian vision of his novel *News from Nowhere* (1890). The Kelmscott Press was an attempt to produce books that were inspired by the craftsmanship of the fifteenth century, the Kelmscott Chaucer being the most noted example.

The Vale, Kings Road, Chelsea SW.

Dear Sir,

It would give us much pleasure to know that one copy of this our half-private magazine should be in your hands. Will you allow our great admiration for The Tragic Mary & some of your other noble plays to be the excuse for our sending it to you.

> Yours very truly
> C. H. Shannon
> C. S. Ricketts[4]

Their interest in 'The Tragic Mary' had been established when Shannon and Ricketts saw an illustrated copy at a fair devoted to items inspired by the Arts and Crafts Movement. They must have seen the opportunity for a mutually satisfying collaboration, the text and art work seen to be part of a common project. However, the initial response from Cooper and Bradley to *The Dial* was critical and negative. The literary content of the magazine aroused their censure. However, it should be noted that the way in which Shannon and Ricketts refer to their magazine as 'half-private' and imagine it in the hands of 'Michael Field' (whose identity they did not at this stage know), personalises the magazine – it has almost become a metaphor for personal contact.

The success of ventures such as this created a taste for lavish portfolio style magazines that lasted into the 1920s with publications such as *Form, The Apple* and *The Golden Hind*. At the same time, there was also a public for equally lavish examples of the fine press publication – W. B. Yeats's (1865–1939) poems, for instance, were published in de-luxe book format. Even before the First World War, the poet Ralph Hodgson (1871–1962) had collaborated with the journalist and book collector Holbrook Jackson (1874–1948) and the artist Claud Lovat Fraser (1890–1921), to establish the *Sign of the Flying Fame* in 1913, a publishing company that produced broadsides and booklets at Fraser's house. In this case the publication was largely based on the principle of independence – independence from the main publishing houses. As even little magazines such as *The Golden Hind* were produced by large commercial houses, in this case Chapman & Hall, true independence could not be guaranteed. In particular it seems that Hodgson was suspicious of any infringement of his copyright. The *Sign of the Flying Fame* therefore was a private venture, that sought to eschew the entanglements that normally attended publication. Indeed the idealism of the *Sign of the Flying Fame* was to evoke the spirit of the 'rough and ready', 'home-brewed' wares of travelling pedlars of the seventeeth century with verses to sell.[5] These publications were known as Chapbooks. Something of the marginality and provisionality of the Chapbook appealed to the writers of this period and was the cause for the revival of the form in modernist culture. Chapbooks – essentially pamphlets containing poetry or fiction – were produced in New York by Guido Bruno (1915–16) and in London by Harold Monro during the First World War and just after. These publications were only partly a reaction against the commercial book trade of mass society, which operated on a mass production basis; contemporary developments in printing allowed for the easy production and sale of such items. Although, when Monro tried to revive the idea after the war with a periodical called the *Chapbook*, he found that it 'fell between two markets, appealing neither to the sort of readership catered for by the Poetry Society nor to the intellectuals who were to support *The Criterion*' [T. S. Eliot's critical review (1922–39)].[6]

The Hogarth Press

One of the best known and most influential independent presses of the early twentieth century was The Hogarth Press, run by Leonard and Virginia Woolf. It began when the Woolfs installed a handpress in the drawing room of their home, Hogarth House, Richmond-upon-Thames, in 1917. They went on to publish the early work of T. S. Eliot, Laura Riding, Katherine Mansfield and John Maynard Keynes, as well as notable translations from Russian authors. Their publishing activities were not limited to poetry and fiction but included works of psychoanalysis and criticism. The intention was to provide an outlet for the printing of books that would not otherwise get published by commercial publishers. It is clear that part of the impetus for the project came from the opportunity to work in the manner of the art for art's sake movement* (indeed the idea of the press was conceived as a form of therapy for Virginia, in which the physical activity of the printing press was an important component), especially as interpreted by William Morris into a celebration of a return to handcrafts.

However, in one important respect the vision of the Woolfs was different. Their intention was to produce books that were read and not de-luxe editions for collectors of fine printed books. Soon, however, the advantages of being freed from the constraints of publishers' deadlines and editorial control became apparent, and showed new directions which the combination of printing and writing could open up. As J. H. Willis has suggested, Virginia Woolf 'could experiment boldly, remaking the form and herself each time she shaped a new fiction, responsible only to herself as writer-editor-publisher' and she was significantly, as she declared, 'the only woman in England free to write what I like'.[7] This provided two important aspects of modernist book production: freedom from censorship and the opportunity to challenge existing gender roles. The fact that the press was independent meant that the Woolfs were not obliged to print work which they felt would compromise their own standards, and were able to reject books that might be profitable but were not to their taste. The first Hogarth Press publication was *Two Stories* (1917), featuring a story by Leonard – 'Three Jews' – and one by Virginia – 'The Mark on the Wall'. The title page made it clear that the functions of writer and printer were regarded as of equal significance. Only 150 copies were produced, some bound in Japanese grass paper, some in light blue, some with a white and red design, and some in yellow paper wrappers. The book was truly collaborative, including four woodcut illustrations by Dora Carrington. Within a month 124 copies of the book had been sold, and the press was established.

* See the section on the Aesthetic Movement in Part Two: 'A Cultural Overview'.

The role of printer created a number of challenges to the Woolfs, and the typesetting of Hope Mirrlees's *Paris: a poem* (1919), which featured eccentric typography, was followed by T. S. Eliot's *The Waste Land* (1922) – the first UK book publication of Eliot's poem. The Woolfs had already published Eliot's poems (1919), and later published his influential book of criticism, *In Homage to John Dryden* (1924), in a series of paperback Hogarth Essays, which was to shape literary opinion far beyond the period of modernism.[8] The style of the Hogarth Press publications was quite distinctive and Virginia Woolf's sister, the artist Vanessa Bell, was responsible for illustrations that contributed to the sense of uniform integrity.

A number of studies of the Hogarth Press have been made, and mention should be made of: Donna E. Rhein, *The Handprinted Books of Leonard and Virginia Woolf at the Hogarth Press, 1917–1932* (1985), Mary Gaither's 'The Hogarth Press' *British Literary Publishing Houses 1881–1965* in *Dictionary of Literary Biography 112* (1991), S. P. Rosenbaum, *Leonard and Virginia Woolf at the Hogarth Press* (1995), Laura Marcus's, 'Virginia Woolf and the Hogarth Press' in Ian Willison, Warwick Gould and Warren Chernaik (editors), *Modernist Writers and the Marketplace* (1996), David Porter, *Virginia Woolf and the Hogarth Press* (2004).

The standard work is J. H. Willis, *Leonard and Virginia Woolf as Publishers: The Hogarth Press 1917–1941* (1992). Memoirs by John Lehmann and Richard Kennedy's *A Boy at the Hogarth Press* (1972) provide insight into the workings of the Press, especially in the late 1920s and 1930s, when it had grown to be something larger than an operation conducted from the Woolfs' drawing room.[9] An important study has been made of the Press's publication of translations from Russian – Stuart Clarke and Laura Marcus (eds), *Translations from the Russian by Virginia Woolf and S. S. Koteliansky* (2006). The Woolfs were important in boosting the interest that had been gathering pace in Russian authors, especially since Constance Garnett's translations had started to appear, particularly in Chekhov, Tolstoy and Dostoevsky – in 1920 the Hogarth Press printed Maxim Gorky's reminisces of Tolstoy; in 1921 they brought out a volume of Chekhov's Note-Books, together with a memoir by Maxim Gorky; and in 1922 suppressed chapters from Dostoevsky's *The Possessed* were published. J. Howard Woolmer's *The Checklist of the Hogarth Press 1917–1946* (1986) is an invaluable research tool.[10]

Small Presses

The Hogarth Press was not the only small press that played a part in the publishing history of modernism. There were many others, of varying significance. Among the noteworthy was Nancy Cunard's Hours Press. Cunard (1896–1965) wanted to publish experimental poetry that would not otherwise get into print. She set up a press in a Normandy farmhouse in 1928, which was a continuation of the American journalist William Bird's Three Mountains Press (founded in 1922). Bird had already published Ezra Pound's *A Draft of XVI Cantos* (1925), Ernest Hemingway's breakthrough collection of short stories, *in our time* (1925), William Carlos Williams's *The Great American Novel* (1923) and Ford Madox Ford's *Women and Men* (1923). These were typically limited to a run of 300 copies. Cunard published Samuel Beckett's poem *Whoroscope* (1930) and Pound's *A Draft of XXX Cantos* (1930, which anticipated the first commercial edition which appeared in 1933). These followed the format established by the Three Mountains Press, being finely printed and bound and limited to 200 or 300 copies, of which perhaps 100 would be signed by the author. Pound's cantos were embellished by woodcut initials by Dorothy Shakespear, his wife.

Harry Crosby (1898–1929) was another American who set up a press in Europe that was to be highly influential and myth-making. Originally called Éditions Narcisse and founded in 1927, the press changed its name to the Black Sun Press the following year. Run with his wife, Caresse Crosby, Black Sun published their own work and that by their friends D. H. Lawrence – *Sun* (1928) and *The Escaped Cock* (1929) – and James Joyce – *Tales Told of Shem and Shaun: Three Fragments from Work in Progress* (1929) – as well as Kay Boyle's first book, *Short Stories* (1929), and the first printing of Hart Crane's *The*

221

Bridge (1930), in an edition that included three photographs by Walker Evans of Brooklyn Bridge. Again these publications were printed on fine paper and kept to limited editions of 100 or 200 copies. Robert Graves's and Laura Riding's Seizin Press (founded in 1927) was a private press that followed a similar pattern, printing their own works and those by other authors in whom they took an interest, such as the poet James Reeves – who's first collection of poetry, *The Natural Need* (1935), they printed – and Gertrude Stein, who's *An Acquaintance with Description* appeared in 1929. Another significant small press was Boriswood (1931–8), a leftist London publisher of among others the South African poet Roy Campbell 1901–57). They also published the first UK edition of *The Collected Poems of Hart Crane* in 1938 (which had originally appeared in the United States in 1933). The publisher is perhaps best remembered for publishing James Hanley's *Boy* in 1931, which involved them in a legal case that resulted in a severe fine.

A later example of the small press was James Laughlin's New Directions, which was founded in 1936 when Laughlin was still a student at Harvard University. The impetus came from Ezra Pound, who Laughlin had visited in Italy, and initially the press concentrated on producing annuals of new and experimental writing. The first of these was titled *New Directions in Prose & Poetry*, and printed work by Wallace Stevens, Ezra Pound and Marianne Moore. Subsequent yearly volumes (1937, 1938, etc.) contained an anthology of work by Gertrude Stein, William Carlos Williams, e. e. cummings, Kay Boyle, Henry Miller and William Saroyan. The commitment to experimental writing in English and other languages remained the cornerstone of New Directions, and the press still survives on this reputation today.

Censorship and Publication

Modernist texts were often difficult to get published. This difficulty was because texts challenged accepted values, which meant that they sometimes were classified as obscene publications. One of the first publishers to combine activities in the publication of pornography and the printing of ground-breaking literary texts was Leonard Smithers (1861–1907). Smithers became one of the most influential publishers of the decadent writers during the 1890s – publishing Aubrey Beardsley, Aleister Crowley, Ernest Dowson, Arthur Symons and Oscar Wilde. With Symons he was responsible for the influential magazine *The Savoy* (1896).[11] In New York, during the period of the First World War and its aftermath, Guido Bruno (real name Curt Kisch, 1884–1942) made his name as a publisher and magazine editor. He was responsible for the first printings of works by Hart Crane and Djuna Barnes. One of the ways in which banned or controversial works could be published was by exploiting legal loop-holes. The Paris-based and Manchester-born publisher Jack Kahane (1887–1939) found one by which works that were banned in the US or Great Britain could be published in Paris. His publishing list included pornography as well as Henry Miller, Anaïs Nin, James Joyce and D. H. Lawrence. He was responsible for the printing of Richard Aldington's *Death of a Hero* in an edition that restored expurgations made to the first British and American trade editions of 1929, which were bowdlerised owing to the obscenity laws that then existed; Frank Harris's *My Life and Loves*; Cyril Connolly's *The Rock Pool* (1936); and the reprinting of James Hanley's *Boy* (1931) in 1935.

However, it was the publication of Henry Miller's *Tropic of Cancer* in 1934 that made the Obelisk Press its name.[12] George Orwell, in the influential essay 'Inside the Whale' (1940), declared: 'I earnestly counsel anyone who has not done so to read at least *Tropic of Cancer*. With a little ingenuity, or by paying a little over the published price, you can get hold of it, and even if parts of it disgust you, it will stick in your memory.'[13] Also in this recommendation is the assumption that the author and the publisher are engaged together in a mutually agreed campaign to make available work that the authorities – whether it be the police or the Customs – have taken steps to prevent reaching the general public, in whose name the preventative measures have been instigated by the state. Kahane, who was friendly with James Joyce and Eugene Jolas, must have realised that during the dark days of the 1930s Great Depression capital could be made from providing 'cellophane-wrapped offerings essential reading for the broad-minded and up-to-date Anglo-Saxon visitor to Paris'.[14]

The contribution to modernism of publishers such as the Obelisk Press represents a challenge to conventional notions of morality and censorship, and publications provided a space in which individuals could find a public outlet for the expression of their search for personal freedom.

The Book as Object

It may be argued that the objects that a culture produces reveal the nature of that culture. What then can we deduce from the books and magazines that were produced by modernist culture? Take, for example, James Joyce's *Ulysses* (1922), one of the most iconic modernist texts. Joyce was famously in despair that no one would publish his book after extracts were printed in the *Little Review*, which was then successfully prosecuted for obscenity in 1921, meaning that the book was banned from publication in the United States. The case was one of those celebrated occasions in the history of modernism when literature is brought before the public in such a manner that it is required to justify itself. Richard Ellmann's account of the trial gives an indication of the non-literary scrutiny that was applied to *Ulysses*. As a result of the publicity that was created by the trial, the book itself became a battle ground for the acceptance of modernist methods. Ellmann states that John Quinn, the New York lawyer representing the defendants:

> summed up with a more wily than brilliant speech: the book was futurist and experimental, not – he was too quick to concede – wholly successful; in effect disgusting rather than lascivious, revolting rather than contaminating.[15]

Quinn, it should be noted, was a patron and collector of modernist manuscripts, so had an awareness and sensitivity to the notion of the unique value of printed matter. Perhaps, a little unwittingly, this defence of Joyce's text may have contributed to the formation of the idea that modernist texts were conducted as experiments – and that, as such, they may not have been fully achieved. The subsequent history of the publication of *Ulysses* indicates a tendency for the work to have become regarded as a special case – written over a seven-year period in three different cities, it had survived bowdlerisation, legal action, bitter controversy and persistent misunderstanding. When Sylvia Beach, an expatriate American living in Paris, asked Joyce whether he would be willing to let her publish the book from her shop, Shakespeare and Company, he readily agreed. Joyce continued to work on the novel almost right up to the publication date, which – as Ellmann points out – was chosen for 'talismatic purposes', being his fortieth birthday, 2 February 1922.[16] To comply with this specification the printer in Dijon arranged for two advance copies to be personally delivered to Sylvia Beach by the engineer on the Dijon–Paris express train. The first edition quickly sold out and the story of later editions is confused, but this history contributed to the status of the modernist text as an item that had its own distinct individuality.

Perhaps the most striking example of a modernist text that is an object is Blaise Cendrars's long poem *The Prose of the Trans-Siberian and of the Little Jehanne of France* (*La prose du Transsibérien et de la Petite Jehanne de France*, 1913). A collaboration between Cendrars (Frédéric Sauser, 1887–1961) and the artist Sonia Delaunay, the work comprises four sheets of paper pasted together and folded into forty-two separate panels. The book was designed as a two metre high object and the whole edition (planned to be 150 copies) if placed end to end would have been as high as the Eiffel Tower, which was regarded as a symbol of modernity. Although only about sixty copies were printed, this is thought to be the first attempt to produce a book based on abstract art. The publication was printed by Cendrars's own private press, the Éditions des Hommes Nouveaux (New Man Editions), which had already printed his *Easter in New York* (*Les Pâques à New-York*, 1912). The name of the press was adopted as Cendrars was seeking the revitalisation of culture which he believed could only come from 'Newness, the New Men' that could provide 'a new impetus and reform

225

whole societies'.[17] These men would be found among those working with the new technology of the time, aircraft and automobiles, and spending their leisure time playing with slot machines. The utility discovered in the production of the new would provide the foundations for the society of the future, or so Cendrars believed. It might seem a contradiction that this utility could be associated with the production of a text that was both an object of beauty and an unwieldy limited edition text. Perhaps the resolution was to be found in the fact that the edition would equal the height of the Eiffel Tower. More pertinently, the text was designed to baffle the bourgeois – and in this respect the alignment with the utility of modern technology was seen to be part of an attack on perceived standards of taste and the book as mass-produced commercial product. Cendrars regarded himself as an international citizen (it should be noted that the cosmopolitanism of the modernist generation was a key feature of their cultural outlook), and led an underground existence, nomadically moving from country to country, and scorning life. His attitude was summed up by his statement in the novel *Moravagine* (1926) that:

> There's no truth. There's only action, action obeying a million different impulses, ephemeral action, action subjected to every possible and imaginable contingency and contradiction, Life. Life is crime, theft, jealousy, hunger, lies, disgust, stupidity, sickness, volcanic eruptions, earthquakes, piles of corpses. (p. 182)

Significantly, he suggests that the contemplation of life, the classification of data, the production of books in which human thought is brought to bear on diverse subjects is a thing of the past, an attempt to impose order on chaos. The text is therefore considered with ironic detachment, the book is considered to belong to a past civilisation. Of course, it should be pointed out that Cendrars went on to write many books, including some novels, and was motivated by a need to make money.

Modernism and the Marketplace

In the 1980s studies began to emerge that reflected the preoccupations of a decade that saw increased focus on business methods and a reliance on the concept of market forces to justify or condemn literary texts. This prompted a number of academics to consider historical art and culture in the same light. In part this was a continuation of the materialist studies that Marxist critics had utilised to investigate literary production. As Marxists were concerned with literary texts as material products, it was necessary to describe them in relation to the historical conditions that controlled their production and consumption. The economic 'base' was important in relation to the surrounding 'superstructure' or collection of beliefs, politics, laws and arts that existed in the particular culture. Among the early studies to appear in the 1980s was Michael Anesko's *Friction with the Market: Henry James and the Profession of Authorship* (1987), which challenged the notion that James was the image of the writer in the Ivory Tower, not subject to the demands of the marketplace. In contrast, Anesko demonstrated that James was often acutely aware of crude economic realities. John Carlos Rowe and David McWhirter's *Henry James's 'New York Edition': The Construction of Authorship* (1996), an edited collection of essays, demonstrated the significance of the New York Edition in positioning James's status in literary culture, and developed the concept of the modernist writer as being engaged in a process of self-monumentalisation which has been a feature of recent criticism. James's Prefaces for the New York Edition provided one of the most influential examples of modernist criticism – they were later reprinted separately in 1934 as *The Art of the Novel*. In addition, photographic frontispieces by Alvin Langdon Coburn were strategically added, indicating a departure from the nineteenth century use of illustration by utilising the still new and controversial medium of photography. In 1996 Ian Willison, Warwick Gould and Warren Chernaik edited a volume of essays on Modernist Writers and the Marketplace. This book looked at a range of ways in which modernist writers engaged with market forces.

Modernist Magazines

It has long been understood that magazines provided an important platform for modernist writers, often allowing them to get published in the first place. Those magazines usually referred to as 'little magazines' were instrumental in providing a platform for the ideas that came to constitute literary and artistic modernism. Apart from publishing many of the major literary figures of the modernist era (including James Joyce, Ezra Pound, Marianne Moore, Ernest Hemingway, Hart Crane, Wyndham Lewis and William Carlos Williams) before they were acceptable to mainstream publishers, they have also been fundamental to the genesis, growth and dissemination of literary and artistic movements from Symbolism, Futurism, Imagism, Expressionism and Surrealism through to Beat literature and concrete poetry.* 'Little magazines' were usually considered to be those that published creative work in literature and the other arts, with little or no regard for commercial gain. Therefore, they often provided an outlet for work that might be seen as exploring or pushing at the boundaries of its given medium or what may be acceptable. In many cases such work may have beeen regarded as innovative or simply too unusual for more mainstream or commercially orientated journals. Little magazines tended to publish a wide variety of different material.

To understand these phenomena it is necessary to give attention to the economic and intellectual conditions that governed the circumstances that gave rise to the production of modernist magazines. The influence of the editors also needs to be explored, along with the relationship between the arts and contemporary developments in philosophy and politics. Magazines offered editors and movements, or coterie groups, the opportunity to develop self definitions through

---

* The Beat generation emerged in New York in the 1950s and expressed dissatisfaction with mainstream culture. This was manifested in experimentation with mystical religious experience, sexuality and drugs. The most significant literature produced by the Beats were Allen Ginsberg's *Howl* (1956), William Burrough's *Naked Lunch* (1959) and Jack Kerouac's *On the Road* (1957). Concrete poetry developed in Brazil in the 1950s and was an attempt to find expression through the visual aspect of a poem.

editorials and manifestos; they also offered up the possibility of the combination of literary and visual interest (word and image). The study of the conditions of production (patronage, printers, small press involvement and advertising) helps our understanding of the crucial networks that underpinned modernist literary activity. The study of modernist periodicals offers the chance to shed new light on the culture of modernism. There have, of course, been other attempts to chart what is a varied and extensive topic.

Early interest in little magazines tended to be fuelled by an interest in the authors themselves. Magazines were the place where many of the most significant works of modernism first appeared. Eliot's *The Waste Land* (1922) in the American *Dial* and the *Criterion*; Joyce's *A Portrait of the Artist as a Young Man* (1916) in the *Egoist*; fragments of *Ulysses* and *Finnegans Wake* in the *Little Review* and *Transition* respectively; Wyndham Lewis's short stories and *Tarr* (1918) in the *English Review* and the *Egoist* respectively; and the early poems by W. H. Auden (1907–73) all made their debuts in periodicals. Magazines that featured work by these and other writers, such as D. G. Rossetti, Ernest Hemingway and Dylan Thomas, quickly assumed an almost mythic status in the history of modernism. As the reputations of the writers increased so the value for collectors of these magazines increased. During the 1930s it became apparent that little magazines were important in the culture of modernism. Sometimes this awareness was apparent and became self-conscious among editors and contributors themselves. For example, writing in *Intermountain Review* in 1937, the American writer Sherwood Anderson wrote a leading article on 'Little Magazines', in which he stressed the relationship between the magazine and the emerging new spirit in literature breaking through the ice of habitual modes of thought in the Middle West in the early years of the twentieth century. This he particularly associated with Margaret Anderson, who edited the *Little Review* from Chicago. For Anderson, the magazine was a medium by which 'eager young men' (he might have added women, too) were able to keep in touch with the new.[18] The new included, among poets, Carl Sandburg, Vachel Lindsay, Edgar Lee Masters and William Carlos Williams. The new theatre was represented by Eugene O'Neill. In prose fiction the new approach included the acceptance of Theodore Dreiser's *Sister Carrie*, which had been published in 1900 but did not receive general recognition until after 1910.* The point about little magazines, Anderson felt, was seen to be the fact that they were not economically self-sustaining in the culture of their time; but were, nonetheless, kept running, by individuals or groups of individuals, who were prepared in a spirit of comradeship to keep open the opportunities for aspiring writers.

Serious academic interest in little magazines can be traced back to the work of Frederick J. Hoffmann in the 1940s. This resulted in the publication of Frederick J. Hoffmann, Charles Allen and Carolyn F. Ulrich, *The Little Magazine: A History and a Bibliography* (revised 1947), which remains one of the standard bibliographies of this fascinating subject. However, it was not until the 1960s that this interest began to result in a widespread evaluation of the phenomenon. Malcolm Bradbury wrote a series of articles on individual magazines for *The London Magazine*, the piece on *The Calendar of Modern Letters* (1961) being particularly notable. Then, in 1964, Cyril Connolly wrote an article on little magazines for *Art and Literature*. This was to celebrate fifty years of little magazines, although in fact the article includes magazines that went back into the nineteenth century, such as *The Yellow Book* and *The Savoy*. Indeed, Connolly states that the first of what we would now call modernist magazines was Ford Madox Ford's *English Review*, which was first published in December 1908. Another problematic definition was the use of the term 'little magazine'. Connolly's essay includes magazines which challenge the meaning of the term – for example, *Life and Letters* was a commercially backed periodical. Some of this confusion continues to this day, with avariety of terms adopted to indicate what is clearly meant to define

---

* *Sister Carrie* was considered to be too shocking for American audiences when it was first published. Part of this reputation was a result of a dispute between the publisher, Doubleday, and the author. The novel had been rejected by Harper's publishing house, but was accepted by the new company of Doubleday at the novelist Frank Norris's suggestion. However, they later tried to get out of their agreement after the publisher's wife apparently considered it too sordid. As a result it was issued to fulfil the contractual agreement, but not promoted in any way.

a particular type of periodical that is likely to offer the opportunity for printing of work that would not find a place in more commercially run magazines.

A number of reprints of entire runs of magazines published by Frank Cass and Kraus Reprint began to appear in the late 1960s; these remain an important resource. The assumption behind these publishing activities was the aura that had begun to attach to modernist 'little magazines', and should probably be seen in the context of the counter-cultural perspectives of the time.* The 1970s saw attempts to provide bibliographic records to supplement the information that had become available in the previous decade. Notable among these publications were J. R. Tye's *Periodicals of the Nineties: A Checklist of Literary Periodicals published in the British Isles at Longer than Fortnightly Intervals, 1890–1900* (1974) and Marion Sader's *Comprehensive Index to English-language Little Magazines, 1890–1970* (1976). These provided invaluable information on a range of periodicals, but were somewhat limited by a perhaps necessarily restricted scope. There was an awareness of the importance of magazines, but sometimes the decisions about which to include and what to leave out seemed arbitrary. In America it was felt necessary to update Hoffmann's earlier work, as well as to stress the continuity between the magazines of the pre-World War Two period with the contemporary scene. The result was the monumental *The Little Magazine in America: A Modern Documentary History* (1978), edited by Elliott Anderson and Mary Kinzie. This originally appeared as part of *TriQuarterly Magazine*. In addition to bibliographic data the volume contained many articles by people who had been involved in the publication of little magazines. In 1979, Francis Mulhern produced his still useful study, *The Moment of 'Scrutiny'*. While the 1980s did not see a significant interest in modernist magazines, Alvin Sullivan's *British Literary Magazines: The Victorian and Edwardian Age, 1837–1913* (1984), and *British Literary Magazines: The Modern Age, 1914–1984*

---

* The 1960s saw the development of a social revolution that has been labelled a counter-culture (a term that originated in sociology). Beginning with the Beats it was marked by a rejection of the cultural values of the 1940s and 1950s by a younger generation.

(1986), attempted to provide 'biographies' for a wide range of periodicals; and these volumes continue to provide a useful starting point for scholars and general readers.

New Responses and Resources

The recent resurgence of interest in modernist periodicals has been an off-shoot of the development of modernist studies within academia. It has been increasingly understood that modernism's diversity has been restricted by narrowly constructed maps of modernism. Books such as Peter Nicholls's *Modernisms* (1995) have pointed the way to a more inclusive interpretation of the period of modernism. This has coincided with the rise in research into social groupings which tended be marginalised in the early histories, and with the wider liberation of feminist and gay viewpoints. Lawrence Rainey's *Institutions of Modernism: Literary Elites & Public Culture* (1998), shifted attention away from the key texts, and examined the processes by which modernism was instituted into cultural discourse by examining where modernism was produced and how it was transmitted.

In 1995 Brown University began a project to make available through technology periodical literature that charted the rise of modernism. This project still continues at the time of writing and is known as the Modernist Journals Project (MJP). A decision was made by the MJP to limit the period to between 1890 and 1922. This was done for reasons of the possible difficulty of copyright issues in material published after 1922. Also it was understood that even by limiting the size of the project to modernist texts in English, the number of publications produced in the period was considerable. Being generally held to signal the moment when modernism had sufficiently consolidated its position within the framework of contemporary literature, 1922 offered a convenient date. This in itself was marked by the publication of Joyce's *Ulysses*, Eliot's *The Waste Land* and Woolf's *Jacob's Room* in that year. It was also the year in which Eliot's *Criterion* was launched. The late 1990s also saw the setting up of Nottingham Trent University's Little

Magazines Project, which provides on-line indexes and bibliographic details relating to post-1945 magazines.

In recent years a number of studies have started to appear, reflecting the growing academic interest in modernist periodicals. Of particular significance have been: Jayne E. Marek's *Women Editing Modernism: 'Little' Magazines and Literary History* (1995), Mark S. Morrisson's *The Public Face of Modernism: Little Magazines, Audiences, and Reception 1905–1920* (2001), Adam McKible's *The Space and Place of Modernism: The Russian Revolution, Little Magazines and New York* (2002), Jason Harding's *'The Criterion': Cultural Politics and Periodical Networks in Interwar Britain* (2002), Suzanne W. Churchill's *The Little Magazine: 'Others' and the Renovation of Modern American Poetry* (2006), David Miller and Richard Price (eds), *British Poetry Magazines 1914–2000: A History and Bibliography of 'Little Magazines'* (2006), and Suzanne W. Churchill and Adam McKible (eds), *Little Magazines and Modernism* (2007). It will be immediately apparent from such a list that magazines have been seen as key indicators of the history of modernism.

Building upon these activities the AHRC-funded Modernist Magazines Project was devised to enable scholars to gain an even more extensive knowledge of the periodicals of the modernist period. The project's website will contain indexes for a wide range of magazines. These will be supplemented by additional information, such as publication details, including sizes and prices, so that comparative analyses can be undertaken. The physical impact of a magazine is something which the project is keen to investigate, so the examination of covers and illustrations plays an important part in developing an understanding of how magazines are situated in the cultural context. One of the advantages of a web-based system is the ability to provide different types of search of the database. This means that a search can be made which is concerned with finding the various publications of a single author, as well as exploring the history of a particular magazine. This enables the investigation of the development of a periodical, while providing cross references to other publications, so that the often complex interrelationships between individuals, groups and the work that they produce can be mapped. The more extensive territory covered in the project's scope allows for references to follow not just through transatlantic publications but also into continental Europe. Magazines often provided the foothold by which international cross-fertilisation was made possible. It has long been seen that modernism was an international movement; with the appearance of details relating to the periodical culture across national boundaries, it should be possible to trace the way in which such internationalism worked. The chronology is as important as the geography, and the database will allow an overview of the way the history of modernism is more about continuity and engagement through a sequence of networks, than a single line of development through one or two outlets. It is hoped that as the project develops more sophisticated statistical analysis will be available.

The Oxford Critical and Cultural History of Modernist Magazines: Vol. 1, Britain and Ireland 1880–1955 (2009), edited by Peter Brooker and Andrew Thacker, is indicative of the current wave of research into modernist periodicals. Some of these are treated individually, but many are considered in relation to clusters of similarity of theme, content or contributors. These essays have been commissioned from internationally recognised experts on modernism and periodical literature. The result will be a comprehensive study of modernism and the magazines in which it found expression, debate and publicity. Previous studies have tended to ignore regional and migrant voices. While *Wales* and some of the Irish magazines that Yeats contributed to have received some attention, magazines such as *Welsh Review*, *The Dublin Magazine*, *The Bell* and the *Modern Scot* have tended to be marginalised. Sometimes this marginalisation has been ignored because these magazines do not easily conform to the label of little magazine. These marginal areas have been opened up in the series of essays published in *The Oxford Critical and Cultural History of Modernist Magazines: Volume I, Britain and Ireland 1880–1955* (2009), to reveal the diversity of debate in the print culture of the time. In one further respect the project highlights an area that has hitherto been unacknowledged. This is the area of commerce and the modernist periodical, in particular the relation of the magazine to advertising. For example, Ford Madox Ford noted, in his capacity as the editor of the *Transatlantic Review*, that the first number of Thackeray's magazine *Cornhill* – along with the serialisation of Trollope's *Framley Parsonage* – printed an advert for 'Ford's Eureka Shirts'. Ford suggested that the inclusion of advertising was 'a milestone in the history of civilization'. Alongside an illustration of 'Ford's Jackets' (printed in facsimile in the *Transatlantic Review*), Ford made the observation that this promotion of his namesake's jackets marked the point when advertising began to encroach on the experience of life to such an extent that Literature itself was compromised.[19] It has been assumed that modernist magazines reacted to the threat of such a compromise by eschewing the commercial opportunities provided by magazine space. This assumption was supported by the fact that advertising pages were sometimes removed from reprint versions of magazines. The modernist magazines project has attempted to engage with this topic by revealing the extent to which advertising formed part of the cultural experience of modernist periodicals.

The project has also been involved in a number of conferences in Britain, America and Europe. In particular, two conferences directly related to the project's concerns have been organised. The first of these, entitled 'The Modernist Atlantic', was held at De Montfort University in Leicester in July 2007. The second, 'Modernism, Cultural Exchange and Transnationality', was hosted by the University of Sussex in Brighton in July 2009. These conferences have offered scholars the chance to engage with emergent ideas developing from the detailed study of a range of modernist magazines, and have been related to the investigation of the cultural role played by the periodical in a dynamic and volatile period.

It is perhaps fitting to conclude with a reference to the Pulitzer Prize-winning* play *The Time of Your Life* (1939) by the Armenian American William Saroyan (1908–81). One of the characters, McCarthy, expresses the individualism that lies behind modernist print culture. He makes the observation that everyone should have the chance to see himself in print.[20] Modernist print culture in the form of little magazines, small

---

* The Pulitzer Prize is awarded annually for outstanding contributions to journalism, literature or music in the United States. It was first awarded in 1917.

presses and pamphlets enabled a large number of individuals to see their work in print. Saroyan was one of these, his early stories appearing in *Story*, a magazine devoted to short fiction, in 1934. The plurality of modernist culture allowed for opportunities for new writers, not just from the avant-garde but reflecting a widely divergent range of perspectives. However, the notion of an anti-conventional bohemia was bound up with this opening up of opportunities and the desire to find publication in a magazine was seen to be at 'the forefront of literary and artistic progress'.[21] Arthur Ransome, in *Bohemia in London* (1907), made it clear how magazine culture was a statement of lifestyle, describing how 'by its payments for my young essays and exuberantly juvenile reviews, [the little newspaper] made it possible for me to adventure by myself and take my first lodging in Chelsea.[22] The modern artist emerging out of the Victorian twilight into the harsh sunlight of contemporary urban modernity adopted a conspicuous bohemianism that was a reaction to commercial and bourgeois society as well as being conditioned by it. As such the dynamic of modernist print culture reflected the tendency of self-creation that was facilitated by the commercial opening up of the book trade and the variety of printed matter being both produced and consumed.

Therefore, the modes of modernist publication reflected this complex need for the unique printed product that announced its individuality and disregard for convention, while negotiating with economic necessity. Key accounts of modernism and publishing can be found by Peter D. McDonald, 'Modernist Publishing: "Nomads and Mapmakers"', in David Bradshaw (ed.), *A Concise Companion to Modernism* (2003) and by Mark S. Morrisson, 'Modernist Publishing', in David Bradshaw and Kevin Dettmar (eds), *A Companion to Modernist Literature and Culture* (2006). Modernist invention, experimentation and publication were bound up together in the melting pot of cultural dislocation that characterised a moment of shifting values. An examination of modernist print culture tells us much about the nature of modernism itself, and the dynamic engagement between culture and society in the early twentieth century.

Notes

1 Mark S. Morrisson, *The Public Face of Modernism: Little Magazines, Audiences, and Reception, 1905–1920* (Madison: University of Wisconsin Press, 2001), p. 3.

2 See Andreas Huyssen, *After the Great Divide: Modernism, Mass Culture, Postmodernism* (Bloomington: Indiana University Press, 1986). See also John Carey's denunciation of modernism's apparent antipathy towards mass consumer culture in his *The Intellectual and the Masses: Pride and Prejudice Among the Literary Intelligentsia, 1880–1939* (London: Faber, 1992).

3 Mark S. Morrisson, *The Public Face of Modernism*, pp. 7–10.

4 Quoted in Paul Delaney, 'Book Design – A nineteenth-century revival', *The Connoisseur*, 198:798 (August, 1978), p. 283.

5 Joy Grant, *Harold Monro & the Poetry Bookshop* (London: Routledge, 1967), p. 108.

6 Dominic Hibberd, *Harold Monro: Poet of the New Age* (Basingstoke: Palgrave, 2001), p. 205.

7 J. H. Willis, *Leonard and Virginia Woolf as Publishers: The Hogarth Press 1917–1941* (Charlottesville: University of Virginia Press, 1992), p. 400.

8 See Jessica Svendsen, 'Hogarth Press', The Modernism Lab at Yale University, http://modernism.research.yale.edu./wiki/index.php/Hogarth_Press.

9 See John Lehmann, *In My Own Time: Memoirs of a Literary Life* (Boston. MA: Little, Brown and Co., 1969) and *Thrown to the Woolfs: Leonard and Virginia Woolf and the Hogarth Press* (London: Weidenfeld and Nicolson, 1978).

10 The interested reader might also consult Helen Southworth, '"Outside the magical (and tyrannical) triangle of London-Oxford-Cambridge": John Hampson, the Woolfs and the Hogarth Press', Anna Burrells, Steven Ellis, Deborah Parsons and Catherine Simpson (eds), *Woolfian Boundaries: Selected Papers from the Sixteenth Annual Woolf Conference* (Clemson: Clemson University Press: 2007).

11 See James G. Nelson, *Publisher to the Decadents: Leonard Smithers in the Careers of Beardsley, Wilde and Dowson* (University Park: Pennsylvania State University Press, 2000).

12   See Neil Pearson, *Obelisk: A History of Jack Kahane and the Obelisk Press* (Liverpool: University of Liverpool Press, 2007).

13   George Orwell, 'Inside the Whale', *Inside the Whale and Other Essays* (Harmondsworth: Penguin, 1982), p. 49.

14   Jeremy Lewis, *Cyril Connolly: A Life* (London: Jonathan Cape, 1997), p. 262.

15   Richard Ellmann, '*Ulysses*: A Short History', in James Joyce, *Ulysses* (Harmondsworth: Penguin, 1982), pp. 712–13.

16   Ibid., p. 714.

17   Blaise Cendrars, *Moravagine* (Harmondsworth: Penguin, 1979), pp. 173–4.

18   Sherwood Anderson, 'Little Magazines', *Intermountain Review*, 2:2 (Fall, 1937), unpaged.

19   Ford Madox Ford, 'Communications', *Transatlantic Review*, 1:5 (May, 1924), p. 360.

20   William Saroyan, *Three Plays* (New York: Harcourt, Brace & Co., 1940), pp. 88–9.

21   Arthur Ransome, *Bohemia in London* (London: Chapman & Hall, 1907), p. 182.

22   Ibid., p. 171.

Literature and War

One of the most significant developments in modernist studies in recent years has been the dialogue between modernism and modernity. There has been a tendency to enlarge the territory occupied by the term modernism to cover all manifestations of the reaction against Victorianism. The subject of the First World War provides an excellent example of the interaction between culture and modernity, and highlights some of the key debates.

Vorticism and Futurism: Modern Art and Modern War

Even before the First World War began in 1914, Modernist writers had begun to express themselves in terms of aggressive violence. Many of the developing ideas about art and literature in the years after 1910 embraced the notion that the Victorian era had extended into the twentieth century and needed to be brought to a brutal end. Wyndham Lewis (1882–1957), a painter and writer, expressed this attitude in bold manifestos written in aggressive language and typography in the first number of his important modernist magazine *Blast*, which appeared in the summer of 1914.

The origins for this attitude can be traced back to the emergence of the avant-garde movement called Futurism. This had begun in Italy, where it was a response to the late influence of mass industrialisation on what had been a traditional and rural economy until the late nineteenth century. Young Italian artists sought to free themselves from the past by embracing the machine in its dynamism as an ideal of beauty. Filippo Marinetti (1876–1944), a poet and self-publicist who would later befriend the Italian dictator Mussolini, was the leader of this movement, and he produced a manifesto which proclaimed his aesthetic of mechanical energy. While in Paris, he published in the French newspaper *Le Figaro*, dated 20 February 1909, an announcement which proclaimed 'a new beauty … a roaring motorcar, which runs like a machine-gun … . We wish to glorify war'. These and other statements expressed a desire to break with the past and delight in the immediate present, glorifying the new technology of the day, such as the aeroplane and the motor car, which liberated man from traditional modes of living. War for Marinetti was to be the violent and necessary test of a people's strength, 'the world's only hygiene'.[1] Further Futurist manifestos followed in 1910, and a Futurist Exhibition was held in Paris in 1912, where it caused a great scandal and outraged the prevailing bourgeoisie with challenging notions of art, before going on to be seen in London and Berlin. Marinetti became a celebrity and was invited to talk about his theories and to recite his poetry all around Europe.

Marinetti visited London several times, and while his Futurist ideas attracted a great amount of interest, and influenced to some extent the work of Wyndham Lewis, Ezra Pound (1885–1972) and D. H. Lawrence (1885–1930), he did not acquire disciples among English writers. Instead, Lewis and Pound founded an Anglo-Saxon rival to the continental Futurism, called Vorticism, which was an energetic avant-garde movement that both developed Marinetti's ideas and also reacted against them. Vorticism, like Futurism, was simultaneously a literary and an art movement, and adopted Futurist-style polemics which were expressed in the magazine *Blast*. The blasting was aimed at Victorian and Edwardian culture, and soon found a bitter counterpart in the outbreak of what was called The Great War on 4 August 1914. Lewis's angular and geometric designs, 'Plan of War' and 'Slow Attack', appeared in *Blast* number 1, demonstrating how prophetically the image of war had entered into the psychology of the period. When the second number of *Blast* came out in 1915 it was a 'War Number', announcing the death of the French sculptor and Vorticist, Henri Gaudier-Brzeska at Neuville St Vaast on 5 June 1915. Gaudier-Brzeska's response to the war was printed in this issue, alarmingly declaring: 'This war is a great remedy, in the individual it kills arrogance, self-esteem, pride. It takes away from the masses numbers upon numbers of unimportant units, whose economic activities become noxious as the recent trade crises have shown us.' This number also printed the first of T. S. Eliot's (1888–1965) poems to be published in England.

War Poetry and Early Responses to Conflict

Today the War is easily associated in the mind with its poets, but at the time this was quite a new thing. 'The very phrase *War Poet*,' wrote Osbert Sitwell (1892–1969),* in *Noble Essences* (1950):

> indicates a strange twentieth century phenomenon, the attempt to combine two incompatibles. There had been no War Poets in the Peninsular, Crimean or Boer wars. But war had suddenly become transformed by the effort of scientist and mechanician into something so infernal, so inhuman, that it was recognised that only their natural enemy, the poet, could pierce through the armour of horror ... to the pity at the human core.[2]

There was another reason for the phenomenon: the First World War was the first war in which the effects were felt by the whole of society, through conscription, the advent of widespread propaganda, the German blockade of English ports and air raids by Zeppelins. This was total war that affected the civilian population and a whole generation of young men was sucked into battle. The only ones who avoided

---

* Sitwell wrote war poetry himself, which was published in the modernist anthology edited by his sister Edith Sitwell, *Wheels*, from 1916 to 1921.

the fighting were those who were medically unfit, such as the author Aldous Huxley.

Osbert Sitwell's comment about war poetry reflects the attitudes that had developed by the end of the war, once the brutality and pointlessness of the conflict had become clear. In August 1914 the reality of modern mechanised warfare was but dimly understood, and it was still possible for the verse occasioned by the war to be innocently patriotic and romantic. Peace in Europe had existed since the end of the Franco-Prussian War in 1871, and it was difficult for either readers or writers to comprehend what the actual experience of war would be like. Rupert Brooke (1887–1915) has become the poet most associated in England with this attitude to the war. He was not alone: in France Charles Péguy (1873–1914), a socialist and nationalist, who had been warning his countrymen of the German menace since 1905, responded to the outbreak of war with the statement, 'Happy are they who died in a just war'.[3] He died in one of the first engagements, on the eve of the battle of the Marne in 1914. Others, like Stefan George (1868–1933) in Germany, regarded the conflict in terms of spiritual regeneration. He saw German youth as corrupted by materialism and hoped for a sort of Holy War that would purge society of its false values. Materialism was also the enemy for Brooke, who similarly longed to see the emergence of a new society from the wreckage of the European conflict.* Both these writers had homosexual or bisexual tendencies and this can be interpreted as contributing to their desire to see changes in society that would allow for greater individual freedom. Brooke's view of the war as 'swimmers into cleanness leaping' reflects this attitude.[4] It should be noted that recent developments in gender studies have enabled greater exploration of the politics of sexuality, and the uncovering of details that earlier critics were reticent to discuss openly. Another gay poet, one of the most famous of the British war poets, was Wilfred Owen (1893–1918), who began as a Keats-inspired romantic, and who had been strongly influenced by his mother's evangelical Anglicanism – he

---

* The term 'materialism' used in this context refers to the perceived decline in spiritual values in the cultures of the major Western democracies during the latter part of the nineteenth century, and their replacement with materialism – the result of the triumph of scientific rationalism.

had served as the lay assistant to a vicar. Before he had encountered actual experience of trench warfare he wrote of 'the need / Of sowings for new Spring, and blood for seed' ('1914' (1914), l. 14).

Rupert Brooke's optimism that the war would be short was shared by many of his generation. There was a widespread opinion that a modern war could not last long, and its effects were expected to be, as we have seen, to purge Western civilisation of its materialism. These beliefs were modern in character and represented the general dissatisfaction with the nineteenth century inheritance. Such dissatisfaction was symptomatic of the modern sensibility, but did not necessarily find expression in stylistically modern ways. Brooke remained essentially a traditional poet. His posthumous fame largely rested on the fact that he had found expression for the thoughts and feelings of the ordinary officer-class recruit. His *1914, Five Sonnets* was printed in 1915 and sold twenty thousand copies. Brooke became an ideal representative of heroic sacrifice; he died in April 1915 from septicaemia on a hospital ship in the Aegean Sea while on route to Gallipoli. He never saw action at the front and remained innocent of the reality of war.

Of the continental poets caught up in the war, some took it as their subject, others, preoccupied by the aesthetic demands of their own conception of poetry, preserved the 'purity' of their art by retreating into silence or writing on other themes. This story is, then, rather the story of individuals than of mass response to the war. However, the writings of Vladimir Mayakovsky (1893–1930) in Russia, condemning the 'capitalist' war, were part of a movement that found a political solution in the Russian Revolution of 1917. It is important to keep an understanding of what was happening in other countries, as modernism transcended national boundaries – rather than being absorbed into the national culture – and much recent critical debate has used the American social critic Randolph Bourne's (1886–1918) concept of transnationalism as a means of investigating this phenomenon.* The rebirth of society, which the poets and artists of different nations had

---

* Randolph Bourne's essay 'Trans-National America' (1917) argues for cultural pluralism. See Randolph Bourne (1886–1918), *War and the Intellectuals: Essays, 1915–1919* (New York: Harper & Row, 1964).

been seeking, seemed to have been successfully achieved by revolution in Russia.

In France, the avant-garde poet Guillaume Apollinaire (1880–1918) served in the artillery and the infantry (he was born in Rome, the illegitimate son of a Polish noble woman, and did not win French nationality until he had served from December 1914 until March 1916). He reported his experiences with a frank acceptance of the contradictory nature of military service. The war was in a sense just another facet of twentieth century modernity, and Apollinaire wrote about the war, as he wrote about everything else, simply because it happened to him. Too humane to glorify it; too honest to suppress its unexpected, casual moments of strange beauty, Apollinaire was able to achieve a remarkable degree of objectivity in his reporting on the experience of war. He managed to remain apart, avoiding the moral engagement adopted by Wilfred Owen. He had already, before the war, been part of the Parisian avant-garde, championing the work of the painters Picasso, Braque, Matisse, Vlaminck and Derain. A wound to the head caused by a shell fragment piercing his helmet ended his war service on 17 March 1916, just days after finally receiving his French citizenship. Apollinaire lived out the war in Paris recovering from his wounds. He became the inspiration for the 'little magazines'* *Sic* and *Nord-Sud*, and of young French poets serving in the army – poets such as André Breton, Paul Eluard and Louis Aragon, who would later found the Surrealist movement. It was for his techniques, his will to experiment with forms, and his modern sensibility that these writers looked to him for leadership, rather than his attitude to the war. His calligrams were poems that took the shape of the subject of the poem, so that, for instance, the 'Calligram for Madeleine (15 May 1915)', with its star shape, reflects the sudden exploding of a shell and the description of the ironic appearance of this jewel in the sky. These poems made use of typography and the appearance and spacing of the poem on the page. One of the most celebrated is in the shape of the Eiffel Tower. Apollinaire himself wrote that, 'As for the calligrams, they are an

* See Part Four: 'Modernist Print Culture'.

idealization of vers-libre poetry and of typographical precision at a time when typography is brilliantly ending its career, at the dawn of new methods of reproduction, the cinema and the gramophone'.[5] In this sense their concerns, and his, were aesthetic. Apollinaire died of Spanish flu on 9 November 1918, and his funeral coincided with the celebrations marking the end of the war.

In the Twentieth Century Fashion

T. S. Eliot once wrote that 'the only good poem I have met with on the subject of the war' was Ford Madox Ford's 'In October 1914 (Antwerp)' (1915).[6] Ford was already established as a prolific novelist, critic, editor and poet, before the war. His *Collected Poems* had appeared in 1913. It is worth quoting some lines from 'Antwerp' (ll. 1–8), from a section entitled 'Gloom!':

> An October like November;
> August a hundred thousand hours,
> And all September,
> A hundred thousand, dragging sunlit days,
> And half October like a thousand years ...
> And doom!
> That then was Antwerp

It is well to remember that during the early years of the war the literary response to the conflict came not from ordinary soldiers at the front, but from established writers. This poem was originally published as a pamphlet by the Poetry Bookshop, with a cover design by Wyndham Lewis, in January 1915. It should be noted then that here was an example of the collaboration of the artist and the writer; indeed between vorticist painter and imagist poet.* Ford later claimed that the poem

---

* See Part Three: 'Modernist Poetry – French Origins, English Settings' for more on Vorticism and Imagism.

had been used by the Ministry of Propaganda to help sustain the war effort. If Ford did not mean the poem to be used propaganda, then the text achieved a different interpretation in the hands of the government officials entrusted with maintaining morale and purpose. The reading of the lines that follow those already quoted switch the attention to the ordinary Belgians who opposed the German advance in 1914:

> In the name of God,
> How could they do it?
> Those souls that usually dived
> Into the dirty caverns of mines;
> Who usually hived
> In whitened hovels; under ragged poplars;
> Who dragged muddy shovels, over the grassy mud,
> Lumbering to work over the greasy sods …
> Those men there, with the appearances of clods
> Were the bravest men that a usually listless priest of God
> Ever shrived (ll. 9–19)

This, therefore, might be seen as an instance where the reader-response approach to literary texts might prove useful. Stanley Fish (b. 1938), the American critic who is particularly associated with reader-response theory, places the emphasis on what a text does rather than what it means. His point of view is that the meaning of a text is determined by what is termed the interpretative community of which the author is also part, so that it is necessary to know something of the community outside the text. This is a branch of cultural criticism because the linguistic resources of the language are shaped by the cultural conditions. In relation to Ford's poem, we may see that the matter can be complicated by the fact that Ford was a man of complex cultural construction, having experience of pre-war Germany through his father and his relations. It is also worth bearing in mind in this context that the novel *The Good Soldier* (1915), which is considered Ford's most accomplished piece of writing, his Great Auk's egg – a final offering to posterity before the creator's extinction – as he liked to joke, was the next work to be published. Ford intended the novel to be called 'The Saddest Story', the name under which the opening section was printed in *Blast* in 1914, but the publisher preferred the title by which the novel is now known. The overt reference to war suggests that the reading public were likely to buy works that, however obliquely, were up-to-date, as long as they were not too depressing. *The Good Soldier* was begun before the war began, and marks a development in the history of modernism. The narrative is rooted in the social fabric of Edwardian England, although significantly the narrative voice is American. It concerns the entangled interactions between two couples, and the subtle revelation of their infidelities. Different points in time are interwoven in such a way as to usurp the traditional order of progressive movement, not only suggesting the limitations of 'well-made' realist novels, but also examining the breakdown of relationships in a way that implicates the whole culture.* Gaps and ellipses play a significant part in this narrative construction, allowing the reader to interpret the text with a degree of freedom. The novel has also been a favourite of formalist critics, who are mainly concerned with the structural aspects of a particular text, and set out to examine the intricacies of the narrative structure. The novel has long been admired by other writers, including Graham Greene (1904–91), for its technical achievement. However, it should not be forgotten that the war provided the context in which the novel was received, and Ford uses 4 August (the day of the outbreak of the First World War) as a recurring theme. Later Ford wrote more directly about the war, in which he served as an officer, in the sequence known as *Parade's End* (1924–8), a work that we will return to.

Ford's friend, Ezra Pound, who was very active in the formation and promotion of modernist aesthetics in pre-war London, also wrote about the war. His collection of poems translated from the Chinese, *Cathay* (1915), provided Pound with the opportunity to write about military

---

* We have used the phrase 'well-made realist novels' here to differentiate between those works which maintained the nineteenth century tradition of the novel and those that were more innovatory. Typical of the novels which might be regarded as essentially of the 'well-made' type would be those by Arnold Bennett, H. G. Wells and John Galsworthy – excellent novels with modern content but not revolutionary in form.

campaigns, but with the objective distance of rendering the experience through time and culture – see his 'Lament of the Frontier Guard' (1915).

Disillusion and Protest

After the Battle of the Somme in 1916, a new group of poets began to make their voices heard. These men – Edmund Blunden (1896–1974), Robert Graves (1895–1985), Wilfred Owen (1893–1918), Herbert Read (1893–1968), Isaac Rosenberg (1890–1918), Siegfried Sassoon (1886–1967) and others – had a number of points in common. They were all, with the exception of Rosenberg, junior officers – a group among whom the casualties were the heaviest. They all came to hate the war, hate the profiteering and the jingoist propaganda of wartime Great Britain, and wished to confound the lies and the complacency with a true vision of the trenches. Blunden described the difficulty in the following terms:

> Among the multitudes of us shipped to the Pas de Calais a few months before the Great Push (or Drive) of the British army in 1916, I was a verse-writer; my interests were not yet changed from what life had formed before all this chaos … In May and June 1916, in my notebooks, the grimness of war began to compete as a subject with the pastorals of peace. By the end of the year, when madness seemed totally to rule the hour, I was almost a part of the shell-holes, of ruin and of mortification. But the stanzas then written were left in the pocket-book: what good were they, who cared, who would agree? National interests were, understandably, in the way.[7]

These sentences, taken from Blunden's pamphlet *War Poets 1914–1918* (1958), reveal the tension that existed between the bewildering experience of war and the difficulty in confronting that experience in a public utterance; and reveals the way in which English poets with traditional casts of mind felt obliged to confront modernity in all its brutality in the context imposed by the war. His memoir, *Undertones of War* (1928), is of significance in that it marked an attempt to record the facts of war in a way that he had not been able in his poetry. That this prose account was written in a Tokyo hotel, where Blunden was Professor of English at Tokyo University, is illustrative of the need to find a distance and perspective on the subject of the war – even beyond the boundaries of the national culture in which he had been brought up.[8]

The precursor of these poets, Charles Hamilton Sorley (1895–1915), who was killed at the battle of Loos in 1915, and who was the first to present an image of the war which came near to comprehending its full horror and futility, left behind him a sonnet, 'When you see millions of the mouthless dead' (*c.* 1915):

> When you see millions of the mouthless dead
> Across your dreams in pale battalions go,
> Say not soft things as other men have said. (ll. 1–3)

His successors had to find a language and a style for the hard things they had to say. Robert Graves was to comment on Sorley's poetry that '[h]is clear, brave words are the best inspiration possible for people who are trying like me after a new and vigorous poetry, and like rain and wind & freedom'.[9] In fact, Sorley was critical of pro-war sentiment even before he saw action. He was critical of the attitude displayed in Brooke's poetry, and the sonnet quoted above was written in direct opposition to Brooke's own. Indeed, Sorley, who had spent time in Germany before the war, wrote that: 'in training to fight for England, I am training to fight for a deliberate hypocrisy, that terrible middle-class sloth of outlook ... Indeed I think that after the war all brave men will renounce their country and confess that they are strangers and pilgrims on the earth.'[10] His attitude, then, was prophetic, and indicates the conditions under which an audience was to be found that would be receptive to international modernists such as T. S. Eliot, whose *The Waste Land* (1922) was seen to reflect this dislocation and the search for new spiritual meanings.

When Graves first met Siegfried Sassoon near Béthune, in the part of the Pas de Calais that formed part òf the Western Front, he showed him some of his poems. Sassoon's reaction was that the war should not be written about in such realistic terms. He had joined the army as soon as the outbreak of war became likely in 1914, and still retained his romantic attitude to it. However, after Sassoon had been in the trenches he soon changed his mind; and by 1917 he was totally opposed to the war. His verses were circulating rapidly among his fellow poets among the soldiery at this time, but had not filtered through to the consciousness of the general public. Sassoon, a reckless and brave soldier, decided to make a direct protest against the war. Having discussed his stand with the editor of *The Nation*, which was banned from foreign circulation on the grounds that its attitude to the war prejudiced recruiting, and with the philosopher Bertrand Russell, whose opposition to the war lost him his Cambridge fellowship, Sassoon made public a statement repudiating the war.

Sassoon's statement was not pacifist in intent, but a protest aimed at the continuation of this particular war. The other trench poets, though they too had turned 'against the war', continued to fight; and even Sassoon, in the end, went back to the front. Wilfred Owen moved close to pacifism; but the desire to stand by his men in the trenches, the feeling that the true protest against the war could come only from those engaged in it, overcame the pacifism.

After his protest, Sassoon was sent to Craiglockhart War Hospital near Edinburgh to convalesce from neurasthenia.* Wilfred Owen was also a patient there, recovering from shell-shock, and showed him his early war poems. Sassoon's approval, and the friendship and support that he offered, gave Owen the encouragement he needed to boost his self-confidence. Owen decided to return to the front in August 1918. He was killed on 4 November, a week before the armistice, while taking his company across the Sambre canal in the face of determined German machine-gun fire. In the few months before his death Owen produced

---

* Shell-shock was treated as a psychiatric illness caused by damage to the nervous system during combat. Neurasthenia is now regarded as a behavioural rather than a physical condition. For more on Sassoon see Max Egremont, *Siegfried Sassoon* (London: Picador, 2006).

most of the poems on which his reputation now stands, as one of the greatest war poets of the First World War. He captured the futility, the waste of life, the boredom, the horror and the pity of the trenches in a vision which has proved perhaps more enduring than the protest poems of Sassoon:

> What passing-bells for these who die as cattle?
> – Only the monstrous anger of the guns.
> Only the stuttering rifles' rapid rattle
> Can patter out their hasty orisons.
> 'Anthem for Doomed Youth' (1917, ll. 1–4)

He saw his function as to warn his generation, by depicting the truth and the pity of war. However, the example of Sassoon's committed anti-war satire – ridiculing the jingoism of the home front – was to remain, suggesting that poetry could be a medium for protest as well as patriotism, as in his poem 'They':

> 'We're none of us the same!' the boys reply.
> For George lost both his legs; and Bill's stone blind;
> Poor Jim's shot through the lungs and like to die;
> And Bert's gone syphilitic: you'll not find
> A chap who's served that hasn't found *some* change.'
> And the Bishop said: 'The ways of God are strange!' (ll. 7–12)

The critic Cyril Connolly (1903–74) claimed that 'the Great War cut across the Movement, deflecting it but unable to stem its vitality.'[11] The Movement in question is what he termed the Modern Movement in the 1960s. This should remind us that terms used to define periods and aesthetic movements can be very fluid. It is only comparatively recently that the label Modernism has come to be accepted with authority, and even today much debate surrounds the limits of this usage. Nonetheless, it is significant that Connolly chose to include Wilfred Owen's posthumous *Poems* (1920) as one of the texts selected in his 100 key books of the Modern Movement.

Much has been made recently of the close involvement of many writers and the way they operated in relation to the major literary groupings of the time. It is worth noting in this context that Owen's poems made their earliest appearance in the periodical anthology edited by Edith Sitwell (1887–1964) called *Wheels* due to his friendship with her brother Osbert. This series of publications were self-consciously modernist in intention, with decorated covers exploiting the style of international modernism – with abstract and machine-inspired motifs. They had been launched to counteract the popular anthologies of 'Georgian' poetry, which were seen as escapist, deriving their inspiration from a lost pastoral world. As a criticism this is probably too simplistic, but it does indicate the nature of the significant oppositions and antagonisms that gave direction to different groupings. Indeed Owen once said that he would be proud to be counted among the Georgians; and Sassoon actually did contribute to the Georgian anthologies. There was in fact no Georgian movement as such, the anthologies merely represent the idiosyncratic taste of Edward Marsh, who acted as editor. The immense popularity of this publication inevitably made enemies, and brought with it the suspicion that such popularity must represent some sort of commercially inspired dumbing-down. In contrast, Owen found his poems appearing in the rival *Wheels*, as we have seen. The poet and critic T. E. Hulme (1883–1917), whose ideas were influential in the formation of a distinctly modernist aesthetic, took an anti-humanist and anti-romantic attitude to modern poetry, and claimed that poetry about war should not be about heroic action. Owen's poems, such as the familiar 'Anthem for Doomed Youth' and 'Dulce Et Decorum Est' (both written 1917; published 1920), similarly express an attitude to war that is devoid of the uplift associated with romanticism.

We have already made mention of the role played by associational groupings. This was of particular importance in relation to Owen's work, especially in relation to issues of sexuality. While at Craiglockhart Sassoon introduced him to a circle of young men with homosexual or homoerotic tendencies – these included Osbert Sitwell and Scott Moncrieff, who would later find fame as the English-language translator of Proust's great modernist novel *À la recherche du temps perdu*

(1913–27). What is important about this set of connections is the way that a gay subculture can be seen to operate within the existing cultural formations in the early twentieth century. In particular, in relation to the war, is the necessity to see this as a questioning of the notion of masculinity. Such debates must take account of the way in which young men were living their lives to some extent estranged from female company. This was exacerbated by the sense that the experience at the front could not translate easily to civilians remote from the trenches. Traditional gender roles had already come under attack with the advent of the 'New Woman' in the 1890s, and the First World War had accelerated the process as women now undertook many of the jobs which had previously been reserved for men only.* Also, many of these junior officers were young men who came from private single-sex schools, and who usually boarded – which started their estrangement from women at an early age. Soldiers also felt that a great gulf had opened up between the front line and the domestic home front. Owen recorded that: 'I wish the Boche would have the pluck to come right in and make a clean sweep of the pleasure boats, and the promenaders on the Spa, and all the stinking Leeds and Bradford war-profiteers, now reading *John Bull* on Scarborough Sands.'[12] As far as gender relations were concerned there was a feeling that women were part of this social situation. In its most crude form this could be seen in the belief that women had encouraged the recruitment process. Misunderstanding therefore added to the sense of impending crisis occasioned by the pre-war suffragette movement.

Other Voices

Examination of contemporary documents can reveal much about social conditions and the changes in manners that occurred during the war.

---

* The 'New Woman' was a term used to describe women who were pushing the boundaries of what was allowed in terms of independence and education in the late nineteenth century. The term is associated with the female characters in Henrik Ibsen's *A Doll's House* (1879) and *Hedda Gabler* (1890). American writer Kate Chopin's *The Awakening* (1899) and H. G. Wells's *Ann Veronica* (1909) were later fictional examples.

The following newspaper extract is a good instance of this:

> Two years ago the boldest would never have predicted the
> adaptability to the most diverse kinds of work that women have
> shown. They have now taken up the work of oxy-acetylene
> welding – an industry which is itself in its early stages. Ever since
> the Active Service Branch of the National Union of Women's
> Suffrage Societies was formed it has kept to the fore a programme
> effort, and in September last opened the first school for the
> teaching of this craft to women.
>
> (*Daily Telegraph*, 7 February 1916)[13]

Texts such as this can be used to contextualise the literature of the
period, providing some historicisation of the cultural moment. Such
readings can be seen as evidence of cultural criticism which opposes the
exclusivity of 'high' culture and examines texts in relation to popular
cultural forms, seen here by the example of a popular newspaper. The
evidence provided by material like this letter enables the critic to
evaluate contemporary political and social dialogues.

However, some attempts to historicise can be misleading, and it is
necessary not to forget that any moment in time is likely to reflect a
complex mix of responses. Edward Thomas (1878–1917) was
established as a writer of miscellaneous books about the countryside and
literary biography before the war, but the freedom from producing
work to order and a meeting with the American poet Robert Frost
(1874–1963) allowed him to concentrate on the writing of poems.
These are now considered to be among the most remarkable of their
time, and can be seen to reflect upon the war in an oblique way. Edna
Longley has written that it is now old fashioned to insist on the city as
the only location in which modern poetry can be modern and
relevant.[14] The modernity of Thomas's poetry was in the way he used
the rhythms of ordinary speech. For instance in lines such as these:

> Now all roads lead to France
> And heavy is the tread

Of the living; but the dead
Returning lightly dance.

'Roads' (1916), ll. 53–6

This was radical and meant that his verse was considered to be unpoetic by the Georgian poets, who did not include Thomas in the anthologies. This was perhaps especially surprising because of the fact that Thomas drew his inspiration from the English countryside, as did many of the Georgians.

Another poet who was, perhaps, neglected because he did not belong to the group of poets associated with Sassoon was Isaac Rosenberg. Rosenberg was brought up in poverty in London's East End among the Jewish community that had made their home in that part of the capital. He was also an artist, and it was as an artist that he first attracted attention, and as a result obtained entry to the Slade School of Art. There he was able to make friends with other artists such as Adrian Allinson (1890–1959), who encouraged his wide reading. As a result of his city-based background, and his interest in his identity as a Jew, Rosenberg was less drawn to rural subjects than the prevailing generation of Georgian poets. However, a notable fragment of a verse play, *Moses* (1916), did find its way into the Georgian anthologies. His work has been more aligned with the modernists, though, because his concern with Jewish myth and legend led him to explore new ways to render contemporary experience. He was also unusual because his decision to enlist (in 1915) was not made out of patriotic fervour or idealism, but simply in order to have a job which would enable him to support his mother. He was in Cape Town when he heard of the outbreak of the war, and recorded his feelings in the poem 'On Receiving News of the War'. Rosenberg reacted against Brooke's rhetorical sonnets, believing that war 'should be approached in a colder way, more abstract, with less of the million feelings everybody feels; or all these should be concentrated in one distinguished emotion'. Unlike Brooke – and for that matter, Owen – Rosenberg enlisted as a private rather than a commissioned officer. The poems 'Break of Day in the Trenches' (1916) and 'Dead Man's Dump' (*c.* 1917) exemplify the virtues of his way of writing. These poems seem to have evolved out of a new consciousness forged by the First World War.

Some key modern works appeared or were being written across the years of the war. H. D.'s (Hilda Doolittle) *Sea Garden* (1916) alluded to it. Pound's *Homage to Sextus Propertius* (1919) was satirical, comparing the British Empire with Imperial Rome. Joyce's *Ulysses* (1922) and Franz Kafka's *The Trial* (1925) were written across the period, as was D. H. Lawrence's *Women in Love* (1920). While these works were not directly related to the war, they all represent the acute sense that the values of the past had become dislocated in the confusions of the contemporary modern experience.

The Delayed Response

The 1920s saw some of the most remarkable writing about the war, but much of this work was not appreciated at the time. Wilfred Owen's and Isaac Rosenberg's posthumous poems were published early in the decade, 1920 and 1922 respectively, but they did not immediately establish a wide readership. At the same time, Ivor Gurney (1890–1937), who suffered from mental instability, was writing poems that did not see publication until much later – indeed Gurney's reputation as a poet (he was also a composer) only gained ground after the publication of a selection of his work in 1954. Significantly, the war so dominated Gurney's psychology that he was convinced that it had not really ended in 1918. Later, an edition, edited by the writer P. J. Kavanagh (b. 1931), *Collected Poems of Ivor Gurney* (1982), went a long way to creating and consolidating an interest in the poet, whose only books of poems to be published in his lifetime were *Severn & Somme* (1917) and *War's Embers* (1919).

Robert Graves began as a war poet, and *Over the Brazier* (1916) and *Fairies and Fusiliers* (1917) were moving accounts of his war experience, although in traditional forms. He suppressed many of these from his later collections of poems, but since his death in 1985 they have come back into print. Graves, not usually known as a modernist, was a pioneer in the use of the psychological approach to poetry. His theoretical text, *On English Poetry* (1922), was an attempt to face up to the scientific analysis of the subconscious, especially as it was understood by Dr W. H. R. Rivers, who had treated, among other patients, Sassoon and Owen. The book was dedicated to both Rivers and T. E. Lawrence, and can be seen as a response to the crisis of the war years.* Sigmund Freud is usually taken to be one of the key influences on modernism, and his *The Interpretation of Dreams* (1900) is of utmost importance in the history of ideas (see Part Two: 'A Cultural Overview'). This was because of the challenge to the notion of the reliability of reason. The war was part of the process by which radical conceptions of the multiplicity of truths and the role of the subconscious undermined traditional views about experience. In fact, although critical, Graves was more open to the discussion of these ideas of the psychoanalytical than either Eliot or Pound. Graves's *Goodbye to All That* (1929) is one of the most noted examples of literary war narratives, describing the development of the poet's mind, and finally his abandonment of England, which he had come to find too stultifying.

Some of the most distinguished prose fiction about the war also appeared in the 1920s. Certainly by the end of the decade there was a new readiness to engage imaginatively with the war and its legacy. However, writers such as Ford Madox Ford, with *Parade's End* (1924–8), and R. H. Mottram (1883–1971), with *The Spanish Farm* trilogy (1924– 6), had already brought the subject into the realm of contemporary novel writing. Indeed, Rebecca West's novel *The Return of the Soldier* (1918), with its psychoanalytical interest, anticipates later fiction, such as Pat Barker's First World War trilogy *Regeneration* (1991–5), by explaining the impact of shell-shock on real-life characters such as Sassoon, Owen and Graves. It is worth noting that West, like Ford, was published in Wyndham Lewis's *Blast* in 1914. *Parade's End*, Ford's masterpiece, was highly regarded by the author and critic Anthony Burgess (1917–93), who believed it was one of the best

---

* T. E. Lawrence (1888–1935) is better known as 'Lawrence of Arabia'. He fought the Turkish army in the Middle East, and became celebrated as a hero. His account of the conflict appeared in the *Seven Pillars of Wisdom* (which has had a complicated publication history).

narratives about war in English. The novel, really four novels, is a sequence that charts the fragmentation of society across the pre-war period with the suffragettes through to the attempt to find new values in the post-war world. The protagonist, Christopher Tietjens, is a hero in an age which has no use for heroes, and yet represents symbolically the High Tory gentleman, who serves in the war, and tries to maintain stability while being beset by the difficulties caused by the flux of public events. The story is told through indirection; everything is elusive and elliptical, displaying a modernist concern with point of view, to produce a compressed narrative of modern society.

It was the change to the harsh economic realities in the late 1920s that seemed to provide the impetus for the sudden flow of books about the war. The rhetoric of politicians such as David Lloyd George, who had been wartime Prime Minister (1916–22), now seemed inadequate as new problems added to the sense of historical disillusionment. The American novelists William Faulkner and Ernest Hemingway also wrote significant fiction arising from the war. As far back as Henry James, American writers had turned to Europe as the source of experience, as a place to escape the provincialism that narrowed the sense of their own cultural heritage. When the USA entered the war, it was seen that here was an opportunity for young American men to test themselves. It also brought with it conscription, which was a challenge to American notions of the liberty of the individual. George Creel, the head of US war propaganda, attempted to turn this erosion of freedom into the expression of positive social engineering, declaring that 'Universal training will jumble the boys of America all together, shoulder to shoulder, smashing all the petty class distinctions that now divide, and promoting a brand of real democracy.'[15] As it happened, the training here referred to, coupled with a lack of sufficient troop ships, meant that American troops did not start arriving in France in appreciable numbers until the summer of 1918, when the war was already approaching its end. Henry James, who adopted British citizenship in 1915, and American novelist Edith Wharton, whose *Fighting France* (1915) was a significant contribution to the support of the French people against German aggression, had already been campaigning for America to enter the war on the side of the Allies. When young Americans became eligible for war service, however, the result was that relatively few saw active service. T. S. Eliot, already based in London, attempted to join the US navy but failed. Ernest Hemingway had joined the ambulance corps in order see the action more closely for himself, and his experiences are fictionalised in the novel, *A Farewell to Arms* (1929). William Faulkner was frustrated from getting to the front line, although he was able to use his experiences in his 1926 novel, *Soldier's Pay*, which originally bore the statement that the book was not a war novel on its cover. The poet e. e. cummings also wrote about the war in the experimental *The Enormous Room* (1922), which dealt with his confinement within a prison in France, a sentence served because of his challenge to authority.

The 1920s also saw the emergence of Edgell Rickword (1898–1982), who became one of the key critical intelligences of the decade through his editorial and review work for *The Calendar of Modern Letters* (1925–7). Rickword had served on the Western Front, but came only later to render these impressions in verse. He needed to encounter the example of French poet Charles Baudelaire to release his artistic vision from the influence of the Victorian poets and novelists (see Part Three: 'Modernist Poetry – French Origins, English Settings'). His war poems, such as 'Trench Poets' (1921), are satiric and also show the effect of the revival of interest in the work of the metaphysical poet John Donne (1572–1631), as a reaction to the Victorian greats such as Alfred Lord Tennyson (famous for a very different war poem – 'The Charge of the Light Brigade', 1854). Rickword's first critical work was *Rimbaud: the Boy and the Poet* (1924), and it was as a critic that he has been most influential. He later edited two volumes of *Scrutinies* (1928 and 1931), which reassessed the reputations of a number of the literary celebrities of the day. In particular, the effect was to call into question the value of work that did not stand up to the experience of a generation that had served in the First World War. F. R. Leavis, one of the most important critics to emerge in the twentieth century, was profoundly affected by Rickword's approach. Until these publications by Rickword, with the exception of some of Pound's and Eliot's essays, the critical standards were still largely those of the Victorian gentleman reviewer. Leavis, under this primary influence of Rickword, went on to produce *New Bearings in English Poetry* (1932), one of the classics of modern criticism, and to edit the highly influential Cambridge-based quarterly critical review, *Scrutiny* (1932–53), which put modernist criticism at the heart of the critic's search for value in literature.

The late 1920s saw a new willingness to engage with the horrors of the war. There had been a silence in the early 1920s, with almost a common conspiracy between authors, publishers and readers against facing up to the memory of the war. It touched upon by Blaise Cendrars (1887–1961), the Swiss-born poet and novelist who became a naturalised French citizen and served in the war in the French Foreign Legion, in his 1926 novel, *Moravagine*, which stresses the pointlessness and destruction caused by the war. In 1927, the German novelist Arnold Zweig published *The Case of Sergeant Grischa*. One of the most celebrated and successful war novels by the German writer Erich Maria Remarque – *All Quiet on the Western Front* – came out in 1928; and was made into a highly acclaimed American film in 1930. Edmund Blunden's *Undertones of War* appeared in 1928, and in 1929 there appeared a spate of publications which sought in one way or another to come to terms with the experience of the Western Front. These included Robert Graves's *Goodbye to All That*, Richard Aldington's *Death of a Hero* (1929), and Hemingway's *A Farewell to Arms*. Sassoon's *Memoirs of an Infantry Officer* appeared in 1930. *Journey's End* (1928/1929) by R. C. Sherriff (1896–1975) should also be mentioned, which was a well-made play about the war – it was criticised at the time for having little action, the entire drama taking place over four days in an officers' dugout in 1918. It perhaps suggests the sense of cultural paralysis that ensued after the war:

> HARDY: Well, damn it, it's pretty dull without *something* to liven people up. I mean, after all – Stanhope is a sort of freak; I mean it is jolly fascinating to see a fellow drink like he does – glass after glass. He didn't go home on his last leave, did he?[16]

Mention should also be made of the Austrian novelist Joseph Roth's masterpiece, *The Radetzky March*, which appeared in 1932, and dealt with the war as part of the collapse of the Habsburg Austro-Hungarian Empire.

Later Attempts to Define the Impact of the War

The decade of the 1930s saw a number of additions to this literature of the war. The modernist painter and writer Wyndham Lewis brought out an autobiography, *Blasting and Bombardiering*, in 1937. David Jones (1895–1974), also an artist and writer, collated his memories of the war in a mixture of verse and prose influenced by Eliot and Joyce, *In Parenthesis* (1937). Jones attempted to see the fact of war as part of a recurrent theme in history, and celebrated the brotherhood of the soldiers amid the destruction of warfare. This reflected the modernist tendency to emphasise the historical moment against a larger pattern of epoch-defining significance.

Anti-heroic depictions of war circulated in the 1960s mood of anti-establishment sentiment. Popular histories, such as A. J. P. Taylor's *The First World War* (1963), contributed to the sense that the war was a potent source of modern experience that still had an influence on contemporary society. Taylor's book makes use of illustrations to convey the grim reality, as he writes: 'the unknown soldier was the hero of the First World War. He has vanished, except as a cipher, from the written records. He lives again in the photographs.'[17] Taylor's book was dedicated to Joan Littlewood, who had devised the satirical musical for the Theatre Workshop, *Oh, What a Lovely War!* (1963). Benjamin Britten (1913–76), an English composer who had been strongly influenced by the modernism of the Austrian Alban Berg (1885–1935) and the Russian Igor Stravinsky (1882–1971), produced *War Requiem* in 1962, which set anti-war poems by Sassoon and Owen to music. Bernard Bergonzi's *Heroes' Twilight* (1965) continued the critical focus on a defining period in cultural and literary experience. Paul Fussell's *The Great War and Modern Memory*, first published in 1975, was to further explore the legacy of the war:

> I have focused on places and situations where literary tradition
> and real life notably transect, and in doing so I have tried to
> understand something of the simultaneous and reciprocal process
> by which life feeds materials to literature while literature returns
> the favor by conferring forms upon life.[18]

Fussell's view here, from the preface to *The Great War and Modern Memory*, is reflected in the decision to establish a special memorial to sixteen of the First World War poets in Westminster Abbey in 1985. In 2000, Edna Longley, in editing *The Bloodaxe Book of 20th Century Poetry*, suggested that the First World War was perhaps the single most important expression of modernity, and as such caused a profound reshaping of poetry, and that this has been why war poetry has become so central to understanding twentieth century poetry as a whole. This was because the experience of war caused people to question traditional notions about religion and the forms by which social life was regulated.

Recent studies have focused on such issues as wartime propaganda and publishing in the war years. There has been a growing awareness about what was read during the war, and the interaction between the reading public and the publishing industry. Shafquat Towheed has noted: 'By November 1915 the market for fiction had rebounded considerably, and sales for novels were if anything higher than immediately before the outbreak of the conflict. Sales figures were, however, as FM [Frederick Macmillan] points out, notoriously difficult to predict during this period.'[19] This uncertainty indicates the shifts that were taking place in British society as the conflict helped to reshape modern consciousness. In 2007 Mary Hammond and Shafquat Towheed edited an influential volume, *Publishing in the First World War: Essays in Book History*, which brought attention to the processes of publication, circulation and reception of literature in the period of the First World War. This, and other studies, have shown how writers such as Sir Arthur Conan Doyle (1859–1930) were used to produce wartime propaganda. The interest in reading experience has opened up an interest in a more inclusive approach to the literature of the First World War, moving away from elitist models of 'high' culture to examine the common experience.

Now that the generation of the First World War has passed away, we still have the complex legacy of the first truly global and mechanised conflict. Charlotte Mew's 'The Cenotaph (September 1919)' expresses something of this complexity by bringing the concept of trade and the tragedy of slaughter together in a poem of memorial. Mew (1869–1928), who wrote stories and poems during the war, and was highly regarded by Thomas Hardy and Walter de la Mare, has enjoyed a revival of interest that has coincided with feminist criticism and the development of gender studies. She was published during the war by the Poetry Book shop, and her collection *The Farmer's Bride* (1916) appeared alongside the publication of Graves's early books of poetry. Her cenotaph poem is typical of her originality and modernity, and is worth quoting:

> Not yet will those measureless fields be green again
> Where only yesterday the wild sweet blood of wonderful youth
> was shed;
> There is a grave whose earth must hold too long, too deep a stain,
> Though for ever over it may we speak as proudly as we may tread.
> But here, where the watchers by lonely hearths from the thrust of
> an inward sword have more slowly bled,
> We shall build the Cenotaph: Victory, winged, with Peace,
> winged too, at the column's head.
> And over the stairway, at the foot – Oh! Here, leave desolate,
> passionate hands to spread
> Violets, roses, and laurel, with the small, sweet, tinkling country
> things
> Speaking so wistfully of other Springs,
> From the little gardens of little places where son or sweetheart
> was born and bred.
>
> ('The Cenotaph', 1919, ll. 1–18)

This poem may well serve to highlight some key features of the experience of the First World War in relation to modernism and literature. There is the sense in which the war was an event of enormous cultural significance, with the stain likely to last much longer than it will take for the grass to grow back over the battlefields. It was not only those soldiers who served on the Western Front who were affected but the whole community, including mothers, wives and girlfriends. Also it is an event that has left its mark on the social and economic environment of daily activity, with a memorial in every marketplace. Mew switches the attention from the public rhetoric of victory to the individual tragedy – which implies that such gestures of patriotism are meaningless. More subtly she suggests that the faith in the pastoral world has been profoundly changed; the country things become tokens for a lost way of life.

T. E. Hulme, who was one of the most significant articulators of modernist aesthetics, in *Speculations* (1924), posthumously edited by Herbert Read, fell in action in 1917. His rejection of romanticism amplified an important aspect of modernity: the discontinuity of ideas and experience. New metaphors were needed to articulate the experience of the modern environment, and it was this that was the problem that was faced by the literature of the First World War. Hulme's death on the Western Front is a reminder of how inextricably linked were modernism and war. Hulme's belief was that romanticism was no longer a possibility because modern life was made not of continuity but of discontinuity; and it is perhaps for this reason that Hulme's works seemed to have a special significance for a generation coming to terms with the breakdown of so many accepted thoughts and feelings in the wake of the chaos of the First World War.

Notes

1   Quoted in Peter and Linda Murray, *The Penguin Dictionary of Art and Artists* (Harmondsworth: Penguin, 1979), pp. 170–1.
2   Osbert Sitwell, *Noble Essences: A Book of Characters* (London: Macmillan, 1950). The fifth volume of Sitwell's autobiography, *Left Hand, Right Hand*.

3   Quoted in Majorie Villiers, *Charles Péguy: A Study in Integrity* (London: Collins, 1965), p. 369.
4   Rupert Brooke, 'Peace' (1914), l. 4, in *New Numbers*, 4 (December 1914), p. 165.
5   Apollinaire to André Billy (1918). Quoted in Apollinaire, *Selected Poems*, translated with an introduction by Oliver Bernard (London: Anvil Press Poetry, 1994), p. 6.
6   Quoted in Ford Madox Ford, *Selected Poems*, ed. by Max Saunders (Manchester: Carcanet, 1997), p. ix.
7   Edmund Blunden, *War Poets 1914–1918* (London: Longmans Green, 1958). pp. 26–7. See also *Undertones of War* (Harmondsworth: Penguin, 2000).
8   See Edmund Blunden, *Overtones of War: Poems of the First World War*, edited with an Introduction by Martin Taylor (London: Duckworth, 1996), p. 17.
9   Graves to Professor W. R. Sorley, 15 March 1917. Quoted in Robert Graves, *Complete Poems*, Volume 1, edited by Beryl Graves and Dunstan Ward (Manchester: Carcanet, 1995, revised 1999), p. 345.
10 Quoted from a letter dated 14 November 1914 in Jon Silkin, *Out of Battle: The Poetry of the Great War* (Harmondsworth, Penguin, 2000), p. 75.
11 Cyril Connolly, *The Modern Movement: A Hundred Key Books from England, France, and America, 1880–1950* (London: Andre Deutsch, 1965).
12 Wilfred Owen, letter dated 1917. See Wilfred Owen, *Collected Letters*, ed. by Harold Owen and John Bell (London: Oxford University Press, 1967).
13 Joyce Marlow (ed), *The Virago Book of Women and the Great War 1914–18* (London: Virago Press, 1998), p. 161.
14 Edna Longley (ed.), *The Bloodaxe Book of Twentieth Century Poetry* (Tarset, Northumberland: Bloodaxe, 2000), p. 17.
15 Quoted in David Reynolds, *Empire of Liberty* (London: Allen Lane, 2009).
16 R. C. Sheriff, *Journey's End* (London: Penguin, 2000), p. 13.
17 A. J. P. Taylor, *The First World War: An Illustrated History* (Harmondsworth: Penguin, 1978), p. 11.
18 Paul Fussell, Preface, *The Great War and Modern Memory* (Oxford: Oxford University Press, 2000).
19 Shafquat Towheed (ed.), *The Correspondence of Edith Wharton and Macmillan* (Basingstoke: Palgrave, 2007), p. 166.

Modernism and its Critics

In this chapter we take a look at responses to modernism at the time and also the effect it generated on the literature that followed. The focus of the chapter is primarily concerned with literary modernism as it was debated in Anglo-American criticism. Many of the writers that we think of as being modernist would probably not have recognised themselves under such a label. They might have signed manifestos for groups and movements which they supported or joined, but the term 'modernism' is something of a blanket term for a variety of new approaches. Modernism implies a radical departure from the past. Famously, and with some exaggeration and half-seriousness, Virginia Woolf declared that 'On or about December 1910 human nature changed.'[1] Retrospectively it is perhaps a little too easy to agree with Woolf's statement; at the time, while it was clear that there was a chaotic ferment of artistic activity and discussion, the recognition and acceptance of modernism was far from assured. Indeed, it might be argued that the notion that new art and literature is necessarily experimental and challenging begins with the appearance of modernism at the start of the twentieth century. Certainly it was a feature of the debate about modernism that much modernist art and literature became immediately part of a climate of controversy and public debate – a fact that was fuelled by the advent of the popular press. Many in society reacted negatively to what they saw as a challenge to the tradition. It was not simply a case of the uninitiated being reluctant to be challenged but also an area hotly debated by writers themselves.

Movements: 1910s

In 1910 modern art and literature was tolerated in London as long as its bohemianism fitted in with the stereotype – created in Paris, especially by the success of Henri Murger's novel *Scènes de la Vie de Bohème* (1851) – of the struggling artist, which still had currency in the early years of the twentieth century. Since the days when the American painter Whistler first arrived in London it was expected that writers and artists would lead unconventional lives.[2] Therefore, when the Post-Impressionist Exhibition opened in London in December 1910 – introducing the work of Van Gogh, Gauguin, Cézanne, Matisse and Picasso to the British public – it marked a watershed in the consciousness of the 'modern' in Edwardian society. There was a general sense in which tension had been growing since the turn of the century. Women had been demanding equal voting rights. There had developed an arms race between Britain and Germany (meaning a significant investment in military power, such as the building of costly dreadnought battleships). The security and confidence provided by Britain's economic and manufacturing dominance was being challenged as other nations, such as America and Germany, modernised themselves. There was also a sense that conventional standards were holding back the expression of the spirit of the age. It was difficult for contemporary writers to find adequate expression for their understanding of this sense of subterranean tensions. John Middleton Murry (1889–1957), one of the most prominent critics of the modernist period, and editor of the influential magazine *Rhythm* (1911–13), in his obituary for H. G. Wells written in 1946, stressed something of the nature of the sense of crisis:

> he was the Englishman of an age when England was undergoing a profound transition – that social upheaval which had its first large-scale political manifestation in the Liberal triumph of 1906. The

speed of the change was indicated by the fact that the unprecedented triumph of the great Liberal party was the immediate prelude to its complete collapse.[3]

Wells was one of Edwardian England's most significant novelists – with novels such as *Kipps* (1905) and *The History of Mr Polly* (1910). His novels, while comic in effect, have a serious purpose by giving expression to the possibility of aspiration and the economic and social challenges that can prevent such an aspiration from becoming realised. Wells believed in social progress, and had been a member of the Fabian Society, and in particular was concerned with the lack of opportunity given to the lower middle class – making a case for the 'crying need for a strenuous, intellectual renewal'.[4] The condition of England in the years around 1910 can be characterised as being dominated by the shifting of the once solid ground of Victorianism, a rise in the power, influence and wealth of the middle classes, and an increasingly individualistic outlook on life.[5] It was a period in which legislation was passed by the Liberal government bringing in pensions and other social and state support. In part this was a response to the agitation for reform stimulated by the increasing literacy of the population and the relative wealth being generated. The Independent Labour Party (ILP) was formed in 1893, campaigning for better conditions for workers and the sick and old, as well as free education, and this tendency was acknowledged in the birth of the Labour Party in 1906. Increasingly, movements were springing up all over the world advocating alternatives to capitalism – movements such as syndicalism, which advocated democratic trade unionism as the basis for the running of national economies. Therefore, the Liberal Party reforms were a response to a range of radical movements threatening to force change on the nations of Europe and America.

There was a slippage between these political discussions and the feeling that progress in the arts was being inhibited by the habits and conventions of the past. When the now nearly forgotten poet and short story writer Richard Middleton (1882–1911) committed suicide in Brussels, Frank Harris, who had previously edited the *Saturday Review* with distinction, and knew of the harsh realities of journalism, wrote in

Middleton Murry's *Rhythm* that, 'I would rather lose a Dreadnought than a Davidson or a Middleton'.[6] The point he was making was that the cultural conditions of the time were extremely unsympathetic to the creative writer – and, it might be argued, the playing out of the role of self-conscious bohemian did not prove to be sufficient. At the same moment, writers and critics were trying to make a case for new work that challenged the critical notions left over from the nineteenth century and still dominating the literary landscape. Middleton Murry himself was an early advocate of the desire for art to embrace the future and throw off the shackles of the past. It was felt necessary at this juncture for writers to make a case for those literary practices which we now think of as modernist. In the essay 'Art and Philosophy', first published in *Rhythm* in 1911, Middleton Murry, basing his ideas on the example of the French philosopher Henri Bergson (1859–1941), who had given lectures at Oxford and Birmingham in that year, put forward the case for an art derived from the current of life at a particular moment of time. He found in favour of a notion of art that is eternal because it lives in the present. He relates this to progress:

> [Art] must go onward and forward. It lives for the present, striving to force fresh paths for its progress across the waste of dull dead matter which it vivifies. It is an evolution because it proceeds only by bringing something to birth. The past is judged by the present, not the present by the past; for in the present alone the past has its being.[7]

The key thing to note here is that this modernism of outlook is derived from French intellectual ideas – which are upheld as being more progressive than British intellectual ideas – and arising from these same sources is the feeling that the past has too great an influence over culture, leading to a stagnation of thought and creativity. At bottom there is here an expression of a need to liberate the consciousness from what has been left over from the Victorian period.

The first wave of the rejection of the Victorian legacy was Georgianism. This was a fairly romantic reaction to late Victorian attitudes, and was largely modelled on the example of the romantic poets – especially Wordsworth – with their reaction from industrialisation, seeking simplicity and celebrating the natural in terms of context as well as language. The term 'Georgian' was coined by Sir Edward Marsh (1872–1953), and was used in a series of extremely popular anthologies of contemporary poetry – the first being *Georgian Poetry 1911–1912* (1912), which was followed by further installments in 1915, 1917, 1919 and 1922. Marsh was an enthusiast for poetry, and he wanted to celebrate what he understood as a rejection of the rather dull verse that had appeared in the first decade of the twentieth century. However, he had no particular programme for reform (and we have already seen in other chapters that it was often necessary for modernist writers and artists to have a plan of action), and so there was no Georgian manifesto. This has caused a great deal of critical confusion, as the term has been applied in a pejorative sense since the Modernists began to gain hegemony over the critical history of modern poetry. Very often the term 'Georgian' has been applied to those writers who appeared in the anthologies regardless of the actual poetry, and as the criterion for inclusion was simply what appealed uncritically to Marsh's temperament, this usage has led to some strange conclusions. For example, D. H. Lawrence's poetry (which was an attempt to break free from conventions of sound and sense) was included in the anthologies; and other poets of genuine quality also appeared, including: Edmund Blunden (1896–1974), W. H. Davies (1871–1940), Walter De La Mare (1873–1956), Robert Graves (1895–1985) and Siegfried Sassoon (1886–1967) – but opinion has varied as to whether these poets are modernist because their techniques were traditional. Also, Marsh's taste in contemporary artists was demonstrated in an interest in the work of Mark Gertler and Duncan Grant, who would hardly belong in the company of anti-modernists. Indeed it is a sign of the way the term 'Georgian' has been appropriated to conform with later ideologies that it now is regarded as indicating the inadequate Edwardian poetic scene as much as the true Georgians. This state of affairs means that the term has come to mean a conservative response to the times, usually a fancy of escapist intention as was usually associated with the outlook of J. C.

Squire (1884–1958), the influential editor of the *London Mercury*, which continued to be a powerful adversary to modernist experiment on to the 1920s.[8]

Perhaps the most high profile debate about what we now know of as literary modernism concerns Imagism. Imagism had a 'programme for deinhibiting poets from poetic conventions' and, therefore, 'it released into poetry material which, before imagism, poets themselves would have rejected'.[9] The result of this inevitably brought into question the very notion of what constituted poetry. For many, the result of Imagism then was the introduction of what had hitherto been regarded as the non-poetic as a possibility for poetry. This was controversial, and a number of contemporary poets entered the discussion. Among these, Harold Monro (1879–1932), the owner of the recently opened Poetry Bookshop, in an essay published in *The Egoist*, in May 1915, declared that, 'poets of the Imagist and other kindred modern schools are no longer "visited by the Muses".'[10] It was felt that this new poetry was a response to the speeding up of modern life – the underground tube train had become a fact in the linking of suburban life with the city centre, the motor car had quickly established itself as a fact of everyday life, even if only the select could afford such a means of transport, and aircraft were to be seen in the skies, suggesting even greater possibilities for transforming the perception of the world. The techniques advocated by the Imagists allowed for a poetry that could describe concisely the rapid impression made by the phenomena of this emerging modernity. The novelist May Sinclair (1863–1946), who was in support of the Suffragette movement (being a member of the Woman Writers Suffrage League), also wrote some significant criticism of modernist poetry at this time.[11] In an article on Imagism, also appearing in *The Egoist* in 1915, she sought to differentiate Imagism from Symbolism (something Ezra Pound would have approved of – see Part Three: 'Modernist Poetry – French Origins, English Settings'), which had been explained to Anglo-American audiences by Arthur Symons in his *The Symbolist Movement in Literature* (1899, revised 1908) and had to some extent been absorbed into the literary consciousness of the educated public – certainly in metropolises such as London. She wrote that, 'what the

Imagists are "out for" is direct naked contact with reality. You must get closer and closer. Imagery must go. Symbolism must go. There must be nothing between you and your object.'[12] It is probable that this sort of explanation was more effective than some of the publicity stunts that Pound thought were necessary to establish an audience for the Imagists. However, without the sense of confusion, and perhaps mystery, that had been occasioned by the statements that had been put out by Pound on behalf of Imagism there would have been no interest and no debate about what it was or was not, or whether it was a serious development in modern poetry.[13]

Contemporary Discussions: 1920s

It has been argued that Modernism achieved official acceptance by the time that T. S. Eliot started to edit the *Criterion* in 1922; it was also of course the year of *The Waste Land*, James Joyce's *Ulysses* and W. B. Yeats's *Later Poems*. For later critics such as Michael Levenson, modernism was an established reality in literary discourse by 1922:

> If we look for a mark of modernism's coming of age, the founding of the *Criterion* in 1922 may prove a better instance than *The Waste Land*, better even than *Ulysses*, because it exemplifies the institutionalization of the movement, the accession to cultural legitimacy.[14]

The rapidly developing doctrines that constituted the evolvement of a single aesthetic seemed to have been consolidated. However, it was only some time later that attempts were made to engage with the nature of modernist activity, to give it some rationale, explanation and effective criticism.

One of the first to make an attempt to write effective criticism in the aftermath of the First World War was Edgell Rickword (1898–1982). He had seen action on the Western Front and immediately after the war enrolled at Oxford to study French literature. A number of writers or would-be writers were attracted to Oxford at that time. The younger generation, of which Rickword was a part, was extremely conscious of the survival of pre-war values among the literary and academic establishment. Their experience on the battlefield contributed to a sense in which dissatisfaction with the prevailing conditions was acutely felt and awakened a social consciousness. Rickword found some inspiration in magazines such as *Art and Letters*, *Coterie* and Holbrook Jackson's *Today*, and the Sitwells's periodical anthology *Wheels* was a self-consciously modern alternative to the stale survivals of the pre-1914 period (*Wheels* was deliberately offered as a modernist alternative to the Georgian anthologies). However, he noted that in the post-war world both Vorticism and Imagism seemed to be spent forces. For those returning from the trenches the experimentation of these movements seemed dead and perhaps rather superficial. It has been suggested that the 'task for criticism during the Twenties was far from easy. These younger writers [like Rickword] knew that the prevailing standards of most of their immediate literary forebears were totally inadequate, but not because they themselves participated in any general cultural consensus.'[15]

The sense that there was no consensus is demonstrated in some remarks extracted from *The Times Literary Supplement* (5 April 1923) by Harold Monro in an editorial in *The Chapbook* (May 1923). The unnamed critic had observed, we are told, that no two critics seemed to be able to agree about the value of any recently published book. In contrast, as Monro records, the *TLS* asked the reader to consider those works that had appeared in the first twenty years of the preceding century (1800–21). The works cited consisted of books by Scott, Wordsworth, Coleridge, Austen, Byron, Keats and Shelley. The critic declared: 'we feel ourselves indeed driven to them, impelled not by calm judgment, but by some imperious need to anchor our instability upon their security ... and frankly if we pit one century against another, the comparison seems overwhelmingly against us.'[16] We can see, then, that even in the early 1920s there was no critical consensus, and the place of modernism was far from assured. The standard of criticism in this period was still largely one derived from the romantic movement of the early nineteenth century.

Robert Graves was one of those who sought to engage with the direction of contemporary poetry, producing *Contemporary Techniques of Poetry: A Political Analogy* (1925) and *Another Future of Poetry* (1926), both in the Hogarth Essays series published by Virginia and Leonard Woolf. These paved the way for the highly influential book that followed, written as a line by line collaboration with the American poet Laura Riding (1901–91), *A Survey of Modernist Poetry* (1927). This study was an attempt to provide an account of the experimentation of writers such as Eliot, Pound and e. e. cummings (1894–1962). It quickly established itself as an illuminating – if at times controversial – critical text, providing close reading of poems and giving an account of the early development of modernist poetry. It is worth noting that Graves had originally been planning to write a book on modern poetry in collaboration with T. S. Eliot. This was to have been published under the title of *Untraditional Elements in Poetry*, which perhaps suggests the uncertainty that existed in the 1920s about how to label the new literary doctrines.[17] It is interesting that the title that Riding and Graves adopted used the word 'modernist' to designate those new literary practices that were often deemed to be baffling to the common reader. Indeed, it should be noted that this book was influential in putting forward a notion of the ordinary reader of poetry. In part this was a response to the charge that was frequently made that modern poetry was obscure.

Some of the most interesting discussion about Modernism appeared in the periodical literature of the inter-war period. *The Decachord*, for example, was a little magazine that was apparently traditional, even reactionary, in terms of its content.[18] However, this publication did contain some perceptive discussion which is important. Edwin Faulkner, a sensible critic, and a regular contributor to *The Decachord*, was one of those that sought to make sense of the opposing forces of modernism and traditionalism. He noted: 'Those who have followed the so-called Modernist movement in poetry will have noted with interest that Hardy is the only Victorian of whom the Modernists speak with respect. Yet there is little of the Modernist in his form.'[19] The contributor who signed himself 'Ettrick' observed that Modernism was not simply experimental, but was a matter of theme and subject, and referred to 'the so-termed Modernists, who commonly clothe a sordid or shallow theme in ill-chosen and unmetrical language'.[20] However, 'Lancastrian' responded: 'Why praise the Romantics for their rebellion, yet find no word of excuse for the 'Modernists?' ... They have only followed the example of the Romantics. They are doing what the Romantics did, viz., *experimenting*.' He went on to suggest that, 'New art often seems crude at first. It *is* crude at first. It needs to find its feet. But it may grow into a strange new beauty and then we may one day awake to find that it and it alone can adequately express the modern world.'[21]

The notion that true poetry was revolutionary in a way that embraced the reality of the modern world was taken up by the Marxist critic and historian A. L. Morton, who expressed the opinion that 'There is one final sense in which all real poetry is modern and revolutionary. The poet is a creator, and all creation is the creation of things new and unique.'[22] In this essay, which adopts the title 'Beauty is not Enough', surely in imitation of Laura Riding's just-published book *Anarchism is Not Enough* (1928), Morton was attempting to situate the new art within a context that would account for textual modernity as an indicator of an engagement with modernity in the widest sense. The contemporary environment was seen to be hostile to art because it was not beautiful in terms of now conventional notions of beauty that had been established by the romantics.

The fact that there was no taste for modernity meant that there was no large public, as the Georgian poets had managed to find through a brand of nostalgic verse, for modernist poetry. 'Ettrick' could claim with justification, as 'Mr. Stephen Spender admits the apparent lack of sympathy between the modern poet ... and the general public' was seen to be a problem. Significantly, he inadvertently reveals the role that the modernist 'little magazine'* had to play in the culture of the 1920s, when he isolates one manifestation of modernist poetry: 'Mr. Eliot's – to take an example of one type – is so palpably detested by all but a certain small school that nothing of the kind is ever found in an ordinary magazine or journal.'[23] In contrast, modernist magazines were

---

* See Part Four: 'Modernist Print Culture'.

defined by not being the ordinary magazine or journal of the day. However, it might be asked what constituted the ordinary.

These discussions were perhaps understandably limited by a provinciality of outlook. Even when the continental movements in art are mentioned, it is clear that they are considered as belonging to the margins. Edwin Faulkner noted that: 'It is true you have Dadaism, and Dadaism is as complete a break-away as is perhaps possible. But outside a small group of pathological eccentrics reinforced by posers with their tongue in their cheeks, there is no following for Dadaism.'[24] In fact, in spite of such assertive statements, continental movements in art were to develop a following during the 1930s.

Edouard Roditi (1910–92), the American poet and translator, noted how provincial he found Oxford when he arrived there as an undergraduate in 1928. Roditi had been brought up in Paris, and understood what was happening on the continent. He had contributed to *Transition* (1927–38) – a Paris-based American periodical, which is noted for the promoting of the concept of the 'Revolution of the Word' and the printing of extracts by James Joyce of what became *Finnegans Wake* (1930). He claimed that the only person who seemed to be open to contemporary avant-garde influences at Oxford was Clere Parsons (1908–31), who died young and has been unjustly neglected.[25] Parsons had co-edited *Oxford Poetry* in 1928, which included a significant editorial – a 'Plea for Better Criticism'. Both Roditi and Parsons contributed to *Sir Galahad* (1929), an Oxford undergraduate literary magazine that lasted for just two issues, and while this publication seems relatively conservative compared with the standard of the European avant-garde in the late 1920s, it did represent an attempt to emulate the Cambridge journal *Experiment* (1928–31). In turn, *Transition* had noted the emergence of *Experiment*, and in June, 1930, had printed some of the poems that had appeared in the Cambridge magazine. So by the end of the 1920s there was a consciousness of what was happening being circulated by the periodicals, and this helped to create a cultural climate that allowed for a mutual interaction of ideas.

A decisive event in the critical appraisal of Modernism was the publication of Edgell Rickword's *Scrutinies* (1928). The background to this volume – which was added to with the publication of a second volume in 1931 – was located in the literary critical review *The Calendar of Modern Letters*. This periodical had been begun in 1925 (it ceased publication in 1927) with the express intention to provide readers with the opportunity to encounter literature which, in the eyes of the editors, reflected the 'spirit of the present day'.[26] It has been suggested that Rickword 'was involved both in recognizing what has become accepted as the canon of modernism, and in offering some of the most significant early criticism of it'.[27] This criticism comprised reviews of books by writers such as T. S. Eliot, Virginia Woolf and Wyndham Lewis. These reviews attempted to provide a thorough analysis of the work with an understanding of the social implications. The volume of *Scrutinies* attempted to reassess the literary landscape, by cutting down the obscuring inflated figures of the Edwardian generation who still tended to dominate the scene. As Rickword wrote in the foreword:

> There is a sluggishness in the communication of ideas in this country and a lack of curiosity about them which make a response to the intellectual situation slower than it is anywhere else. Such a disturbance as the War, and the consequent economic troubles, undoubtedly helped to aggravate this tendency, increasing the prestige of reputations established before the catastrophe, and the repugnance to modify an attitude once adopted – helped directly, because half a generation of potential rivals and critics was bodily eliminated.[28]

He noted that the reassessment was about ten years overdue and that what was needed was an engagement with the ideas that were circulating on the continent, among the European avant-garde and the American expatriates. We can see, then, that critics were slow, in Britain at least, to respond to the emergence of modernist literary activity.

Modernism Becomes Political: 1930s

However, with the emergence of the Cambridge-based magazine *Experiment*, the modernist magazine was firmly established in Britain; and the magazines that kept the discussion about modernism alive that followed in the 1930s, such as Geoffrey Grigson's *New Verse* (1933–9), Roger Roughton's *Contemporary Poetry and Prose* (1936–7) and Julian Symons's *Twentieth Century Verse* (1937–9), concerned themselves with the modern and the new without looking backwards into an idealised Georgian past.

Undoubtedly one of the key books that earned Modernism academic acceptance, through the reputations of some of the movement's most notable writers, was F. R. Leavis's *New Bearings in English Poetry* in 1932. Leavis had been influenced by Edgell Rickword's criticism, and published a selection of critical pieces taken from *The Calendar of Modern Letters*, with the significant title, *Towards Standards of Criticism* (1933). In fact Leavis was inspired by the example of the *Calendar* to start a critical journal of his own in Cambridge, where he was employed in university teaching. This was *Scrutiny* – which first appeared in 1932 (and continued until 1953). Leavis was initially greatly influenced by the criticism of T. S. Eliot (later he was to come to the view that D. H. Lawrence provided a better example of a writer engaged in a mature engagement with life), and his standpoint was based upon an understanding of 'high seriousness' in relation to literature and the values it represented.

Another key book in the critical history of Modernism that first appeared in the 1930s was Michael Roberts's anthology, *The Faber Book of Modern Verse* (1936). Roberts (1902–48) had already produced anthologies called *New Signatures* (1932) and *New Country* (1933), which had printed young poets who were communist in outlook – W. H. Auden, John Lehmann and Stephen Spender. The Faber anthology made a case for modern poetry on the basis that it was necessary for the poet to be 'compelled to make … notable development[s] of poetic technique' which sprang directly from 'a change or development of subject-matter'.[29] This belief – that technical innovation adapted to specifically modern subject matter was the criterion by which the contemporary poet could be judged – gained wide acceptance. Writing in 1981, the poet David Wright commented that Roberts's anthology had had the effect of 'divid[ing] the modernist sheep from the traditionalist goats'.[30] Roberts was concerned with the difficult concept of the accuracy with which the poet was able to render contemporary experience, and interpreted this as an attempt to get beyond the 'poetical' by engagement with modernity. In this sense Modernism was accepted as a rallying cry for what was new and original.

1940s and 1950s: The New Criticism and Modernism

New Criticism, which was the dominant critical approach in the 1940s and 1950s, had its origins in and emerged from modernism. T. S. Eliot's early criticism, to be found for instance in the essay 'Tradition and the Individual Talent' (1919), has been taken as an example of the method at the point of its foundation. Others, like William Empson, who was influenced by some of the critical procedures used by Laura Riding and Robert Graves in *A Survey of Modernist Poetry* (1927), were working out similar methods of analysis for themselves – *Seven Types of Ambiguity* (1930) being an important instance. The new critical approach, which was based on close reading (at the expense of contextual analysis) is most clearly associated with the group of Southern Agrarian poet critics – all associated at some point with Vanderbilt University in Nashville. Among these was Cleanth Brooks (1906–94), who in a number of important critical articles and books sought to examine modernist texts. In *Modern Poetry and the Tradition* (1939), he articulates the view that modern poets are those 'who, if they are accepted at all, demand a radical revision of the existing conception of poetry'. He finds that in modernist literary activity, 'we are witnessing (or perhaps have just witnessed) a critical revolution of the order of the Romantic Revolt'.[31] His analysis provides an apology for modernism by seeking to tackle the issue of the difficulty and obscurity of modernist poetry for the ordinary reader by attempting to give it a genealogy in seventeenth century metaphysical poetry and French symbolism.

By the 1950s literary modernism had won acceptance, and was consolidated into academic literary discourse. This was still, however, largely a matter of individual reputations. This monumental account of Modernism was beginning to take shape and a 'new critical canon' was being established.[32] However, there were voices of dissent. The poet Robert Graves was one of these, and he used the opportunity provided by being invited to give the Clark Lectures at Cambridge in 1954–5, to question the effects of the process by which the reputations of individual Modernists were being enhanced by institutional recognition. He regarded the establishment of the modern poet as a sort of canonised figure as being a symptom of the contemporary fascination with celebrity writers. Graves phrased this obsession as 'a modernism' and noted that there was a growing tendency to absorb contemporary literature into the academic critical discourses that had once been reserved for the analysis and discussion of literature that belonged to remoter periods of history. The result of this process is, he claims, the 'setting up of five living idols – namely Yeats, Pound, Eliot, Auden, and Dylan Thomas'. He further notes that, if you have any pretence towards being cultured, 'you are expected not only to regard these five as the most "significant" modern writers but to have read all the "significant" literature that has grown up about them; because "Age of Consolidation" implies "Age of Criticism".'[33] Clearly, this was an attack on the way in which academia had been instrumental in constructing a critical orthodoxy that accepted modernist writers as key indicators of the shifts in culture that had occurred in the twentieth century. Graves was suspicious – and understandably envious – of this attention; equally he stuck to the notion of poetic inspiration being derived from a muse, and felt that modernist poets were given artificial status according to their ability to articulate their rhetoric. These ideas are closely associated with one of Graves's most influential and well known books, *The White Goddess: A Historic Grammar of Poetic Myth* (1948, rev. 1952, 1961). The romantic myth of inspiration that was crucial to Graves's poetic practice was combined with what was understood in the 1950s as his rational wit, which was partly an influence on some of the British poets that emerged to public notice at that time – now usually referred to as the 'Movement'.

Later Modernism: 1960s and Beyond

During the 1960s experimentation re-emerged and embraced ideas borrowed from conceptual art, and new ways to explore transient mediums such as the periodical were attempted. The mode of the transmission of 'literature' was questioned in ways that allowed for a self-conscious provisionality, so that 'Work in Progress' (the title adopted by Ford's *Transatlantic Review* and Jolas's *Transition* for Joyce's *Finnegans Wake* [1939]) became 'process-showing'. This begs the question – echoing Raymond Williams's famous remark, 'when was modernism?' (1987) – when was the modernist magazine, or, indeed, when was the post-modernist magazine?[34] The situation was different in Britain to that in the USA, which was different to that in Europe. Stephen Spender, in *The Struggle of the Modern* (1963), suggested that there was by the early 1960s a distinction between the modern and the now, because writers no longer sought to 'create works which expressed the experience of a present which was distinct from all the past' and from which there was no escape.[35] Peter Gay, in his recent study, *Modernism: The Lure of Heresy – From Baudelaire to Beckett and Beyond* (2007), has put forward the view that the modernist rebellion against bourgeois society came to an end amid the emergence of Pop Art.* At this time modernism was increasingly interpreted by critics as a platform for revolutionary literary engagement and experiment.

Cyril Connolly (1903–74), a critic who had come to prominence with *The Enemies of Promise* (1938), produced a controversial and influential popular guide to modernist literature in 1965, during this period of counter-cultural re-evaluation. His book, *The Modern Movement: 100 Key Books from England, France and America,*

---

* Pop Art emerged in the 1950s and is particularly associated with the use of mass-produced images from popular culture. Protagonists include Andy Warhol and Roy Lichtenstein.

1880–1950, located the key period of modernist experiment in the early years of the twentieth century. The choice of key works was surprising to many at the time, especially academic critics such as Frank Kermode – including for instance D. H. Lawrence's *Sea and Sardinia* (1921), but not *Women in Love* (1921). The tone was manifestly backward looking and regretfully nostalgic, although internationalist in outlook, declaring that once modernism had successfully achieved its ends, 'the complacent hypocrisy of the nineteenth century punctured, its materialism exposed', the movement 'ground to a halt … technical innovations were by-passed, originality incorporated into the norm, until rebellion grew meaningless' in all but the most authoritarian countries.[36] The first exhibition organised by the Harry Ransom Center at the University of Texas, in 1971, was *One Hundred Modern Books*, based on Connolly's list, and perhaps marks a point in time when modernism became a subject for research.

As a reaction against the widespread institutional acceptance of modernism and its influence over the discussion of poetry, the poet Philip Larkin wrote critically and publicly of the modern movement. He noted that a gap had occurred between the reading public and contemporary poets. His argument, in a 1971 article on one of the few modern poets who was popular, John Betjeman (who nonetheless was also included among Connolly's key books of the modern movement, for *Selected Poems*, 1948), blamed modernism for the fact that, 'in this century English poetry went off on a loop-line that took it away from the general reader.'[37] There is an element of nostalgia in Larkin's perspective, a nostalgia that looks back to the popularity enjoyed by poets at the beginning of the twentieth century, by Rudyard Kipling, A. E. Housman and Rupert Brooke. It is therefore a viewpoint that takes issue with the advent of modernism. What Larkin was able to tap into – and was temperamentally attuned for – was the mood of post-war Britain. Such an analysis reflected the hardships of the period in which Britain's role in the world was being reduced in line with the economic realities of the change in the global power base, and the ascendancy of American culture. Modernism was seen by Larkin to be part of this larger process of Americanisation. The narrowness of this view of modernism was challenged by Hugh Kenner (1923–2003), a Canadian academic who had met Pound in 1948 at St Elizabeth's Hospital for the Criminally Insane, Washington, D.C., where Pound was incarcerated after the Second World War for his controversial views on the Italian regime. Kenner had, in the summer of 1949, written *The Poetry of Ezra Pound* (1951), which tried to rehabilitate Pound's reputation. He later wrote extensively about James Joyce, Wyndham Lewis, Samuel Beckett and T. S. Eliot, as well as Pound, and returned to the subject of Britain's apparent failure to respond to the lessons of modernism in *A Sinking Island: The Modern English Writers* (1988).

Modernism and the University

By 1975 critics were increasingly trying to locate an understanding of modernism in the broad cultural changes of the twentieth century rather than with any individuals or groups of individuals. In that year Ian Hamilton (1938–2001), the poet and critic, devoted part of an issue of *The New Review* to 'Modernism: A Symposium'. This was introduced by Brian Finney, and included articles by Jonathan Culler, Anthony Quinton and John Weightman. The symposium was conceived as a cross-disciplinary approach to the subject, allowing specialists from different areas to engage with the central concept.

The mid 1970s saw the emergence of modernism as an established discourse in academic debate. Peter Faulkner's study guide, *Modernism*, appeared in 1977, and confidently claimed that 'Modernism has come to seem a broadly homogeneous movement, with roots in Romanticism and a flowering in the first third of this century.'[38]

One of the most influential books in the history of the academic discussion of modernism is Malcolm Bradbury and James McFarlane's *Modernism: A Guide to European Literature 1890–1930*, which was first published in 1976. Since that date it has become a standard textbook on the subject of modernism. Indeed, it has become central to the teaching of modernism in the universities of Britain and the USA. It has also probably helped to provide the basis for the consensus that has adopted the use of 'modernism' as the main term for labelling certain experimental tendencies in the literature of the late nineteenth and early twentieth centuries. Perhaps the inclusion of the decade of the 1890s in the study can be viewed as being open to question. Even the date of 1930 can be viewed as of only approximate value. These issues are acknowledged in the preface added to the 1991 reissue, where the editors note that 'it is precisely because Modernism is still, in some fashion, a shaping art behind the art of our own times that, for all our exhibitions and archives, the task must stay provisional.'[39]

This provisional nature of modernism has lead critics to question the assumptions that have been made about it. Peter Nicholls, in *Modernisms: A Literary Guide* (1995), has made a convincing case for a plural form of the usage of the term modernism. It has become apparent that modernism is as various as the practitioners themselves. While Eliot and Joyce, and thanks to Hugh Kenner, Ezra Pound (see *The Pound Era*, 1971), have quickly gained canonical status, it is now clear that any discussion of modernism should take account of the achievements of many others, including Ford Madox Ford, Wyndham Lewis and Gertrude Stein at the very least. The work of Virginia Woolf and H. D., for example, has been examined with emphasis on the way in which these writers negotiate the moment of modernism with a feminist concern for gendered linguistic experiment, as well as a radical questioning of sexuality and gender roles. Jane Goldman has shown how the aesthetic strategies that Woolf evolved in her novels have not only similarities to the experiments of James Joyce and Marcel Proust, but a specific relationship to her concerns as a woman.[40] In addition to Woolf there has been a great rediscovery of the Women of 1914 (and beyond) in response to feminist studies; and the work of Dorothy Richardson, May Sinclair, Rebecca West, Marianne Moore, Jean Rhys, Djuna Barnes, Laura Riding and Mina Loy – among others – has received increasing amounts of close attention. Studies worthy of mention are Jean Radford's *Dorothy Richardson* (1991), Helen Carr's *Jean Rhys* (1996), Suzanne Raitt's *May Sinclair: A Modern Victorian* (2000), Laura Marcus's *Virginia Woolf* (rev. 2004), and Elizabeth Friedmann's *A Mannered Grace: the Life of Laura (Riding) Jackson* (2005).

The research undertaken by Bonnie Kime Scott has led to a greater understanding of the development of modernism, and has stressed the importance of looking at the work of women in the 1920s and 1930s to get a more complete picture of the period. Her ground-breaking *Refiguring Modernism: The Women of 1928* (1995) and *Refiguring Modernism: Postmodern Feminist Readings of Woolf, West and Barnes* (1995) have alerted critics to the limitation of existing male-orientated readings of modernism. Susan Gubar and Sandra M. Gilbert, in *No Man's Land: The Place of the Woman Writer in the Twentieth Century* (1988), have demonstrated that modernist writers have been profoundly influenced by radically conceived gender roles among the avant-garde. Jayne E. Marek has brought attention to the women who as editors were responsible for furthering the modernist cause through such generally recognised little magazines as *Poetry (Chicago)*, the *Little Review* and the *Dial*, in *Women Editing Modernism: 'Little' Magazines and Literary History* (1995). She examines the influence of Harriet Monroe and Alice Corbin Henderson on *Poetry*, Margaret Anderson and Jane Heap on the *Little Review*, and of Marianne Moore on the *Dial*.

Lesbian and Gay studies have also enriched our understanding of the extent that modernism was more than just a period of literary experimentation. The focus that has been given to modernism in queer theory has been relatively slight in comparison. The lives and loves of Virginia Woolf, Gertrude Stein, H. D., and more latterly Mary Butts, have provided opportunities to explore lesbian constructions of modernism. The exploration of male homosexuality in this respect has tended to lag behind – perhaps as a result of feminist alternative readings. Accounts of the lives of, for example, Henry James, E. M. Forster, Lytton Strachey, Ronald Firbank, Wilfred Owen, Hart Crane, W. H. Auden, John Lehmann and Stephen Spender, have partly contributed to an awareness of the possibilities of other queer readings of modernism. One study that has questioned the process of the development of modernism as a literary discourse in relation to male sexuality is Langdon Hammer's *Hart Crane and Allen Tate: Janus-Faced Modernism* (1993).

The influential cultural critic Raymond Williams (1921–88) placed a stress on the importance of immigration as a factor that contributed to the cultural hybridity of modernism in the posthumously published *The Politics of Modernism* (1989). These 'immigrants' were largely attracted to cities such as London, Paris or New York because these urban centres allowed for a large ebb and flow of social movement, and with this movement came the spread of new ideas. One result of this understanding of modernism's plurality has been a growing awareness of the way issues of alienation and marginality contribute to the formation of counter-culture in the metropolian space. African-American critics, such as Houston A. Baker Jr. in *Modernism and the Harlem Renaissance* (1987), have taken the given literary discourses of modernism to explore the way that national and racial identity interacts with literature.

Recent critical discussion has been concerned with how modernism is defined and what the extent of its scope should be. This is an ongoing discourse, but it is clear that increasingly critics are taking a broader view of modernism than just an account of the 'high modernism' of Eliot, Joyce and Woolf, as we have seen. Indeed, it might be argued that the term has been adopted to refer to any post-Victorian literature. More precisely, perhaps, the term has been interpreted in relation to the idea of an emerging consciousness of modernity. This has included refiguring modernism around places and spaces, the cities of modernism discussed in the Bradbury and McFarlane volume. An excellent example of this approach is provided in Peter Brooker and Andrew Thacker (eds), *The Geographies of Modernism: Literatures, Cultures, Spaces* (2005), which also draws upon current trends in postcolonial studies. The academic journal *Modernism/modernity* (the official journal of the Modernist Studies Association) is a good source of the use of current critical approaches to modernism.

Notes

1   Widely quoted, in this case from Walter Allen's still useful survey *The English and American Novel From the Twenties to Our Time* (London:

Phoenix House, 1964), p. 2. Woolf's comment originally appeared in her essay 'Mr. Bennett and Mrs. Brown' (The Hogarth Essays, First Series, No. 1, 1924), a defence of Georgian novelists from an attack by Arnold Bennett, one of the leading Edwardian novelists. Virginia Woolf, *Collected Essays*, Vol. 3 (London: Hogarth Press, 1966), pp. 422–3.

2   See Donald Davie, *Ezra Pound* (Chicago IL: The University of Chicago Press, 1982), pp. 27–30. See also Peter Brooker, *Bohemia in London* (Basingstoke: Palgrave, 2004).

3   John Middleton Murry, 'H. G. Wells', in the *Adelphi*, 30 (October–December, 1946), pp. 1–5.

4   H. G. Wells, *The History of Mr Polly* (London: Penguin, 2005), p. 122.

5   For a more detailed and useful account of the social background to Modernism, see Malcolm Bradbury's *The Social Context to Modern English Literature* (Oxford: Basil Blackwell, 1971).

6   Frank Harris, 'Richard Middleton', *Rhythm*, 2:7 (August, 1912), p. 83. The poet John Davidson, who was something of a rebel, committed suicide in 1909.

7   John Middleton Murry, 'Art and Philosophy', *Rhythm*, 1:1 (Summer, 1911), p. 10.

8   For a more detailed history of the Georgians see Robert H. Ross, *The Georgian Revolt* (London: Faber & Faber, 1967) and James Reeves (ed.), *Georgian Poetry* (Harmondsworth: Penguin, 1981).

9   Stephen Spender, *The Struggle of the Modern* (London: Methuen, 1965), p. 113.

10   Harold Monro, 'The Imagists Discussed', *The Egoist* (1 May 1915), p. 78. For more on Harold Monro see Dominic Hibberd, *Harold Monro: Poet of the New Age* (Basingstoke: Palgrave, 2001).

11   See Suzanne Raitt, *May Sinclair: A Modern Victorian* (Oxford: Clarendon Press, 2000).

12   May Sinclair, 'Two Notes: II. On Imagism', *The Egoist* (1 June, 1915), p. 88.

13   The history of Imagism can be traced most fully in Glenn Hughes's *Imagism and the Imagists: A Study in Modern Poetry* (Stanford, CT: Stanford University Press, 1931), which provides an interesting insight, having been written so close to the period being discussed. See also the introduction to Peter Jones's anthology *Imagist Poetry* (Harmondsworth: Penguin, 1981).

14   Michael Levenson, *A Genealogy of Modernism: A Study of English Literary Doctrine 1908-1922* (Cambridge: Cambridge University Press, 1995), p. 213.

15 Alan Young's introduction to Edgell Rickword, *Essays and Opinions 1921–31* (Manchester: Carcanet, 1974), p. 2. For more on Rickword consult Charles Hobday, *Edgell Rickword: A Poet at War* (Manchester: Carcanet, 1989).

16 Quoted in 'Editor's Notes', *The Chapbook*, 37 (May 1923), p. 2.

17 See Richard Perceval Graves, *Robert Graves: The Years with Laura, 1926–40* (London: Weidenfeld and Nicolson, 1990), pp. 23–4.

18 This magazine has been discussed further in Stephen Rogers, 'Nostalgia and Reaction: Austin Osman Spare, and *Form*, *The Golden Hind*, and *The Decachord*', Peter Brooker and Andrew Thacker (eds), *The Oxford Critical and Cultural History of Modernist Magazines: Britain and Ireland, 1880–1955* (Oxford: Oxford University Press, 2009), pp. 570–90.

19 Edwin Faulkner, 'The Poetry of Thomas Hardy: The Dynasts', *The Decachord*, 4:16 (September–October, 1928), p. 100.

20 'Ettrick', 'Modernist and Traditional Poetry', *The Decachord* , 4:17 (November–December, 1928), p. 166.

21 'Lancastrian', 'Ettrick Again Answered', *The Decachord*, 4:17 (November–December, 1928), p. 172.

22 A. L. Morton, 'Beauty is not Enough', *The Decachord*, 4:17 (November–December, 1928), p. 177.

23 'Ettrick', 'The Poet and the Public', *The Decachord*, 5:19 (September–October, 1929), p. 83.

24 Edwin Faulkner, 'Browning and the Modernists', *The Decachord*, 5:19 (September–October, 1929), p. 87.

25 See Clere Parsons, *The Air Between: Poems of Clere Parsons*, with an afterword by Edouard Roditi (Newcastle: Cloud, 1989).

26 'Editorial', *The Calendar of Modern Letters*, 1:1 (March, 1925), p. ii.

27 Alan Munton, 'Edgell Rickword', *P.N. Review*, 9:2 (1982), p. 7.

28 Edgell Rickword, *Scrutinies* (London: Wishart & Co., 1928), p. v.

29 Michael Roberts, *The Faber Book of Modern Verse* (London: Faber & Faber, 1946), pp. 1–7.

30 David Wright, *Edward Thomas: Selected Poems and Prose* (Harmondsworth: Penguin, 1981), p. 14.

31 Cleanth Brooks, *Modern Poetry and the Tradition* (London: Editions Poetry London, 1948), pp. vii–viii.

32 Francis Mulhern, *The Moment of 'Scrutiny'* (London: New Left Books, 1979), p. 16.

33 Robert Graves, *The Crowning Privilege: The Clark Lectures 1954–1955* (London: Cassell, 1955), pp. 113–14.

34   See Raymond Williams, *The Politics of Modernism*, ed. by Tony Pinkney (London: Verso, 1989)

35   Stephen Spender, *The Struggle of the Modern* (London: Methuen, 1965), pp. 256–7.

36   Cyril Connolly, *The Modern Movement: 100 Key Books from England, France and America, 1880–1950* (London: André Deutsch, 1965), p. 15.

37   Philip Larkin, *Required Writing* (London: Faber & Faber, 1983), pp. 216–17.

38   Peter Faulkner, *Modernism* (London: Methuen, 1977), p. 74.

39   Malcolm Bradbury and James McFarlane, 'Preface to the 1991 Reprint', Malcolm Bradbury and James McFarlane (eds), *Modernism: A Guide to European Literature 1890–1930* (Harmondsworth: Penguin, 1991), p. 12.

40   See Jane Goldman, *The Feminist Aesthetics of Virginia Woolf: Modernism, Post-Impressionism and the Politics of the Visual* (Cambridge: Cambridge University Press, 1998).

Part Five
References and Resources

Timeline

	Historical Events	Literary Events
1891		Thomas Hardy, *Tess of the D'Urbervilles*; Oscar Wilde, *The Picture of Dorian Gray*
1895	Marconi invents 'wireless' technology; Roentgen's discovery of X-rays; trial of Oscar Wilde	Oscar Wilde, *The Importance of Being Ernest*; Joseph Conrad, *Alymayer's Folly*
1896	*Daily Mail* founded	Anton Chekhov, *The Seagull*
1897	Queen Victoria's Diamond Jubilee	
1898	Spanish–American War; the Curies discover radium and plutonium	H. G. Wells, *War of the Worlds*
1899	Anglo–Boer War begins	
1900		Joseph Conrad, *Lord Jim*; Sigmund Freud, *The Interpretation of Dreams*
1901	Queen Victoria dies	
1902	Anglo–Boer War ends	
1903	Emmeline Pankhurst founds Women's Social and Political Union; first successful flight of the Wright brothers	

Timeline

	Historical Events	Literary Events
1904		Anton Chekhov, *The Cherry Orchard*
1905	Albert Einstein proposes the theory of relativity	
1906	British Liberal Party wins election and begins programme of social and class reform	
1907	Cubist exhibition in Paris	
1908	Protests for women's rights in London	
1910	King Edward VII dies; George V succeeds the throne; Union of South Africa	E. M. Forster, *Howard's End*; Henry James, *The Finer Grain*; Ezra Pound, *The Spirit of Romance*; W. B. Yeats, *The Green Helmet and other poems*
1911	National Insurance Act, UK; beginning of several years of industrial unrest (miners and shipworkers) UK	Joseph Conrad, *Under Western Eyes*; D. H. Lawrence, *The White Peacock*; Katherine Mansfield, *In a German Pension*
1912	Sinking of the ill-fated ship *Titanic*; start of suffragette window-breaking campaign; first Balkan War; Woodrow Wilson elected as President of the USA; Futurist exhibition in Paris	Joseph Conrad, *'Twixt Land and Sea*; T. E. Hulme, *The Complete Poetical Works*; D. H. Lawrence, *The Trepasser*; Ezra Pound, *Ripostes*
1913	London Psychoanalytical Society founded; Second Balkan War	Ford Madox Ford, *Collected Poems*; D. H. Lawrence, *Sons and Lovers*; Leonard Woolf, *The Village in the Jungle*
1914	First World War breaks out (August); Britain and France occupy German Colonies in West Africa	Joseph Conrad, *Chance*; James Joyce, *Dubliners*; Wyndham Lewis (ed.), *Blast*; Gertrude Stein, *Tender Buttons*; W. B. Yeats, *Responsibilities*

	Historical Events	Literary Events
1915	Zeppelins attack London; Wartime Coalition government formed in UK; Italy enters the War; Battle of Gallipoli	Richard Aldington, *Images, 1910–15*; Rupert Brooke *1914, Five Sonnets*; Joseph Conrad, *Victory*; Ford Madox Ford, *The Good Soldier*; D. H. Lawrence, *The Rainbow*; Ezra Pound, *Cathay*; Dorothy Richardson, *Pointed Roofs*; Virginia Woolf, *The Voyage Out*
1916	University Conscription introduced in the UK; Battles of Verdun and the Somme; David Lloyd George becomes Prime Minister; Easter rising in Ireland (August)	H. D., *Sea Garden*; James Joyce, *A Portrait of the Artist as a Young Man*; Ezra Pound, *Lustra, Gaudier-Brzeska*; Dorothy Richardson, *Backwater*; W. B. Yeats, *Reveries Over Childhood and Youth*
1917	USA enters the war; Russian Revolution	Joseph Conrad, *The Shadow Line: A Confession*; T. S. Eliot, *Prufock and Other Observations*; D. H. Lawrence, *Look! We Have Come Through*; Dorothy Richardson, *Honeycomb*; May Sinclair, *The Tree of Heaven*; W. B. Yeats, *The Wild Swans at Coole*
1918	Armistice brings the end of War (11 November); Women granted limited voting rights in UK	James Joyce, *Exiles*; Wyndham Lewis, *Tarr*; Katherine Mansfield, *Prelude*; Rebecca West, *The Return of the Soldier*
1919	Treaty of Versailles allocates reparations to the aggressor parties in the War; Non-Co-operation protests led by Ghandi in India; Amritsar massacre; Ernest Rutherford splits the atom	Joseph Conrad, *The Arrow of Gold*; T. S. Eliot, *Poems*; Ezra Pound, *Quia Pauper Amavi*; Dorothy Richardson, *Interim, The Tunnel*; Virginia Woolf, *Night and Day*

Timeline

	Historical Events	Literary Events
1920	League of Nations created; US Constitution amended to give women the vote; Palestine becomes British mandate; Prohibition of alcohol sale begins in US; Oxford University admits women students	Joseph Conrad, *The Rescue*; T. S. Eliot, *The Sacred Wood: Essays on Poetry and Criticism*; D. H. Lawrence, *The Lost Girl*; Katherine Mansfield, *Bliss, and Other Stories*; Wilfred Owen, *Poems*; Ezra Pound, *Hugh Selwyn Mauberley*
1921	Irish Free State founded	John Dos Passos, *Three Soldiers*; Aldous Huxley, *Chrome Yellow*; D. H. Lawrence, *Women in Love*; Dorothy Richardson, *Deadlock*; W. B. Yeats, *Michael Robartes and the Dancer*
1922	Mussolini comes to power in Italy	T. S. Eliot, *The Waste Land*; James Joyce, *Ulysses*; D. H. Lawrence, *Aaron's Rod*; Katherine Mansfield, *The Garden Party, and Other Stories*; May Sinclair, *Life and Death of Harriet Frean*; Virginia Woolf, *Jacob's Room*; W. B. Yeats, *The Trembling of the Veil, Later Poems*
1923		Elizabeth Bowen, *Encounters*; Joseph Conrad, *The Rover*; D. H. Lawrence, *Psychoanalysis and the Unconscious, Fantasia of the Unconscious, Kangaroo*; Katherine Mansfield, *The Dove's Nest*; Dorothy Richardson, *Revolving Lights*; Wallace Stevens, *Harmonium*; William Carlos Williams, *Spring and All*

	Historical Events	Literary Events
1924	Lenin dies; First (minority) Labour government in the UK elected	T. S. Eliot, *Homage to John Dryden*; Ford Madox Ford, *Some Do Not*; E. M. Forster, *A Passage to India*; T. E. Hulme, *Speculations*; D. H. Lawrence, *England, My England, Studies in Classic American Literature*; Katherine Mansfield, *Something Childish, and Other Stories*
1925		John Dos Passos, *Manhatten Transfer*; T. S. Eliot, *Poems 1905–25*; F. Scott Fitzgerald, *The Great Gatsby*; Ford Madox Ford, *No More Parades*; Ernest Hemingway, *In Our Time*; Aldous Huxley, *Those Barren Leaves*; Hugh MacDiarmid, *Sangshaw*; Gertrude Stein, *The Making of Americans*; Virginia Woolf, *Mrs Dalloway, The Common Reader*; W. B. Yeats, *A Vision*
1926	General strike in UK; John Logie Baird invents television	Ford Madox Ford, *A Man Could Stand Up*; Henry Green, *Blindness*; D. H. Lawrence, *The Plumed Serpent*; May Sinclair, *Far End*; Gertrude Stein, *Composition as Explanation*
1927		E. M. Forster, *Aspects of the Novel*; Wyndham Lewis, *Time and Western Man*; William Plomer, *I Speak of Africa*; Jean Rhys, *The Left Bank, and Other Stories*; Dorothy Richardson, *Oberland*; Virginia Woolf, *To The Lighthouse*

Timeline

	Historical Events	Literary Events
1928	Vote given to women over 21 in UK for the first time	T. S. Eliot, *For Lancelot Andrewes: Essays on Style and Order*; Ford Madox Ford, *Last Post*; Radclyffe Hall, *The Well of Loneliness*; Aldous Huxley, *Point Counter Point*; D. H. Lawrence, *The Woman Who Rode Away and Other Stories*, *Lady Chatterley's Lover*; William Carlos Williams, *The Descent of Winter*; Virginia Woolf, *Orlando*; W. B. Yeats, *The Tower*
1929	Wall Street Crash, New York	Richard Aldington, *Death of a Hero*; Elizabeth Bowen, *The Last September*; William Faulkner, *The Sound and the Fury*; Henry Green, *Living*; Ernest Hemingway, *A Farewell to Arms*; Virginia Woolf, *A Room of One's Own*; W. B. Yeats, *A Packet for Ezra Pound*
1930	Beginning of widespread civil disobedience in India	W. H. Auden, *Poems*; Evelyn Waugh, *Vile Bodies*; John Dos Passos, *The 42nd Parallel*; T. S. Eliot, *Ash Wednesday*; James Joyce, *Anna Livia Plurabelle*
1931		Virginia Woolf, *The Waves*; Samuel Beckett, *Proust*
1932	James Chadwick discovers the neutron	Aldous Huxley, *Brave New World*; Stella Gibbons, *Cold Comfort Farm*
1933	Hitler appointed as Chancellor of Germany	George Orwell, *Down and Out in Paris and London*; Gertrude Stein, *Autobiography of Alice B. Toklas*

	Historical Events	Literary Events
1934		Evelyn Waugh, *A Handful of Dust*
1935		George Orwell, *Burmese Days*
1936	George V dies, Edward VIII becomes king and then abdicates; Spanish Civil War	Dylan Thomas, *Twenty-Five Poems*
1937	George VI's coronation	Virginia Woolf, *The Years*; J. R. R. Tolkien, *The Hobbit*; George Orwell, *The Road to Wigan Pier*
1938	Germany occupies Austria	Evelyn Waugh, *Scoop*; Virginia Woolf, *Three Guineas*
1939	Start of Second World War (September)	James Joyce, *Finnegans Wake*; John Steinbeck, *The Grapes of Wrath*
1940	Churchill becomes Prime Minister; Blitz on London	W. H Auden, *Another Time*; Dylan Thomas, *Portrait of the Artist as a Young Dog*
1941	Pearl Harbour attacked by Japan	Noel Coward, *Blithe Spirit*
1942	First thousand RAF bomber raid (May)	
1943	Fall of Mussolini (July)	
1944	D-Day Landings in Normandy	T. S. Eliot, *Four Quartets*
1945	End of Second World War	Evelyn Waugh, *Brideshead Revisited*; George Orwell, *Animal Farm*
1946		Dylan Thomas, *Deaths and Entrances*
1947	The Queen marries the Duke of Edinburgh (November); Britain's Coal Industry nationalised (January)	
1948	NHS formed; Olympics held in London	Graham Greene, *The Heart of the Matter*
1949		George Orwell, *1984*
1950	Princess Anne born	Bertrand Russell, *Unpopular Essays*

Further Reading

General Books on Modernism

Ayers, David, *English Literature of the 1920's* (Edinburgh: Edinburgh University Press, 1999)

> The chapter entitled 'Sex, Satire and the Jazz Age' tries to move away from Freudian theory to expose lesser known authors and their ideas; a very interesting read

—, *Modernism – A Short Introduction* (Oxford: Blackwell, 2004)

> Clear and concise chapters on a selection of key modernist authors and texts. Particularly good chapter on James Joyce's *Ulysses*

Bell, Kevin, *Ashes Taken For Fire – Aesthetic Modernism and the Critique of Identity* (London: University of Minnesota Press, 2007)

> A complex but rewarding text. Chapter two addresses the issue of the impossibility of language to represent reality

Bell, Michael (ed.), *The Context of English Literature 1900–1930* (London: Methuen, 1980)

> Provides wider context for modernism. Cyril Barrett's chapter looks at what was happening aside from literature within the arts world

Bloom, Clive (ed.), *Literature and Culture in Modern Britain (Volume 1: 1900–1929)* (Harlow: Longman House, 1993)

> Jim Reilly's 'The Novel as an Art Form' looks at the effect the period 1900–29, such as the impact of the First World War, on the novel

Bradbury, Malcolm and McFarlane, James (eds), *Modernism – A Guide to European Literature 1890–1930* (London: Penguin, 1976)

> Informative chapters on the different geographies of modernism. The text also covers most areas of modernism but considers them from different European angles

Bradshaw, David (ed.), *A Concise Companion to Modernism* (Oxford: Blackwell, 2003)

> Addresses the diverse issues of modernism. The chapter 'Reading' looks at the readers of modernist literature and the issue of elitism

Brooker, Peter (ed.), *Modernism/Post Modernism* (Harlow: Longman, 1992)

> Each chapter in the first section contains extracts of essays written by critics; these are useful and cover a wide range of areas of modernism

—, *Bohemia in London – The Social Scene of Early Modernism* (Basingstoke: Palgrave Macmillan, 2007)

> Brooker looks at the geography of London and establishes the social activity of the period, such as the relationships between the artists and where they were formed

Brooker, Peter and Thacker, Andrew (eds) *Geographies of Modernism* (Abingdon: Routledge, 2005)

> An interesting look at geographical locations and their connection with modernism. See, particularly, Anna Snaith's chapter 'Jean Rhys and London', which draws on the disjointed relationship between geography and identity that the author experienced

Campbell, Kate (ed.), *Journalism, Literature and Modernity – From Hazlitt to Modernism* (Edinburgh: Edinburgh University Press, 2004)

> An informative look at the relationship between modernism and journalism. The latter chapters are particularly concerned with modernist magazines

Childs, Peter, *Modernism* (London: Routledge, 2000)

> An easy to understand text, looks at the key events and thinkers of modernism

Eksteins, Modris, *Rites of Spring – The Great War and the Birth of the Modern Age* (New York: Houghton Mifflin, 1989)

> Eksteins looks predominantly at European history. 'Journey to the Exterior' examines how World War One influenced modernism, including Dadaism

Faulkner, Peter (ed.), *A Modernist Reader – Modernism in England 1910–1930* (London: BT Batsford, 1986)

Offers readers key extracts from modernist writers' works

—, *Modernism* (London: Routledge, 1990)

A small but interesting look at modernism, covering key authors and subjects. The section entitled 'Virginia Woolf's Critical Essays' provides an overview of Woolf's thoughts and opinions

Ford, Boris (ed.), *Early 20th Century Britain – The Cambridge Cultural History* (Cambridge: Cambridge University Press, 1989)

Ford edits this collection of chapters covering a wide range of topics from Literature to Music; it also looks at the social and cultural events of the period and the impact these had on society

Gillie, Christopher, *Movements in English Literature 1900–1940* (Cambridge: Cambridge University Press, 1975)

Easy to digest text which provides a good overview of modernism. Chapter five, 'Diversification of the novel 1920–1930', looks at how the novel changed shape through this period

Goldman, Jane, *Modernism, 1910–1945 Image to Apocalypse* (Basingstoke: Palgrave Macmillan, 2004)

A useful text, in which the preface and introduction provide a clear overview of modernism

Jaffe, Aaron, *Modernism and the Culture of Celebrity* (Cambridge: Cambridge University Press, 2005)

Jaffe draws on the links between modernism and contemporary culture, particularly celebrity culture

Kolocotroni, V., Goldman, J. and Taxidou, O. (eds), *Modernism – An Anthology of Sources and Documents* (Edinburgh: Edinburgh University Press, 1998)

Excellent resource for all students of modernism as it identifies, in chronological order, the key areas of modernism, including the key thinkers and their essays

Levenson, Michael (ed.), *The Cambridge Companion to Modernism* (Cambridge: Cambridge University Press, 1999)

> The introduction highlights the main issues and themes in a clear and direct way. Each chapter draws on a different strand of modernism, making it a useful tool for students

Mahaffey, Vicki, *Modernist Literature – Challenging Fictions* (Oxford: Blackwell, 2007)

> Separated into three chapters, Mahaffey's book directly addresses the issue of the common misconceptions that exist about 'challenging' literature

Matthews, Steven (ed.), *Modernism – A Sourcebook* (Basingstoke: Palgrave Macmillan, 2008)

> A good basic starting point that gives a clear overview of modernism. Easy to read, and covers a wide range of topics

Nicholls, Peter, *Modernisms – A Literary Guide* (Berkeley: University of California Press, 1995)

> Contains an interesting section about Italian Futurism and Filippo Tommaso Marinetti

Randall, Bryony, *Modernism, Daily Time and Everyday Life* (Cambridge: Cambridge University Press, 2007)

> Drawing on the idea of time and modernism, Randall's book discusses the idea that if there are new concepts occurring in the world then there must be new ways of living

Sherry, Vincent, *The Great War and the Language of Modernism* (Oxford: Oxford University Press, 2003)

> Sherry covers a wide range of topics, including the links between the war and modernism

Smart, John, *Modernism and After: English Literature 1910–1939* (Cambridge: Cambridge University Press, 2008)

> Great starting point for students, easy to read with clearly defined sections. Provides a good grounding with its clear style and approach

Surrette, Leon, *The Birth of Modernism – Ezra Pound, T.S. Eliot, W.B. Yeats and the Occult* (London: McGill-Queens University Press, 1993)

    Surrette deviates from the norm by assessing the links between the three poets and the idea of the occult

Tew, Phillip and Murray, Alex (eds), *The Modernism Handbook* (London: Continuum, 2009)

    An excellent staring point for any student of modernism. Tew and Murray's book offers a wide selection of material in an accessible style

Trotter, David, *Paranoid Modernism – Literary Experiment, Psychosis, and the Professionalization of English Society* (Oxford: Oxford University Press, 2001)

    For students who are interested in looking at modernism and psychology. Trotter's is a really excellent book that addresses the idea of paranoia in both writers and their work

Modernism and Art

Bricker Balken, Debra, *Debating American Modernism – Stieglitz, Duchamp, and the New York Avant-Garde* (New York: American Federation of Arts, 2003)

    A fascinating visual aid for students wishing to understand more about the New York avant-garde

Black, Jonathon, et al., *Blasting the Future – Vorticism in Britain 1910–1920* (London: Philip Wilson, 2004)

    Contains a selection of examples of futurist and vorticist works of art, including sculptures

Crunden, Robert M., *American Salons – Encounters with European Modernism 1885–1917* (Oxford: Oxford University Press, 1993)

    The chapter 'London and Ezra Pound' provides an interesting look at Pound's life and his relationship with London

Deepwell, Katy (ed.), *Women Artists and Modernism* (Manchester: Manchester University Press, 1998)

A collection of essays focusing on the challenges women faced in the modernist period

Edwards, Paul (ed.), Blast – *Vorticism 1914–1918* (Aldershot: Ashgate, 2000)

The introduction provides a clear and concise history of Vorticism, consisting of essays from different critics complete with illustrations

Golding, John, *Visions of the Modern* (London: Thames and Hudson, 1994)

An invaluable tool for students of modernist art, Golding surveys the different arts movements of the early twentieth century, including Surrealism, Futurism and Cubism

Graver, David, *The Aesthetics of Disturbance – Anti-Art in Avant-Garde Drama* (Michigan, MI: The University of Michigan Press, 1995)

The first chapter, 'Defining the Avant-Garde', provides a useful look at what is meant by the term

Joachimides, Christos M. and Rosenthal, Norman (eds), *The Age of Modernism – Art in the 20th Century* (London: Thames and Hudson, 1997)

Includes a useful introduction entitled 'The Age of Modernism' which addresses and defines what is meant by modernism in the art world and whether this differs to the literary world

Kalaidjian, Walter, *American Culture Between the Wars – Revisionary Modernism and Postmodern Critique* (New York: Columbia University Press, 1993)

Kalaidjian's illustrated book contains examples of modernist art depicting machinery and the city

Lasko, Peter, *The Expressionist Roots of Modernism* (Manchester: Manchester University Press, 2003)

Lasko's book draws on the subject of modernism in German art, specifically the roots of Expressionism and its role within German Modernism

Meskimmon, Marsha, *We Weren't Modern Enough – Women Artists and the Limits of German Modernism* (London: I. B. Tauris, 1999)

> Accessible, with interesting chapters such as 'The Prostitute', which looks at the symbolic role of the prostitute in German modernist art

Middleton Wagner, Anne, *Three Artists (Three Women) – Modernism and the Art of Hesse, Krasner, and O'Keeffe* (London: University of California Press, 1996)

> A really useful book looking at the relationship between feminism and modernist art. Although Wagner concentrates on three artists the book is an excellent way of establishing what was happening in the world of art, especially for female artists

Perry, Gill, *Women Artists and the Parisian Avant-Garde* (Manchester: Manchester University Press, 1995)

> Perry's chapter 'The Art Market and the School of Paris: "Marketing a Feminine Style"' provides an interesting look at working mothers as artists and how they balanced motherhood and art

Pyne, Kathleen, *Modernism and the Feminine Voice – O'Keeffe and the Women of the Stieglitz Circle* (Berkeley: University of California Press, 2007)

> Pyne's book looks at the women who were part of the Stieglitz Circle and the impact of Georgia O'Keeffe as an icon

Wilson, Simon, *Surrealist Painting* (London: Phaidon Press, 1991)

> Wilson's book provides a useful introduction charting both the beginnings and the development of Surrealism

Wolff, Janet, *AngloModern – Painting and Modernity in Britain and the United States* (London: Cornell University Press, 2003)

> Wolff provides readers with a selection of essays on different topics. Chapter four, 'The Feminine in Modern Art', looks at what is meant by feminine art, as well as defining the terminology of words such as modernism and modernity

Modernism and Drama

Fuchs, Elinor, *The Death of Character – Perspectives on Theater after Modernism* (Bloomington: Indiana University Press, 1996)
> This book addresses key influences from the modernist period. In Chapter five, the focus is on the relationship between landscape and Gertrude Stein and the influence this had on drama

Graver, David, *The Aesthetics of Disturbance: Anti-Art in Avant-Garde Drama* (Michigan, MI: The University of Michigan Press, 1995)
> Graver looks at, among other subjects, the relationship between 'Anti-Art', Dadaism and drama

Krutch, Joseph Wood, *'Modernism' in Modern Drama* (Ithaca, NY: Cornell University Press, 1953)
> A good book for students wishing to find out more about drama and modernism. Contains a chapter that surveys the work of George Bernard Shaw and his influences

Lewis, Pericles, *The Cambridge Introduction to Modernism* (Cambridge: Cambridge University Press, 2007)
> Lewis discusses the major themes of modernism, including the controversy surrounding portrayals of sexuality

Marker, Frederick J. and Innes, Christopher, *Ibsen, Strindberg, Pirandello, Beckett – Essays from Modern Drama* (Toronto: University of Toronto Press, 1998)
> Benjamin K. Bennett's chapter, 'Strindberg and Ibsen: Toward a Cubism of Time in Drama', provides an interesting discussion of the subject of time and drama and Cubism

Modernism and Gender

Clark, Suzanne, *Sentimental Modernism* (Bloomington: Indiana University Press, 1991)
> Looking at the issue of sentimentality in modernism, Suzanne Clark provides some interesting debates

Dickie, Margaret and Travisano, Thomas (eds), *Gendered Modernisms – American Women Poets and their Readers* (Philadelphia: University of Pennsylvania Press, 1996)
> A series of essays on key American modernists. Dianne Chisholm's chapter draws on the idea of H. D.'s poems as being predominantly sexual

Dowson, Jane, *Women, Modernism and British Poetry, 1910–1939 – Resisting Femininity* (Aldershot: Ashgate, 2002)
> Contains a useful chronology of women's publications

Feldman, Jessica R., *Gender on the Divide – The Dandy in Modernist Literature* (Ithaca, NY: Cornell University Press, 1993)
> Feldman's book provides an interesting and intriguing look at the subject of 'dandies'. She sets out the characteristics of the term, and their relationship with gender

Fraser, Kathleen, *Translating the Unspeakable – Poetry and the Innovative Necessity* (London: The University of Alabama Press, 2000)
> Fraser provides an appealing selection of essays about poetry

Galvin, Mary E., *Queer Poetics – Five Modernist Women Writers* (West Point, NY: Praeger, 1999)
> Provides a debate on the subject of lesbianism within modernist poetry; in her introduction Galvin addresses a number of issues such as the reaction against lesbian writers by the literary cannon

Hanscombe, Gillian and Smyers, Virginia L., *Writing for their Lives – The Modernist Women 1910–1940* (London: The Women's Press, 1987)
> Addresses topics such as why other female writers/editors and contributors are overlooked in favour of Virginia Woolf

Kahane, Claire, *Passions of the Voice – Hysteria, Narrative, and the Figure of the Speaking Woman 1850–1915* (London: The Johns Hopkins University Press, 1995)
> Kahane explores the subject of narrative voice within the text, with a psychological approach

Kaplan, Sydney Janet, *Katherine Mansfield and the Origins of Modernist Fiction* (Ithaca, NY: Cornell University Press, 1991)

> Although the text is primarily concerned with Katherine Mansfield it is a useful source for those students wishing to expand their knowledge of modernist fiction

Kime Scott, Bonnie (ed.), *The Gender of Modernism – A Critical Anthology* (Bloomington: Indiana University Press, 1990)

> Kime Scott's introduction provides a good discussion on the gender debate, defining what is meant by the term as well as how it directly affected modernist literature

—, *Refiguring Modernism – Volume 1 – The Women of 1928* (Bloomington: Indiana University Press, 1995)

> The chapter entitled 'Midwives of Modernism' gives an insight into the women who helped shape modernism

—, *Gender in Modernism – New Geographies, Complex Intersections* (Urbana: University of Illinois Press, 2007)

> An excellent resource for all students of modernism, especially the introductions to the chapters

Miller, Cristianne, *Cultures of Modernism – Marianne Moore, Mina Loy, and Else Lasker-Schüler* (Michigan, MI: The University of Michigan Press, 2005)

> Miller focuses on gender within the text, with reference to Moore, Loy and Lasker-Schüler

Miller, Jane Eldridge, *Rebel Women – Feminism, Modernism and the Edwardian Novel* (Chicago, IL: The University of Chicago Press, 1997)

> Details developments between the Victorian and modernist periods, providing a sound contextual history

Rossen, Janice, *Women Writing Modern Fiction – A Passion for Ideas* (Basingstoke: Palgrave Macmillan, 2003)

> Discusses particularly how the idea of romance changed within novels yet remained true to the traditions of the Victorian romance in terms of its happy endings

Taylor, Georgina, *H.D. and the Public Sphere of Modernist Women Writers, 1913–1946* (Oxford: Oxford University Press, 2001)
> Primarily focuses on the life and works of Hilda Doolittle (H. D.), Taylor's book also comments on the situation of women poets between the years 1913 and 1946

Trodd, Anthea, *Women's Writing in English – Britain 1900–1945* (Harlow: Addison Wesley Longman, 1998)
> Trodd explores the argument that modernist women writers felt the need to break away from the domestic realism of the nineteenth century, and the opposition they faced from the male literary world

Wheeler, Kathleen, *'Modernist' Women Writers and Narrative Art* (Basingstoke: Macmillan, 1994)
> Wheeler explores the role of women writers and how they helped to shape modernism

Modernism and Poetry

Albright, Daniel, *Quantum Poetics – Yeats, Pound, Eliot, and the Science of Modernism* (Cambridge: Cambridge University Press, 1997)
> Albright's text usefully concentrates on W. B. Yeats, Ezra Pound and T. S. Eliot

Beasley, Rebecca, *Theorists of Modern Poetry – T. S. Eliot, T. E. Hulme, Ezra Pound* (Abingdon: Routledge, 2007)
> Beasley draws on the biographies of Eliot, Hulme and Pound as well as analysing the relationships between the poets and other important literary figures such as Bergson

Bloom, Clive and Docherty, Brian (eds), *American Poetry – The Modernist Ideal* (Basingstoke: Macmillan, 1995)
> Draws on a wide range of poets, some well known, others less so

Churchill, Suzanne, *The Little Magazine 'Others' and the Renovation of Modern Poetry* (Aldershot: Ashgate, 2006)
> Churchill celebrates how much impact the magazines had on the world of poetry in terms of promoting careers and new concepts such as free verse

Davidson, Ian, *Ideas of Space in Contemporary Poetry* (Basingstoke: Palgrave Macmillan, 2007)

> Davidson's text draws on the idea of space, a concept that recurs within modernist poetry/ literature

Davis, Alex and Jenkins, Lee (eds), *The Cambridge Companion to Modernist Poetry* (Cambridge: Cambridge University Press, 2007)

> Discusses a broad range of issues surrounding modernist poetry such as how it was received in the period and also how the canon has evolved over time

Day, Gary and Docherty, Brian (eds), *British Poetry 1900–50 – Aspects of Tradition* (Basingstoke: Macmillan, 1995)

> A really useful tool for all students studying modernist poetry as the text covers a wide range of topics in easy to read essays

Emig, Rainer, *Modernism in Poetry – Motivations, Structures and Limits* (Harlow: Longman, 1995)

> Emig provides the reader with clearly defined chapters, and looks at the 'friendship' between poetry and psychoanalysis, indicating that there are positive links between the two disciplines

Larissy, Edward, *Reading Twentieth Century Poetry – The Language of Gender and Objects* (Oxford: Blackwell, 1990)

> Larrissy's text analyses the works of several of the key modernist poets such as Ezra Pound. Chapter two draws on Ezra Pound and Imagist movement, particularly in relation to arguments about gender

Lentricchia, Frank, *Modernist Quartet* (Cambridge: Cambridge University Press, 1994)

> Looks behind the scenes of the American modernist poetry scene, for example the quarrel between Robert Frost and Ezra Pound about mass circulation and the little magazines

Lucas, John, *Starting to Explain: Essays on Twentieth Century British and Irish Poetry* (Nottingham: Trent Editions, 2003)

> A good sourcebook written in an accessible style. The essay entitled 'D.H. Lawrence as Poet' is especially useful

McCabe, Susan, *Cinematic Modernism – Modernist Poetry and Film* (Cambridge: Cambridge University Press, 2005)
> An interesting resource for students wishing to deviate from the usual confines of modernism

Perkins, David, *A History of Modern Poetry – From the 1890's to the High Modernist Mode* (Cambridge: The Belknap Press, 1976)
> Perkins's text covers a wide range of topics such as the rise of the little magazines, how they were important in strengthening the poetry movement and movements such as Imagism

—, *A History of Modern Poetry – Modernism and After* (Cambridge: The Belknapp Press, 1987)
> Perkins discusses the careers of poets such as W. H. Auden and how they were viewed by their contemporaries, and the contrasting reception of poets of the 1920s and 1930s

Perloff, Marjorie, *The Dance of the Intellect – Studies in the Poetry of the Pound Tradition* (Evanston, IL: Northwestern University Press, 1985)
> Perloff dissects the arguments of the supporters of Ezra Pound and Wallace Stevens

—, *21st-Century Modernism – The 'New' Poetics* (Oxford: Blackwell, 2002)
> The chapter 'The Conceptual Poetics of Marcel Duchamp' provides an interesting look at the link between mass production and art

Persoon, James, *Modern British Poetry 1900–1939* (New York: Twayne, 1999)
> A chronological look at British poetry. Persoon covers all of the predominant poets of the period as well as looking at how the war influenced modernism

Sisson, C. H., *An Assessment – English Poetry 1900–1950* (London: Methuen, 1971)
> Each chapter is clearly defined and sectioned according to the poet under discussion

Stead, C. K., *The New Poetic – Yeats to Eliot* (London: The Athlone Press, 1998)

> Stead covers a broad subject area of modernist poetry, analysing the relationship between modernist poets and their audience as well as the readership of modernist poetry

Modernism and the Novel

Briganti, Chiara and Mezei, Kathy, *Domestic Modernism, The Interwar Novel, and E.H. Young* (Aldershot: Ashgate, 2006)

> Briganti and Mezei focus on the domestic novel, charting the change from earlier ideas through to modernist incarnations

Cappetti, Carla, *Writing Chicago – Modernism, Ethnography, and the Novel* (New York: Columbia University Press, 1993)

> Cappetti takes an interesting look at the modernist novel, specifically centring around the Chicago and the idea of 'the city'

Miracky, James J., *Regenerating The Novel – Gender and Genre in Woolf, Forster, Sinclair, and Lawrence* (London: Routledge, 2003)

> Clearly divided into sub genres, and covering a wide range of issues

Parsons, Deborah, *Theorists of the Modernist Novel – James Joyce, Dorothy Richardson, Virginia Woolf* (Abingdon: Routledge, 2007)

> Parson's chapter on Virginia Woolf provides an excellent starting point, breaking the key themes of Woolf's work down into accessible sections

Shiach, Morag (ed.), *The Cambridge Companion to the Modernist Novel* (Cambridge: Cambridge University Press, 2007)

> Anne Fernihough's chapter looks at the origins of the stream of consciousness style of writing

Movements and Authors

Cubism, Symbolism and Imagism

Chadwick, Charles, *Symbolism* (London: Methuen, 1971)

A good starting point for students of Symbolism, Chadwick's first chapter explains in detail what is meant by the term, and its origins

Cottingham, David, *Cubism and its Histories* (Manchester: Manchester University Press, 2004)

Cottingham's book looks at how Cubism evolved onto the modernist scene within France. It also draws on other inspirations for cubist art in France such as the media (billboards and advertising) and music hall revue shows

Golding, John, *Cubism – A History and an Analysis 1907–1914* (London: Faber and Faber, 1959)

Golding's book provides a useful review of the history of Cubism. Chapter one, 'The History and Chronology of Cubism', focuses on the relationship between the works of Pablo Picasso and Georges Braque

Harrison, Charles, Franscina, Francis and Perry, Gill, *Primitivism, Cubism, Abstraction – The Early Twentieth Century* (London: Yale University Press, 1993)

Separated into three clearly defined chapters, each author concentrates on a different subject matter. Franscina's section, 'Realism, ideology and the "discursive" in Cubism' analyses what is considered to be the language of Cubism

Peyre, Henri, *What is Symbolism?* (Tuscaloosa: The University of Alabama Press, 1980)

Emmett Parker's translation of Henri Peyre's book opens with a discussion of the origins of Symbolism and is an interesting and informative text

Pratt, William and Richardson, Robert (eds), *Homage to Imagism* (New York: Ams Press, 1992)

An essential tool for those wishing to find out more about Imagism. The introduction is clear and concise in its explanation of what Imagism is, its sources and the driving forces behind it nons, Arthur and Ellman, Richard, *The Symbolist Movement in* ;rature (Whitefish, MT: Kessinger, 2004)

Reprinted edition of Symons's original text about Symbolism, providing a ood original introduction to Symbolism

Futurism

Apollonio, Umbro (ed.), *Futurist Manifestos* (London: Thames and Hudson, 1973)

An essential guide for students studying Futurism and futurist manifestos

Clough, Rosa Trillo, *Futurism* (New York: Greenwood Press, 1961)

Chapter two draws on the ideas of Futurism and its relationship with literature, which provides points of discussion such as Filippo Tommaso Marinetti's opinion of poetry

Lista, Giovanni, *Futurism* (Paris: Terrail, 2001)

A good starting point for those studying Futurism. Contains excellent colour illustrations that help to exemplify Futurism and its artwork

Nash, J. M., *Cubism, Futurism and Constructivism* (London: Thames and Hudson, 1974)

Nash looks at the relationship between the three movements, as well as at the key figures of each of them

Ottinger, Didier (ed.), *Futurism* (Paris: Éditions du Centre Pompidou, 2009)

An excellent up to date sourcebook for students, clearly separated into two definitive parts. The first of these provides a series of essays on Futurism, such as the relationship between Futurism and Cubism that Ottinger refers to as 'Cubofuturism'

Rye, Jane, *Futurism* (London: Studio Vista, 1972)

Rye's book provides all levels of students and readers with a good overview of Futurism, including key sections from the futurist manifestos, as well as providing relevant historical context as to how the movement began

Tisdall, Caroline and Bozzola, Angela, *Futurism* (London: Thames and Hudson, 1977)

> A clear and concise book that covers a wide variety of issues surrounding Futurism. Chapter four looks at the relationship between Futurism, literature and theatre

Individual Authors

T. S. Eliot

Chiari, Joseph, *T. S. Eliot – Poet and Dramatist* (London: Vision Press, 1972)

> A well rounded book which covers the biographical details of Eliot's life as well as drawing on his works. Particularly good for those students who are new to the author

Cooper, John Xiros, *The Cambridge Introduction to T.S. Eliot* (Cambridge: Cambridge University Press, 2006)

> Cooper's book provides students with a wide range of biographical information in an easy to comprehend style. As well as analysing Eliot's works, Cooper draws on ideas about the influences on it. Particularly good for beginners

Gardner, Helen, *The Art of T.S. Eliot* (London: Faber and Faber, 1968)

> Gardner focuses on Eliot's work (with an emphasis on *Four Quartets*) rather than on biographical details, which is good for those wishing to explore his works further

Gish, Nancy K., *Time in the Poetry of T.S. Eliot* (New Jersey: Barnes and Noble Books, 1981)

> Gish draws on the idea of time, which is a theme often connected with Modernism, within several of Eliot's key works including *The Waste Land*. Recommended for intermediate to advanced readers due to the concentration of subject matter

Kenner, Hugh (ed.), *T.S. Eliot – A Collection of Critical Essays* (Englewood Cliffs, NJ: Prentice-Hall, 1962)

> A really useful source for those wishing to learn more about Eliot, this includes essays from his fellow writers and poets such as Wyndham Lewis. An informative resource for intermediate to advanced students of modernism

Miller, James E. Jr, *T.S. Eliot's Personal Waste Land –Exorcism of the Demons* (London: The Pennsylvania State University Press, 1977)

> An interesting read for the more advanced student who is looking for an unusual topic of discussion about Eliot. Miller looks at the secretive personal life of Eliot and how this influenced his work. A really good read for those wishing to understand more about the author

Pearce, T. S., *T.S. Eliot* (London: Evans Brothers, 1975)

> A really good starting point for students who are beginners to both modernism and Eliot himself. With clearly defined chapters covering both biographical details and his work, such as the imagery and language he uses and the effect this has

Schuchard, Ronald, *Eliot's Dark Angel – Intersections of Life and Art* (Oxford: Oxford University Press, 1999)

> A look at Eliot's intriguing and often complex psychological themes, especially that of the 'Dark Angel', which, Schuchard writes, appears in the work of other writers such as Matthew Arnold. More suitable for the advanced reader due to the complex nature of the themes discussed

Southam, B. C., *A Student's Guide to the Selected Poems of T.S. Eliot* (London: Faber and Faber, 1981)

> Southam's book is separated into clearly defined chapters on each of the poems. Good for providing students with an overview that acknowledges the difficulty of Eliot's work

Spender, Stephen, *Eliot* (London: Fontana, 1975)

> Spender draws on the idea that T. S. Eliot went through three different phases as a poet and these phases are reflected within his work, from creative poet through to critic poet. In each of the chapters Spender looks at different themes and issues within his work, such as Eliot's defiance in keeping his private life from his readers

James Joyce

Costello, Peter, *James Joyce – The Years of Growth 1882–1915 – A Biography* (Lanham, MD: Roberts Rinehart, 1992)

> Costello's book draws on the biographical details of Joyce's life, particularly the influence his native Ireland had on his work

Gross, John, *Joyce* (London: Collins, 1971)

> A concise but informed look at both the biographical details of Joyce's life and selected works. Gross analyses the response to *Ulysses* by both the media and the public

Hodgart, Matthew, *James Joyce – A Student's Guide* (London: Routledge & Kegan Paul, 1978)

> A really good book for those who are new to Joyce and his work. Hodgart looks at biographical details as well as analysing texts such as *Dubliners*. He also looks at Joyce's relationship with Ireland and how this is reflected in his work

Thacker, Andrew, *Dubliners* (Basingstoke: Palgrave Macmillan, 2006)

> A good resource for those students wishing to explore Joyce's short stories. Contains a selection of essays analysing each short story, drawing on different aspects

D. H. Lawrence

Hamalian, Leo (ed.), *D. H. Lawrence* (New York: McGraw-Hill, 1973)

> Excellent resource for students concentrating on Lawrence. It looks at both the biographical aspects of his life as well as critically analysing selected works

Widdowson, Peter (ed), *D.H. Lawrence* (Harlow: Longman, 1992)

> A rich and extremely useful resource for students looking at Lawrence. In the essays, each critic analyses a different aspect of Lawrence's work

Ezra Pound

Sullivan, J. P. (ed.), *Ezra Pound* (Harmondsworth: Penguin, 1970)

> A key text with a selection of information, from excerpts of letters both to and from the author and extracts from essays written by critics of Pound

Virginia Woolf

Briggs, Julia, *Virginia Woolf – An Inner Life* (London: Penguin, 2005)

> Briggs takes an interesting exploration through Woolf's life and works, focusing on her relationship with the 'inner life'

Books on Other Notable Authors

Alpers, Anthony, *The Life of Katherine Mansfield* (London: Jonathan Cape, 1980)

> A biographical look at the life of Katherine Mansfield, together with her influences

Burke, Caroline, *Becoming Modern – The Life of Mina Loy* (Berkeley: University of California Press, 1996)

> Burke draws on the places where Loy spent her life, emphasising the relevance of geographical location to modernism

Gillie, Christopher, *A Preface to Forster* (Harlow: Longman, 1983)

> An excellent starting point for all students, charting the biographical details of Forster's life and providing critical analysis his work, drawing on other poets/writers of the period

Rapport, Nigel, *The Prose and the Passion – Anthropology, Literature and the Writing of E.M. Forster* (Manchester: Manchester University Press, 1994)

> Contains an excellent bibliographical section including the influences behind Forster's writing, such as his education and childhood. Good for exploring more about the author's thoughts and ideas

Index

Index

Index

Index

Index

Index

Index

Index

Acknowledgements

Extracts from Richard Aldington's poem IMAGES © The Estate of Richard Aldington. Reproduced by kind permission of the Estate of Richard Aldington c/o Rosica Colin Limited, London

George Antheil, excerpt from *The Bad Boy of Music* (Doubleday Doran, 1945), reproduced by kind permission of the Estate of George Antheil

Excerpt by Edmund Blunden from *Undertones of War* (©Edmund Blunden, 1964) is reproduced by permission of PFD (www.pfd.co.uk) and HarperCollins Publishers Ltd

Basil Bunting, published in the April (1966) 'Diary' of the North Eastern Association for the Arts, Newcastle-upon-Tyne. Quoted in Herbert Read, *Basil Bunting: Music or Meaning?*, Agenda, Vol 4 Nos. 5 & 6 (Autumn 1966), p. 4. Reproduced by permission of Bloodaxe Books, on behalf of John Halliday (Estate of Basil Bunting)

Blaise Cendrars, excerpt from *Moravagine* (Penguin, 1979), reproduced by permission of Peter Owen Ltd, London

Noel Coward, excerpt from *Private Lives* (Methuen, 2002) © NC Aventales AG, successor in title to the Estate of Noel Coward. Reproduced by permission of Methuen Drama, an imprint of A&C Black Publishers Ltd and Alan Brodie Representation Ltd; www.alanbrodie.com

The extract from 'sh estiffl' is reprinted from COMPLETE POEMS 1904-1962, by E. E. Cummings, edited by George J. Firmage, by permission of W. W. Norton & Company. Copyright © 1991 by the Trustees for the E. E. Cummings Trust and George James Firmage

Acknowledgements

F. S. Flint, extract from 'Beggar' (1917) in Peter Jones (ed.), *Imagist Poetry* (Penguin, 2001) reproduced by kind permission of the Estate of F. S. Flint

Thomas Mann, excerpts from *Tristan* and *Tonio Kröger* in *Death in Venice/Tristan/Tonio Kröger* (Penguin, 1980), originally from *Stories of a Lifetime, Volume 1* published by Secker & Warburg, Reprinted by permission of The Random House Group, Ltd and Random House, Inc.

Charlotte Mew, 'The Cenotaph' (1919), in *Collected Poems and Selected Prose* (Carcanet, 2003), reproduced by permission of Carcanet Press Limited

John Middleton Murry, excerpts from 'Obituary of H. G. Wells', in *Adelphi*, XXX (October–December, 1946), pp. 1–5, 57; and 'Art and Philosophy', in *Rhythm*, Vol. I, No. I (Summer, 1911), p. 10, reproduced by permission of The Society of Authors as the Literary Representative of the Estate of John Middleton Murry

Alfred Noyes, excerpt from 'Art', in *Collected Poems: Volume 1* (William Blackwood and Sons, 1925), reproduced by permission of The Society of Authors as the Literary Representative of the Estate of Alfred Noyes

Edgell Rickword, excerpt from *Scrutinies* (Wishart & Co., 1928), reproduced by kind permission of Dr P. Jane Grubb

'They', from COLLECTED POEMS OF SIEGFRIED SASSOON by Siegfried Sassoon, copyright 918, 1920 by E. P. Dutton. Copyright 1936, 1946, 1947, 1948 by Siegfried Sassoon. Used by permission of Viking Penguin, a division of Penguin Group (USA) inc. and Barbara Levy Literary Agency, representing the Estate of George Sassoon

Osbert Sitwell, excerpt from *Wheels*, in *Noble Essences: A Book of Characters* (Macmillan, 1950), reproduced by permission of David Higham Associates Limited

YORK NOTES **COMPANIONS**

Texts, Contexts and Connections from York Notes
to help you through your literature degree ...

- ✔ **Medieval Literature**, Carole Maddern
  ISBN: 9781408204757 | £10.99

- ✔ **Renaissance Poetry and Prose**, June Waudby
  ISBN: 9781408204788 | £10.99

- ✔ **Shakespeare and Renaissance Drama**, Hugh Mackay
  ISBN: 9781408204801 | £10.99

- ✔ **The Long Eighteenth Century: Literature from 1660 to 1790**
  Penny Pritchard
  ISBN: 9781408204733 | £10.99

- ✔ **Romantic Literature**, John Gilroy
  ISBN: 9781408204795 | £10.99

- ✔ **Victorian Literature**, Beth Palmer
  ISBN: 9781408204818 | £10.99

- ✔ **Modernist Literature: 1890 to 1950**, Gary Day
  ISBN: 9781408204764 | £10.99

- ✔ **Postwar Literature: 1950 to 1990**, William May
  ISBN: 9781408204740 | £10.99

- ✔ **New Directions: Writing Post 1990**, Fiona Tolan
  ISBN: 9781408204771 | £10.99

Available from all good bookshops

For a 20% discount on any title in the series visit
www.yorknotes.com/companions and
enter discount code JB001A at the checkout!

The best books ever written

PENGUIN CLASSICS

SINCE 1946

20% discount on your essential reading from
Penguin Classics, only with *York Notes Companions*

A Portrait of the Artist as a Young Man
James Joyce
Edited with an Introduction and Notes by Seamus Deane
Paperback | 384 pages | ISBN 9780141182667 | 24 Feb 2000 | £7.99

Women in Love
D. H. Lawrence
Edited by David Farmer and Lindeth Vasey, Introduction by Amit Chaudhuri
Paperback | 592 pages | ISBN 9780141441542 | 29 Mar 2007 | £9.99

Ghosts, A Public Enemy, When We Dead Wake
Henrik Ibsen
Translated and Edited by Peter Watts
Paperback | 304 pages | ISBN 9780140441352 | 25 Jan 1973 | £9.99

Three Plays: The Father; Miss Julia; Easter
August Strindberg
Translated and Edited with an Introduction by Peter Watts
Paperback | 176 pages | ISBN 9780140440829 | 27 Mar 1975 | 2003 | £9.99

The Importance of Being Earnest and Other Plays
Oscar Wilde
Edited with an Introduction and Notes by Richard Allen Cave
Paperback | 464 pages | ISBN 9780140436068 | 25 May 2000 | £8.99

To The Lighthouse
Virginia Woolf
Edited by Stella McNichol, Introduction and Notes by Hermione Lee
Paperback | 320 pages | ISBN 9780141183411 | 26 Oct 2000 | £7.99

To claim your 20% discount on any of these titles
visit **www.penguinclassics.co.uk** and use
discount code **YORK20**

YORK PRESS, 322 Old Brompton Road,
London SW5 9JH

PEARSON EDUCATION LIMITED
Edinburgh Gate, Harlow CM20 2JE
United Kingdom
Tel: +44 (0)1279 623623
Fax: +44 (0)1279 431059
Website: www.pearsoned.co.uk

First edition published in Great Britain in 2010

© Librairie du Liban *Publishers* 2010

The right of Gary Day to be identified as author
of this work has been asserted by him in accordance
with the Copyright, Designs and Patents Act 1988.

The author and Publishers would like to thank Stephen Rogers for
his contribution to the volume. Thanks also to Sally Mason

ISBN: 978–1–4082–0476–4

British Library Cataloguing in Publication Data
A CIP catalogue record for this book can be obtained from the British Library

Library of Congress Cataloging in Publication Data
Day, Gary, 1956-
   Modernist literature, 1890-1950 / Gary Day. -- 1st ed.
       p. cm. -- (York notes companions)
   Includes bibliographical references and index.
   ISBN 978-1-4082-0476-4 (pbk. : alk. paper)
   1. Modernism (Literature)--Handbooks, manuals, etc. 2. Literature,
Modern--20th century--History and criticism--Handbooks, manuals, etc. 3.
Literature, Modern--19th century--History and criticism--Handbooks, manuals,
etc. I. Title.
   PN56.M54D39 2010
   809'.9112--dc22
                                                                   201001136

10 9 8 7 6 5 4 3 2 1
14 13 12 11 10
Phototypeset by Chat Noir Design, France
Printed in Malaysia, CTP KHL

YORK NOTES COMPANIONS

ture

Please renew/return this item by the last date
shown. Please call the number below:

Renewals and enquiries: 0300 123 4049

Textphone for hearing or   0300 123 4041
speech impaired users:

www.hertsdirect.org/librarycatalogue

Hertfordshire

Longman
is an imprint of

PEARSON

Harlow, England • London
Sydney • Tokyo • Singapor
Cape Town • Madrid • Mex

York Press